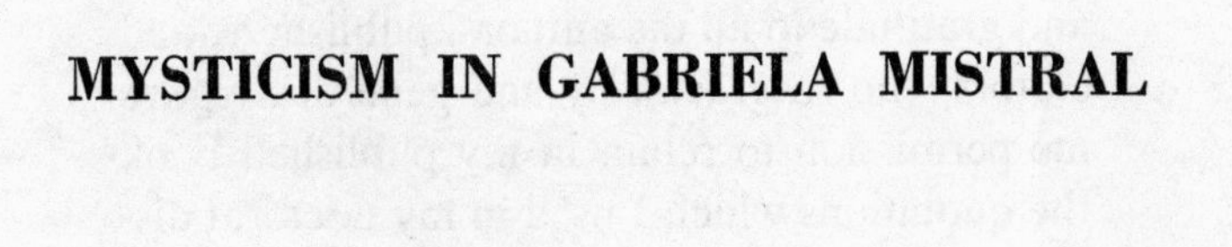

MYSTICISM IN GABRIELA MISTRAL

ACKNOWLEDGMENTS

I wish to express my sincere appreciation and gratitude to all the authors, publishers, and editors who so graciously and generously gave me permission to retain in my published book the quotations which I used in my doctoral dissertation. I am especially grateful to Rev. Richard J. Devine, C.M., Dean of the Graduate School of Arts and Sciences, St. John's University, for his kind permission to have my dissertation published.

MYSTICISM IN GABRIELA MISTRAL

by

SISTER ROSE AQUIN CAIMANO, O.P., Ph.D.
Chairman—Department of Humanities
Dominican College of Blauvelt
Blauvelt, New York

Pageant Press International Corp. **New York, N. Y.**

Library of Congress Catalog Card Number: 73-76582

First Edition

Published by Pageant Press International Corp.
101 Fifth Avenue, New York, N. Y. 10003

Manufactured in the United States of America

To *Reverend Mother Lawrence Marie,* my Mother General

To *Sister M. de la Salle,* my friend

I lovingly and gratefully dedicate my book

AUTHOR'S NOTE

In order to initiate the non-Spanish reader into the study of Gabriela Mistral, I have translated the quotations which appeared only in the original in the dissertation form of this book. My translations of la Mistral's poetry do not pretend to reproduce poetic patterns, rhythm, or rhyme in English, but simply to keep as close as possible to the thoughts which she poetically expresses in her native Spanish. To risk changing her thought for the sake of rhythm or rhyme would be to destroy the study of mysticism in this remarkable woman of our times. Chronologically, she belongs to our time. In spirit, mind, and heart, she is "a woman for all seasons."

CONTENTS

PREFACE

Interest in Gabriela Mistral, especially since her death in 1957, has become increasingly more widespread. The obscure rural school mistress from the Valley of Elqui, Vicuña, Chile, has attracted the attention of scholars and literary critics who hail her as Latin America's contribution to poetry and to international renown. Carlos D. Hamilton calls her "el alma poética de Hispanoamérica" (the poetic soul of Hispanic America), and Gregorio Marañón proclaims her "la América autóctona infundida de universalidad" (aboriginal America imbued with universality). Torres Ríoseco acclaims her "la figura literaria más alta de América" (the most eminent literary figure of America), and Larco Herrera declares her "el símbolo de América" (the symbol of America). José Mora identifies her anguish with "la angustia de un continente que busca adecuada respuesta a todos los interrogantes que plantea un mundo en formación" (the anguish of a continent which searches for an adequate answer to all the questions which a world in formation propounds), and Carlos Clavería alleges that for her "América es valor humano o intuición poética" (America is either human worth or poetic intuition).

That Gabriela herself was aware of this contribution, and of this renown, may be gleaned from the words she pronounced on receiving, in 1945, the Nobel Prize for Literature: "Hoy Suecia se vuelve hacia la lejana América Ibera para honrarla en uno de los muchos trabajadores de su cultura. El espíritu universalista de Alfredo Nobel estaría contento de incluir en el radio de su obra protectora de la vida cultural al hemisferio sur del Continente Americano tan poco y tan mal conocido" (Today, Sweden turns toward distant Iberian America in order to honor her in one of the many fashioners of her culture. The universal spirit of Alfred Nobel would be content to include, in the radius of his protective work of cultural life, the Southern Hemisphere of the American Continent, so little and so poorly understood). She remained, until October, 1967, the only Latin American ever to have received such recognition. Guatemala's Miguel Angel Asturias, novelist of the poor and oppressed, has become Latin America's second Nobel Prize winner.

In the numerous articles and several books which have been written concerning her, the most pivotal point studied and discussed is her religious sensibility. No one, it is true, can come into contact with Gabriela Mistral the woman or Gabriela Mistral the poet without becoming aware of the fact that religion permeates every fiber of her being, every line of her writing. She may be called, what Walter Kaufmann terms "movers and shakers of religion." To her may be applied the words which Julián Marías spoke in praise of Unamuno: "All the work . . . is steeped in an atmosphere of religion; whatever his theme, it ends by showing his religious roots or culminates in a last reference to God. And at bottom nothing interested him if he was not able to convert it in some way into the ever present theme of his thoughts." Some critics, however, in their understandable enthusiasm for this remarkably religious woman, have gone so far as to label her a mystic and her writings mysticism.

Interest in mysticism and curiosity about such labels gave birth to my desire to investigate mysticism in Gabriela Mistral. The interest in mysticism stems from the research and writing of the thesis which I presented in 1958 to the Romance Language Department of Fordham University, in partial fulfillment of the requirements for the degree of Master of Arts. This thesis, *The Antithetical Parallelism between "El cántico espiritual" of San Juan de la Cruz and "The Hound of Heaven" of Francis Thompson,* written under the guidance of my scholarly professor and friend, Dr. John J. Devlin, received the Huntington Award from the New York Chapter of the American Association of Teachers of Spanish and Portuguese.

Although the term "mysticism" has been applied by many to Gabriela Mistral, few have ventured beyond the label. Some, to justify the label, specify mystical tendencies in her personality, her life, or her work. Sister John Berchmans, O.P., in her article, "Gabriela Mistral and the Franciscan Concept of Life," *Renascence,* V (1952), 40-46 and 95, restricts her clarification of mysticism to a comparison between Gabriela Mistral and St. Francis of Assisi. However, to date, no detailed and systematic effort has yet been made to investigate to what extent Gabriela Mistral may or may not be termed a mystic.

The purpose of this study, therefore, is not to prove something that nobody has seen before, but to examine in detail something that many Mistralian critics have talked about but have never proved, either positively or negatively. The scope of this study is confined to an attempt to answer definitively two questions: Was Gabriela Mistral a mystic? Can her writings be classified as mysticism?

The topic has received approbation from literary critics of the stature of Federico de Onís, who was responsible for the first publication of *Desolación,* Hispanic Institute, 1922; Germán Arciniegas, whose letter of congratulations and encouragement reached me from *Cuadernos,* Paris; Angel Valbuena Briones, in whose class of Latin American Literature, University of Madrid, I was privileged to be; Ester de Cáceres, who wrote from Montevideo, Uruguay, gratified that I had selected "tan hermoso tema" (such a beautiful topic); and Jacques Maritain, Toulouse, France, who with his wife, Raïssa, shared Gabriela's confidence.

This investigation, to my knowledge, is the fourth doctoral dissertation to be written on Gabriela Mistral. The first, *Pensamiento y forma en la prosa de Gabriela Mistral (Thought and Form in the Prose of Gabriela Mistral),* accepted in 1963 by the University of Madrid, was written by Luis de Arrigoitia, former pupil and colleague of Federico de Onís, Estudios Hispánicos, Universidad de Puerto Rico. This study is being published by Editorial Gredos, Madrid. The second, *A Study of the Significant Variants in the Poetry of Gabriela Mistral,* accepted and published in 1964 by the Catholic University of America and directed by the scholar, Dr. Margaret Bates, was written by Sister Mary Charles Ann Preston, S.S.N.D. The third, *Religious Sensibility in the Life and Poetry of Gabriela Mistral,* accepted and published on microfilm, in 1964, by the University of California, Los Angeles, and directed by Donald F. Fogelquist, was written by Martin C. Taylor, Lecturer in Spanish, Department of Romance Languages and Literatures, University of Michigan, Ann Arbor, Michigan.

I am particularly grateful to Martin C. Taylor for his prompt and encouraging reply to my inquiries concerning the scope of his study. Since he did not treat the problem of mysticism, I trust that my study of it in Gabriela Mistral will not only complement his study of her religious sensibility, but also live up to his wish that I may build of it "a beautiful 'Church Triumphant.' "

I should like to acknowledge my indebtedness to Dr. Philip L. Astuto, director of this dissertation, and to all at St. John's

University who have helped to make this work possible; to Rev. Mother Lawrence Marie, Mother General of the Dominican Sisters of Blauvelt, and to all my religious Superiors for the time and opportunity given me to pursue graduate studies, and to all the Dominican Sisters of Blauvelt for their sisterly encouragement and understanding. A special word of thanks is due to Professors Andrés Iduarte and Eugenio Florit of Columbia University for their kindly interest and advice, and to Professor Ricardo Florit and his gracious co-workers in the Casa Hispánica for permission to examine and study the valuable articles in their Mistralian files.

Doris Dana, trusted secretary and friend of Gabriela Mistral and now literary heir and executrix of the Mistralian estate, received me as her guest in her home at Pound Ridge, New York. Here, her gracious hospitality reflected the warmth and the interest of her beloved Gabriela. Besides answering any questions I wished to ask her, she placed at my disposal several articles written by Gabriela Mistral and authorized Mr. Robert Hill, Keeper of Manuscripts, New York Public Library, to permit me to read and to study the Gabriela Mistral microfilm collection. These works include the unpublished *Recado de Chile* and *Lagar II*. It was she who made it possible for me to contact and to receive a reply from Jacques Maritain and Ester de Cáceres.

To Miss Dana, therefore, I extend the gratitude of one who feels that, in communicating with her, she has touched the spirit of Gabriela Mistral.

ABSTRACT OF THE DISSERTATION

The purpose of the present study is to explore the intense interior life of Gabriela Mistral and thereby attempt (1) to clarify the meaning of the term "mysticism" when applied to her, and (2) to determine to what extent Gabriela Mistral may be called a mystic.

The examination, while apparently closely related to that made by Martin C. Taylor, University of California, in his Ph.D. dissertation, *Religious Sensibility in the Life and Poetry of Gabriela Mistral,* is a distinct and unique investigation. Dr. Taylor's work ". . . examines in detail, for the first time, Gabriela Mistral's quest for the meaning of God, a quest which unifies her life and poetry." The present study examines in detail, for the first time, the end of the suffering and love which molded her spirit and sublimated her particular love to a universal one. The ultimate end of this suffering and love can alone authoritatively and definitively fix the precise connotation of the term "mysticism" when applied to Gabriela Mistral.

Many sympathetic critics, lacking a clear understanding of what is meant when the term "mystic" is applied to a man or woman, have failed to see that the mystic way, the method by which Gabriela Mistral strives to achieve her goal, is at many points very different from the mystic way of Catholicism and that of other religions. Therefore, they have used the term in reference to the mystery which radiates from her interior solitude, her tragic sense of life and death, her concept of love, her feeling for the desolate aspect of nature, and the religious allusions in her poetry.

Consequently, it is clear that every facet of her personality, life, and poetry must be explored. While it is true that she is one of the most interesting and most prolific prose writers of Hispanic letters, only those prose articles which have a direct bearing on the development of the chapters have been selected, and are listed in the bibliography. Accordingly, the introductory chapter is divided into two parts. The first part places Gabriela Mistral in her literary environment; the second outlines the many and varied "mystical" evaluations which elicited the reasons for a need for clarification of the concept.

The second chapter is a study of mysticism. The study aims to offer the norms by which Gabriela Mistral may or may not be measured as a mystic. The norms are selected from the Catholic connotation of the term "mysticism," from the connotation given to it in other great religions, and from its frequent identification with poetry.

The third, fourth, and fifth chapters examine her multifaceted personality, her complex religion, and the great motifs of her poetry. These chapters, set up against the second, attempt to provide an illuminating comparison between her and the mystics of great religions.

The concluding chapter is divided into two parts. The first part summarizes the potentialities in Gabriela Mistral which, if they had been directed toward the goal of the true mystic, i.e., union with the Beloved, would have justified the use of the term "mysticism" when applied to her. The second part shows that these potentialities were not directed toward union with the Beloved, but rather, toward herself and creatures. Therefore, Gabriela Mistral is not a mystic.

chapter I

INTRODUCTION

1. Place of Gabriela Mistral

> Ésta que aquí yace tras el cristal de un féretro, llamó a su carne Lucila Godoy; el nombre de su espíritu fué Gabriela Mistral.[1]
>
> (She who lies here behind the crystal of a coffin, called her flesh Lucila Godoy; the name of her spirit was Gabriela Mistral.)

This was the last presentation of Gabriela Mistral to the world. The man who presented her was Juan Gómez Millas, Rector of the University of Chile. So great was the impact of his wonder that he found it necessary to direct his words to God. So moved and inspired was he that his farewell address became an ardent prayer which revealed the mystery of the love and suffering of this tremendous woman:

> . . . a aquel que es capaz de sublimar su propio dolor lo haces asumir el dolor de su pueblo y sobre sus débiles hombros cargas el peso de sus culpas; exaltas al justo haciéndolo pagar por el pecador y quieres que el cáliz se vacie en sus labios hasta la última gota.[2]
>
> (. . . you force him who is capable of sublimating his own sorrow to assume the sorrow of his people and on his weak shoulders you impose the weight of their guilt;

you exalt the just one by making him pay for the sinner, and you require that on his lips the chalice be emptied to the last drop.)

Thus had Gabriela been the elect of God. Once again, He had "regarded the humility of His handmaid," and it would seem, "from henceforth all generations would call her blessed. For He that is mighty had done great things for her." Once again, "He had filled the hungry with good things, and had exalted the humble"[3] *maestra rural* (rural school teacher). The Rector, then, could not but separate her flesh from her spirit. The flesh, though an earthen vessel, had housed a boundless spirit capable of scaling the heights of ecstasy and plumbing the depths of despair, for thus does the "Designer Infinite char the wood"[4] of His prey:

> . . . si labras el vaso del cuerpo en frágil cristal, reclamas del espíritu fortaleza diamantina que sobreviva al tiempo y quieres que las cosas por él creadas tengan valor de eternidad; . . .[5]
>
> (. . . if you hew the vessel of the body in fragile crystal, you demand of the spirit adamantine fortitude which will outlive time and you require that the things created by it bear the price of eternity; . . .)

An attempt, therefore, to place the spirit of Gabriela Mistral in time and space would be an essay to capture the Archangel and to harness the wind, whose names she bore.[6] To situate Lucila Godoy is the possible task of the critic.

It was on April 7, 1889,[7] in Vicuña in the valley of Elqui, province of Coquimbo, Chile, that Lucila Godoy y Alcayaga[8] was born. The literary movement called Modernism was then ascending toward its apogee. One year before, in Valparaíso, Rubén Darío had launched his *Azul,* the impact of whose symbolism shook two continents and impelled their poets to echo the cry of Mallarmé: "Je suis hanté! L'Azur! L'Azur! L'Azur!" ("I am haunted! Blue! Blue! Blue!")

An anxiety for novelty in exquisiteness gave to the partisans of the new doctrine the impetus toward a search for the unknown where the sensorial predominated over the ideological. Doubt, melancholy, disillusion, and escape to unreal worlds shook off the declamatory guise of Romanticism and donned the purely esthetic garb of generating Beauty. The device of synesthesia impregnated words with new delights as it charged them with color, fragrance, and tactility, as well as harmony. Poets heard the music of stars and watched the color of symphonies; they touched the aroma of a flower and smelled its hues. Literary expression seemed to be reduced to an ingenious play of artificiality in perfecting form and devising symbols: "el cisne," "el pavo real," "el lis," "el jardín," la torre de marfil," "la princesa que está triste" (the swan, the peacock, the lily, the garden, the ivory tower, the princess who is sad). Thus did the French Parnassians and Symbolists wield their scepters over this American-born movement.

By 1896, *Prosas Profanas* ("Profane Prose") had carried the movement to its apex. *Cantos de vida y esperanza* ("Songs of Life and Hope"), 1905, strengthened its position, supported later by *Canto errante* ("Roving Song"), 1907, and *Poema del otoño* ("Poem of Autumn"), 1910. In these fifteen years of its full flowering, Ricardo Jaimes Freyre sang of Nordic shores in his *Castalia bárbara* ("Barbarous Castalia"). Leopoldo Lugones reached esthetic zones of pure poetry, subtle sensations, and voluptuous love in *Lunario sentimental* ("Sentimental Lunation"), *Odas seculares* ("Secular Odes"), and *Los crepúsculos del jardín* ("Garden Twilights"). Amado

Nervo arrived at the lyrical formula for the Mexican ambient in *El éxodo y las flores del camino* ("The End and the Flowers of the Road"). José Santos Chocano initiated the creole trend in *Alma América* ("Beloved America"), and Julio Herrera y Reissig manifested an intensification of the power of the metaphor in *Los éxtasis de la montaña* ("Mountain Ecstasies").

In 1911, the first cry of rebellion against Modernism came from Enrique González Martínez, as he twisted the neck of the sumptuous and artificial swan and enthroned the wise owl, symbol of introspection, silence, and mystery. He became the leader of young poets who, discontented with the superficiality of Modernism and preoccupied with the eternal mystery of life and death, intensified their personal lyricism and captured the life and landscape of the American people, their inquietudes, their ideals, and their hopes, without abandoning the artistic cultivation of language and form.

The Modernist masters had lost their power. In 1916, their leader, Rubén Darío, died; in 1917, their great critic, José Enrique Rodó followed; and, in 1919, Amado Nervo, with his mystic tendency. Over their tombs there arose a new generation of poets which critics have labeled Postmodernists, but which the great critic and professor, Federico de Onís, separates into two consecutive moments, "post" and "ultra." These men and women who produced between the two world wars and after them searched for depth in reality.[9] Their stamp is neither the artificial nor the exotic, but the real and the tangible, for theirs is a generation of existential anguish and metaphysical doubt.

Perhaps the most significant aspect of this generation is the emergence of women in the field of letters. Modernism can boast of not one of them, since the pre-war Latin American woman still bore the mark of *La perfecta casada* ("The Perfect Married Woman") of Fray Luis de León. The absence of men proved her worth outside the domain of her household. With this new challenge, there came her independence and desire for creativity. Many are these women and varied are their talents:

> Su aparición en las letras de aquel Continente a principios de siglo constituye uno de los hechos más notables de toda la historia de la cultura hispánica. Y no sólo por la calidad de los productos, que rivalizan con los mejores de la época anterior, sino también por la cantidad, que se puede sin exageración calificar de asombrosa. Ya Matilde Muñoz, en su *Antología,* incluye ciento quince poetisas de diversos países, y todas ellas posteriores al modernismo; y recientemente ha podido publicarse un estudio sobre la poesía femenina argentina con referencias de más de ciento cincuenta autoras.[10]
>
> (Their appearance in the literature of that continent at the beginning of the century constitutes one of the most notable events of the entire history of Hispanic culture. And not only for the quality of the production, which rivals the best of the previous epoch, but also for the quantity which, without exaggeration, can be qualified as astonishing. Matilde Muñoz, in her *Anthology,* already includes one hundred fifteen poetesses of different countries, and all of them subsequent to Modernism; and recently a study of Argentine feminine poetry was published with reference to more than one hundred fifty authors.)

Suffice it here to mention the four whom critics usually proclaim the most inspired. From Uruguay came the ardent and voluptuous temperament of Delmira Agustini (1890?-

1914) and the officially heralded "Juana de América" (Juana of America), Juana de Ibarbourou (1895-); from Argentina, the rebellious and semi-savage Alfonsina Storni (1892-1938); and from Chile, "la voz directa de los poetas de mi raza y la indirecta de las muy nobles lenguas española y portuguesa"[11] (the direct voice of the poets of my race and the indirect voice of the very noble Spanish and Portuguese tongues), Gabriela Mistral (1889-1957).

Delmira Agustini, while still an adolescent, shocked and scandalized the bourgeois society of the River Plate with her books of poems: *El libro blanco* ("The Blank Book"), 1907; *Cantos de la mañana* ("Morning Songs"), 1910; *Los cálices vacíos* ("Empty Chalices"), 1913, in which, breaking down all barriers of reserve and modesty, she sang of love in its most turbulent moments. Her language, daring and suggestive, as well as poetic, revealed her most intimate desires. Conscious of her physical beauty and alive with *joie de vivre* (the joy of living), she gave vent to unheard-of concupiscence and libido heretofore merely insinuated or clothed in modest metaphor. She was a woman born to love, but her unbridled passion received the reward which she seemed to presage in:

Yo muero extrañamente . . .
No me mata la Vida,
no me mata la Muerte,
no me mata el Amor;
muero de un pensamiento mudo como una herida . . .

¿No habéis sentido nunca el extraño dolor
de un pensamiento inmenso
que se arraiga en la vida
devorando alma y carne
y no alcanza a dar flor?[12]

(I die strangely . . .
Life does not slay me,
Death does not slay me,
Love does not slay me;
I die of a thought mute as a wound . . .

Have you never felt the strange sorrow
of an immense thought
which takes root in life,
devouring soul and body,
and never succeeds in blossoming?)

Her marriage was short-lived. Her husband, incapable of understanding such a turbulent creature, soon murdered her and then put an end to his own life: "Tristeza, inseparable del placer, se derrama en *Mis amores*"[13] (Sadness, inseparable from pleasure, is poured out in My Loves).

A breath of pagan joy blows through the verses of Juana de Ibarbourou. She describes herself as "libre, sana, alegre, juvenil y morena" (free, healthy, happy, young, brunette). Her poetry is a constant temptation and authentic invitation, underlined by an apparent narcissism. Unamuno calls it "castísima desnudez espiritual" (most chaste spiritual nudity), and Díez Echarri and Roca Franquesa declare that it is a unique interpretation of the *carpe diem* (seize the day) theme:

> Nunca, al menos en castellano, el "carpe diem" había tenido un intérprete como éste . . . un júbilo dionisíaco; los hay que delatan la satisfacción plena de vivir, un hedonismo integral, y los hay también que constituyen una ofrenda de goces, . . . Plenitud de vida . . . la mujer satisfecha de sí misma, que se encuentra perfecta, tanto en lo corporal como en lo psíquico, nadando a brazados

> en el mar sin fondo de la Naturaleza, y queriendo hacer partícipes a los demás de su júbilo.[14]
>
> (Never, at least not in Castilian, has the *carpe diem* theme had an interpreter such as this . . . a Bacchic merriment; there are those that expound the full satisfaction of living, an integral hedonism, and there are those also which constitute an offering of pleasures, . . . Plenitude of life . . . the woman satisfied with herself, who finds herself perfect, in the corporal as well as the psychical, floating with arms wide open in the bottomless sea of Nature and wishing to make others participators of her joy.)

This exuberance is evident in her first poems: "Tómame ahora, que aun es temprano" (Take me now, for it is still early); "Crecí para ti, Tálame. Mi acacia implora a tus manos un golpe de gracia" (I grew for you, Bridal Chamber. My acacia implores from your hands a stroke of grace); and "Te doy mi alma" (I give you my soul). Her later poems, however, reveal the meditative spirit of a maturing woman as she reflects on the fleetingness of joyful hours and the transitoriness of lovely things. Anguish and death supplant pleasure and life as her *carpe diem* theme is drowned in the lament of Jorge Manrique: "¿Qué se hizo del rey don Juan?" (What has become of King John?).

Some critics have compared the progressive transformation in the life and work of "Juana de América" to the four seasons of the year: *Las lenguas de diamante* ("Tongues of Diamond")—spring; *Raíz salvaje* ("Savage Root")—summer; *La rosa de los vientos* ("Rose of the Winds")—autumn; Perdida ("Lost")—winter. Her religious sentiments are poured out into two prose works: *Los loores de Nuestra*

Señora ("Praises of Our Lady") and *Estampas de la Biblia* ("Bible Scenes").

Alfonsina Storni also leaves a self-portrait, the direct antithesis of that left by Juana de Ibarbourou "in the rash lustihood of her young powers,"[15] for Alfonsina considered herself "colorada, redonda, chatilla y fea" (colored, round, flat-nosed, and ugly). Her very personal poetry seems but a reflection of her interior struggle, of her failures and her triumphs. She is resentful of her femininity because it makes her inferior to man whom she despises while she desires and envies him:

En los ojos, la carga de una enorme tristeza;
en el seno, la carga del hijo para nacer;
al pie del blanco Cristo, que está sangrando, reza:
"¡Señor, el hijo mío que no nazca mujer!"[16]

(In her eyes, the weight of an enormous sadness;
In her bosom, the weight of a child about to be born;
At the feet of the blanched Christ, who is bleeding, she prays:
"Oh Lord, this child of mine, may it not be born a woman!")

Her rebellious spirit and life of contradiction and disillusion led her to the fatal decision of suicide.

The sea has always attracted and inspired the poet. Alfonsina dreamed of its magnetic power and poured her dream into verse:

> Voy a dormir, nodriza mía, acuéstame,
> Ponme una lámpara a la cabecera;
> una constelación, la que te guste;
> todas son buenas; bájala un poquito.[17]

(I am going to sleep, my nurse, lay me to rest.
Place a lamp at my head;
a constellation, whatever you wish;
all are good; lower it a little.)

Then, on the morning of October 25, 1938, her dream became a reality. She surrendered to its lure and hurled herself into the waves.[18] On the spot where her body was found floating, a mausoleum was built in her honor. The epitaph, she had already written for herself:

Aquí descanso yo: dice Alfonsina
el epitafio claro, al que se inclina.
. . . . . .
Como es mujer, grabó en su sepultura
una mentira aún: la de su hartura.[19]

(Here I repose: Alfonsina states
her clear epitaph, to him who there inclines.
. . . . . .
Being a woman, she engraved on her tomb
one more deceit: that of her satiety.)

She who had so ironically saluted man:

Con mayúscula escribo tu nombre, y te saludo,
Hombre, mientras depongo mi femenino escudo
en sencilla y valiente confesión de derrota.
. . . . . .
¡Salud! En versos te hago mi fina reverencia.[20]

(With a capital I write your name, and I salute you,
O Man, while I put aside my feminine shield

in simple and valiant confession of my defeat.

. . . . . .

Hail! In verses I make to you my delicate obeisance.)

now stands, glorious and immortal, among the most prominent of them:

> Alfonsina Storni quedaba de este modo incorporada a las glorias nacionales argentinas como lo que es: una de las más inspiradas poetisas de lengua española, y la mayor, sin duda, de su país.[21]
>
> (Alfonsina Storni was in this manner incorporated with national Argentine splendors, befitting what she is: one of the most inspired poetesses of the Spanish language and, undoubtedly, the greatest of her country.)

The poetic life of Gabriela Mistral became public on December 22, 1914. That evening, she sat in the gallery of the Teatro Municipal de Santiago (The Municipal Theatre of Santiago), and watched another woman, María Letelier del Campo, crowned queen of the *Juegos Florales* (Floral Games) and receive the *Flor Natural* (National Flower) and a gold medal. The man who crowned the queen was the poet Julio Munizaga Ossandón. Proud and satisfied, he presented her to the hushed spectators who did not know that the burning words of the "Sonetos de la muerte" ("Sonnets on Death") had erupted from a heart broken from the knowledge that her lover had committed suicide and that this broken heart belonged to the rural school mistress, Lucila Godoy:

Del nicho helado en que los hombres te pusieron,
te bajaré a la tierra humilde y soleada.

Que he de dormirme en ella los hombres no supieron,
y que hemos de soñar sobre la misma almohada.[22]

(From the frozen niche in which men laid you to rest,
I shall lower you to the lowly and sun-dried earth.
That I must sleep in it, men did not know,
And that we must dream upon the same pillow.)

Although she had used her pseudonym, she was still the timid, reserved Lucila Godoy who feared that she had neither the dignity nor the attire to appear in public. From the gallery, she watched and listened to the *Reina de los Juegos* (Queen of the Games), and later described the scene in verse:

El poeta avanzó hacia la florida
guirnalda de mujeres. Pagano, turbador,
el cerco le envolvió en su aliento de amor.
Se hizo un vasto silencio, y él nombró a la elegida.

Y fué lento hacia el ser melodioso y dilecto;
tomó su mano como si tomara una flor.
(En la diestra del bardo alguien notó un temblor . . .)
La mostró con orgullo, como un verso perfecto.

Cual un verso exquisito la mostró satisfecho,
esbelta como un ala, suave como un alcor.
Afuera, de la noche horadaron el pecho

tres estrellas fugaces, con rápidas saetas.
Yo recibí temblando el signo anunciador,
y suspiré: "¡ya tienen su Reina los poetas!"[23]

(The poet advanced toward the flowery

garland of women. Outsider, intruder,
the circle enveloped him in its breath of love.
A deep silence ensued, and he named the chosen one.

And he went slowly toward the melodious, lovely creature;
he took her hand as he would a flower.
[In the right hand of the bard, a tremor was noted . . .]
With pride he showed her, as a perfect verse.

As an exquisite verse, he showed her, gratified,
slender as a wing, soft as a dune.
Outside, there pierced the night's bosom

three scintillating stars, with rapid darts.
Trembling, I received the herald sign,
and I sighed: "Now the poets have their Queen!")

Yes, the poets now had their queen, a queen who had loved and lost and who would carry to eternity and bequeath to posterity the "sombra amada" (beloved spirit) whom she had laid to rest "con una dulcedumbre de madre para el hijo dormido"[24] (with the tenderness of a mother for her sleeping child).

The vigorous voice of this queen from the valley of Elqui was heard at a propitious moment. A bitter experience, hurled at the universe in anguished cries, was transformed into the desired change of esthetics. It was the impetus which she, too, had been seeking:

> He querido hacer una poesía escolar nueva, porque la que hay en boga no me satisface: una poesía escolar que no por ser escolar deje de ser poesía, que lo sea, y más delicada que cualquier otra, más honda, más impregnada

de cosas de corazón, más estremecida de soplo de alma . . .[25]

(I have wished to compose a new scholarly poetry, because that which is in vogue does not satisfy me: a scholarly poetry which, because it is scholarly, does not cease to be poetry. Let it be poetry, and more delicate than any other, more profound, more impregnated with the things of the heart, trembling more with the breath of the soul . . .)

Hers is a talent which must be studied apart, for as Matilde Ladrón de Guevara puts it: "Su tremenda soledad interior era su más hondo poema"[26] (Her tremendous interior solitude was her most profound poem). Alfonso Reyes affirms: "La serenidad de Gabriela está hecha de terremotos interiores, y de aquí que sea más madura . . . ¿Qué latido de nuestra América no ha pasado por su corazón?"[27] (The serenity of Gabriela is made of interior earthquakes, and hence is it more mature . . . What heartbeat of our America has not pulsated through her heart?). Yet, the fact that she lived in time and space and made use of the rhymes and meters at her disposal cannot be overlooked. With natural talent alone she could not have arrived at that which Alfonso Reyes calls "un índice sumo del pensamiento y del sentimiento americanos"[28] (the highest index of American thought and sentiment). The observation of Díez Echarri and Roca Franquesa should be considered here:

Hay muchos más elementos modernistas en la gran poetisa que los que vulgarmente se dice, y desde luego, nos atrevemos a afirmarlo, su obra está infinitamente más vinculada al movimiento rubeniano de última hora que a las tendencias subsiguientes. Del dada, del surrealismo, del ultra, nada o muy poco llegó a *Desolación,* el libro más representativo de la Mistral. Lo que sucede es que nos hemos empeñado en ver sólo del modernismo la primera fase, la de los cisnes y princesas, y esta limitación nos ha impedido establecer nexos, por otra parte bien patentes. La Mistral, luego habremos de verlo, se benefició por lo pronto de toda la métrica modernista, de la que no supo o no quiso desprenderse, y en cambio, no utilizó, o sólo utilizó muy moderadamente, los recursos métricos y estilísticos de las poéticas posteriores.[29]

(There are many more elements of Modernism in the great poetess than one ordinarily observes, and at once, we dare to affirm that her work is more infinitely linked to the last phase of the Rubén Darío movement than to subsequent tendencies. Little or nothing of Dada, Surrealism, or Ultra reached *Desolation,* Mistral's most representative book. What happens is that we have persisted in seeing only the first phase of Modernism, that of swans and princesses, and this limitation has hindered us from establishing bonds that are otherwise quite manifest. Mistral, as we shall see later, profited meanwhile from all the Modernist metrical art from which she either could not or would not extricate herself, and on the other hand, she did not utilize, or utilized only very moderately, the metrical and stylistic resources of later poetics.)

She had admired Rubén Darío and he, in turn, had admired her. He had published some of her poetic and prose compositions, accompanied by special praise. The Modernist figure however who satisfied the yearning of her spirit was Amado

Nervo:[30] "Le hallo a usted, Amado Nervo, en cada día y en cada llanto mío. Con sus versos en los labios fuí yo hacia el amor; ellos me ayudaron a querer, y cuando se fué el amor, ellos también me ayudaron a sollozar 'de modo sosegado y acerbo' "[31] (I find you, Amado Nervo, in every day and in every cry of mine. With your verses on my lips, I went toward love; they helped me to love, and when love was gone, they also helped me to sob "in a quiet but cruel manner").

The spirit of Gabriela Mistral was molded from love and sorrow. Love begot sorrow and sorrow begot love. She understood the purifying quality of love and knew the difference between love and an amorous adventure: ". . . guarde los jugos de su corazón para uno o dos grandes amores que le beban la vida. No se desmenuce en aventuras; cuando se dé, dése bien. . . . un grande amor es una cumbre ardida de sol; las esencias más intensas y terribles de la vida se beben en él. El que quiso así, 'no pasó en vano por los caminos de los hombres' " (. . . guard the affections of your heart for one or two great loves which may drain your life. Do not destroy yourself in adventures; when you give yourself, give well. . . . A great love is a peak burnt by the sun; the most intense and the most terrible essences of life are drunk in it. He who has so loved, "has not passed in vain along the roads of men"). She continues her counsel with a severe warning: "Hay algo peor que la mujer impura y es la insípida. Húyala"[32] (There is something worse than an impure woman, and it is the insipid one. Flee her).

Her tremendous capacity for love had no room for bitterness. When love wounded her, she cried: "Amo amor" (I love love). When it destroyed itself, she pleaded: "¿Que fue cruel? Olvidas, Señor, que le quería, / que él sabía suya la entraña que llagaba"[33] (That he was cruel? You forget, O Lord, that I loved him, / and that he knew that the heart he was wounding belonged to him). When it denied her a child, she embraced the children of the world and raised the state of motherhood to a dignity bordering on that of a sacrament:

Apacenté los hijos ajenos, colmé el troje
con los trigos divinos, y solo de Ti espero, . . .[34]

(I have fed the children of others; I have heaped up the granary with divine crops, and I hope only from You, . . .)

> Como los vasos que las mujeres ponen para recoger el rocío de la noche, pongo yo mi pecho ante Dios; le doy un nombre nuevo, le llamo el Henchidor, y le pido el licor de la vida, abundoso. Aquél llegará buscándolo con sed.[35]
>
> (Like the vases which the women set in order to gather the night's dew, so do I place my breast before God; I give Him a new name; I call Him the Filler, and I beg of Him the liquor of life in abundance. That one will come looking for it with thirst.)

Her invincible courage enabled her to surmount profound and repeated sorrows and to translate them into sublime expressions of beauty until she became another valiant woman, the "mujer fuerte" whom she sought and admired: "¡y aun te sigo en los surcos la sombra con mi canto!"[36] (and in the furrows I still follow your spirit with my song!). Indeed, as she herself put it in her tribute to "la maestra señorita Brígida Walker" (The School Mistress Miss Brigid Walker):

Esta alma de mujer, viril y delicada,
dulce en la gravedad, severa en el amor,

es una encina espléndida de sombra perfumada,
por cuyos brazos rudos trepara un mirto en flor.

. . . . . .
de tanto dar servicio, y tanto dar amor,

todo tu leño heroico se ha vuelto, encina, santo.
Se te ha hecho en la fronda inmortal la belleza,
¡y pasará el otoño sin tocar tu verdor![37]

(This soul of woman, virile and delicate,
gentle in gravity, severe in love,
is a splendid oak of perfumed shade,
through whose rude arms a blossoming myrtle would creep.

. . . . . .
from so much service-giving and so much love-giving,

all your heroic timber has become, Oak, saintly.
In your immortal foliage you have fashioned beauty,
and autumn will pass without touching your verdure!)

The autumn of life for this valiant woman came on January 10, 1957, in Hempstead Hospital, Long Island, New York. The springtime of her spirit continues to blossom in fragrant verdure, for love is eternal, and Gabriela Mistral lived and died in and for love.

2. Mysticism applied to Gabriela Mistral

When death came to Gabriela Mistral, she had reached cosmopolitan stature.[38] Apart from the renown accorded her through the Nobel Prize, Chile had honored her with many diplomatic positions. She was named *Consul Vitalicio por ley de la República* (Consul for Life by Law of the Republic). In Italy, Spain, Portugal, Latin America, and the United States, she became the symbol of her country and the pride of her people. Federico de Onís refers to her as "la excelsa mujer chilena, en la que he visto siempre la más viva personificación de América"[39] (The sublime Chilean woman in whom I have always seen the most vivid personification of America).

New York mourned her loss, then generously returned her body to Chile who received it with mingled awe and sorrow. Newspapers acclaimed her "beata" (blessed one), and an enthusiastic group spoke of a move toward the process of her canonization.[40] Even while she was still alive, works were published which attributed to the Chilean woman concepts of mysticism. In 1933, Virgilio Figueroa wrote *La divina Gabriela,* published in Santiago, Chile. In 1941, Mariano Latorre, in his *La literatura chilena,* devoted a section to "Coquimbo o el misticismo en la poesía chilena" ("Coquimbo or Mysticism in Chilean Poetry"). Here, he refutes "Alone's" thesis that Gabriela Mistral's mystical tendencies are derived from the Bible and attempts to prove that they stem from her environment.[41]

In 1956, Benjamín Carrión compiled a series of eight meditations and published them under the title "Santa Gabriela Mistral." In the first of these meditations, "En el principio fue el dolor" ("In the Beginning There Was Sorrow"), he compares the suffering of Gabriela to the stigmata of Saint Francis of Assisi:

> El sagrado estigma de Gabriela fue el de la maternidad de los hijos de los otros. Pero es tan encarnado, jubiloso y doloroso a la vez el paso por la maternidad carnal,

contado por ella en sus "Poemas de la madres," que solamente el milagro de la transubstanciación pudo dar logros de hondura y ternura como este:

> Por el niño dormido que llevo,
> mi paso se ha vuelto sigiloso,
> y es religioso todo mi corazón
> desde que llevo el misterio.[42]

(The sacred stigmata of Gabriela was that of mothering the children of others. But so incarnate, jubilant, and at the same time, painful is the passage through carnal motherhood related by her in her "Poems for Mothers," that only the miracle of transubstantiation could give rise to depth and tenderness such as this:

> Because of the sleeping child I carry,
> my step has become reserved,
> and religious is all my heart
> since I carry the mystery.)

His second meditation dwells on "La buena pastora" ("The Good Shepherdess"). He qualifies it as "el segundo estigma maravilloso: ser la apacentadora de los corderillos de Dios, de los hijos ajenos. Ser la maestra"[43] (the second marvelous stigmata: to be the shepherdess of the little lambs of God, of the children of others. To be the teacher). In the following six, he continues to laud the woman, the mother, the teacher, and the poet, as he extols the sanctifying virtues which made her holy.

In April of 1956, an article appeared in *Revista Hispánica Moderna* in which Concha Zardoya, Tulane University of Louisiana, classified *Desolación* as "meditatio mortis" (meditation on death), and affirmed that the Chilean poetess here "casi llega a una culminación mística"[44] (almost reaches a mystical culmination).

After her death, this mystical enthusiasm became even more vehement. Julio Saavedra Molina studied and analyzed this facet of Gabriela's personality. In his "Prólogo" to her *Poesías completas* (Complete Poetry), he states that her mysticism emerges from her contemplation of the problem of good and evil, as well as from her contemplation of the mystery of love and death, as she portrays in her sonnet "El pensador de Rodin" ("The Thinker of Rodin"):

Con el mentón caído sobre la mano ruda,
el Pensador se acuerda que es carne de la huesa,
carne fatal, delante del destino desnuda,
carne que odia la muerte, y tembló de belleza.[45]

(With his chin fallen over his rough hand,
the Thinker remembers that he is flesh for the grave,
fatal flesh, before naked destiny.
flesh which despises death, and he trembled with beauty.)

Hers is another "sentimiento trágico de la vida" (tragic sentiment of life), and the spiritual disposition of the enlightened poet who feels that he is in communication with supernatural beings. The true mystic, however, seeks union with God, and to this end he directs all his conduct and all his energies. It is his constant preoccupation.[46] With Gabriela Mistral, it is the result of a momentary crisis; a recourse to the Supreme Power to demand surcease from pain:

> Tal misticismo no es, al menos en sus poemas, una disposición permanente ni la etapa última de una evolución espiritual en que un alma se instala en Dios para

arrobarse en él y gozarlo; sino que es la crisis momentánea de un estado de desesperación, en que la poetisa . . . recurre a Dios, al poder sobrenatural, cuando siente que no hay poder humano que pueda satisfacer sus anhelos. Dios viene siempre a nuestros labios en el extremo dolor; . . . Nadie ha llamado místico a Rubén Darío, sino pagano; sin embargo, al fin de sus días, en la extrema congoja de su experiencia del vivir consciente, no vió otra esperanza de salud para su sed de vida que confiar en Dios.[47]

(Such mysticism is not, at least in her poems, a permanent disposition, nor is it the last state of a spiritual evolution in which a soul is immersed in God to be enraptured by Him and find delight in Him; but it is a momentary crisis of a state of desperation, in which the poetess . . . has recourse to God, to a supernatural power when she feels that there is no human power that can satisfy her yearnings. God always comes to our lips in extreme sorrow; . . . No one has called Rubén Darío a mystic, but a pagan; nevertheless, at the end of his days, in the last agony of his experience of conscious living, he saw no other hope of salvation for his thirst for life than to confide in God.)

He concludes, therefore, that mysticism in Gabriela Mistral is something more human and more comprehensible than "el estado de gracia perenne a que no podemos aspirar los mortales corrientes y molientes"[48] (the state of perennial grace to which we ordinary and weak mortals cannot aspire). For this reason, he feels closer to her than to the old mystical poets, and more impressed with her plaintive verses. Hence he falls on the knees of his soul and accompanies Gabriela with tear-filled eyes when he hears her pray the "Padre nuestro" ("Our Father").

Cora Santandreu, in her detailed and penetrating study, "Aspectos del estilo en la poesía de Gabriela Mistral" ("Aspects of Style in the Poetry of Gabriela Mistral"), tosses "mística" and "misticismo" (mystic and mysticism) around so that all other aspects pale in its blinding light:

> Gabriela Mistral, por sobre los otros aspectos de su personalidad, es una mística. Misticismo que emerge del problema de la vida frente al problema de la muerte. Es la tragedia que atormenta su espíritu.
>
> De este conflicto interior determinado por lo que quiso ser y no logró ser—entraña de su tragedia—surge el cálido misticismo de este espíritu atormentado, patente en *Desolación*. Renunciamiento. Austeridad. Honda raigambre y fuerte tradición española. Evocación de Santa Teresa de Avila. Pero el misticismo de Gabriela se sublima en amor universal que irradia sobre las cosas y los seres de su mundo inmediato. Misticismo impregnado de una mansa filosofía oriental (bien hindú, bien hebraica) de preferencia hacia los seres dolientes—Cristo, la madre desamparada, la maestra rural y hacia los débiles. . . . Misticismo que se traduce también en éxtasis, en arrobamiento panteísta ante el perenne milagro de la naturaleza para quien no escatima sus más fervorosos cantos. Misticismo que va envolviendo a la poetisa como "gajos de niebla" y tornándose más sutil e incorpóreo a medida que avanza el proceso de desrealización, que hemos captado a través de un minucioso análisis de *Tala* y de *Lagar;* fenómeno tal vez el más apasionado de los surgidos en este breve ensayo de estilística, y que por lo tanto merece capítulo especial.[49]

(Gabriela Mistral, above the other aspects of her personality, is a mystic. Mysticism which emerges from the problem of life face to face with the problem of death. It is the tragedy that torments her spirit.

From this interior conflict, determined by that which she wished to be and did not succeed in being—the entrail of her tragedy—there arises the ardent mysticism of this tormented spirit, manifest in *Desolation*. Surrender. Austerity. Deep-rooted and strong Spanish tradition. Evocation of Saint Teresa of Avila. But the mysticism of Gabriela Mistral is sublimated in universal love which radiates over the things and creatures of her immediate world. Mysticism impregnated with a gentle oriental philosophy [Hindu as well as Hebrew], with preference for sorrowing creatures—Christ, the abandoned mother, the rural school mistress, and the weak.... Mysticism which is also translated into ecstasy, in pantheistic rapture before the perennial miracle of nature for which she does not lessen her most fervent songs. Mysticism which envelops the poetess as a spray of mist and becomes more subtle and incorporate as the process of unreality advances, which we captured during a minute analysis of *Felling of Trees* and of *Wine Press;* the most impassioned phenomenon, perhaps, of those raised in this brief essay of stylistics, and for that reason, it deserves a special chapter.)

The nature of the mysticism to which Cora Santandreu refers should be carefully considered. She states that it is the emergence of the problem of life before the problem of death; that it is the tragedy that torments her spirit; that it arises from an interior conflict between that which she desired to be and that to which she did not arrive at being; that it is a mysticism impregnated with oriental philosophy, as intensely Hindu as Hebrew, with an inclination toward weak and suffering creatures, among them, Christ; that it is transformed into ecstasy of pantheistic rapture before the perennial miracle of nature.

Can this be an evocation of Saint Teresa of Avila? Can it recall that "living flame of love," Saint John of the Cross? Cora Santandreu sees a comparison and quotes Américo Castro to substantiate her opinion: "Lo místico nos pone en contacto con almas anhelosas y torturadas, que tras un áspero peregrinar a través de la tiniebla y el aniquilamiento obtiene reposo de claridades emotivas. El estilo de Santa Teresa o en Juan de la Cruz llega a proyectarse sobre irradiantes perspectivas" (*Santa Teresa de Jesús y otros ensayos,* Ed. Historia Nueva, 1929)[50] (Mysticism brings us into contact with desirous and tortured souls who, after arduous journeying through darkness and annihilation, obtain the repose of emotive clarities. The style of Saint Teresa or that of John of the Cross succeeds in projecting itself over radiant perspectives. *Saint Teresa of Jesus and Other Essays,* Ed. Historia Nueva, 1929).

"Fenomeno semejante observamos en Gabriela" (A similar phenomenon we observe in Gabriela), Cora Santandreu continues, and then, unwittingly, she proceeds to draw the specific difference between Gabriela Mistral and the true mystics: "A través del dolor y de la angustia trocados en misticismo Gabriela se encuentra a sí misma para el arte y para la vida"[51] (Through sorrow and anguish, transformed into mysticism, Gabriela finds herself for art and for life).

Gabriela finds herself; the mystics find God. The mystics die to themselves. "Vivo sin vivir en mí, que muero porque no muero"[52] (I live without living in me, for I die because I do not die), cries Saint John of the Cross. They lose themselves in order to find Him:

> Pues ya si en el ejido
> de hoy más no fuere vista ni hallada,
> diréis que me he perdido,
> que andando enamorada,
> me hice perdidiza, y fuí ganada.[53]
>
> (For, now, if on the common land,
> from this day forth, I am neither seen nor found,
> you will say that I have lost myself,
> that going about lovesick,
> I became lost, and was won.)

It is the fundamental dissimilarity, pointed out by Sister John Berchmans, O.P., between St. Francis's mystic apprehension of God and Gabriela's egotistical one.[54] But Cora Santandreu, in her loyalty to her Chilean compatriot, continues to see the similarity: "No obstante, ningún otro poeta de la lengua española—acaso se le aproxime la mística Santa Teresa de Jesús—ha expresado sus vivencias con más ardor, con más quemantes imágenes. Y para ello su lenguaje se torna térmico, dinámico, impresionista"[55] (Nevertheless, no other poet of the Spanish language—perhaps the mystic Saint Teresa of Avila approaches her—has expressed her experiences with more ardor, with more burning images. And for this reason, her language becomes thermic, dynamic, impressionistic). Her final tribute to the great poetess is a boast of affinity: ". . . nos enseñó a romper el tabú de las palabras, y a aventar la paja para coger el 'grano de oro' de la verdad. Lección que tenemos muy presente las mujeres de Chile"[56] (. . . she taught us to break the taboo of words, and to winnow the chaff in order to find the golden kernel of truth; a lesson which we Chilean women hold quite present).

Enrique Espinoza envisions Gabriela Mistral, as the "Mujer del Viejo Testamento" (The woman of the Old Testament), and declares that not since Sor Juana Inés de la Cruz, that seventeenth-century Mexican genius, has Latin American letters produced a poet of such manifest mysticism, in the classical meaning of the word. He admits, however, that a comparison between them would prove to be idle theorizing: "Ocioso resulta establecer la distancia que media entre la formación erudita de la humilde monja de México y el instinto maravilloso de la soberbia maestra chilena"[57] (Fruitless it is to establish the distance which lies between the erudite formation of the humble Mexican nun and the marvelous instinct of the superb Chilean school mistress).

Espinoza records that Gabriela cried bitterly when she learned of Figueroa's publication in Santiago of *La divina Gabriela.* He, teasing, reminded her of Lugones' verse for D'Annunzio: "el divino Gabriele del ojo herido" (the divine Gabriele with the injured eye). She retaliated with: "Es un solo verso contra todo un libro que me pone en ridículo"[58] (It is a single verse against an entire book which places me in ridicule). A mystic, however, does not weep bitterly when he is placed in a ridiculous situation. He welcomes the occasion to punish his pride; to become aware of his nothingness and God's allness. It is the summary of the doctrine of San Juan de la Cruz: "nada—Todo" (nothing—All).

The Cuban, Dulce María Loynaz, recalls that Gabriela Mistral had a way of losing contact with her surroundings, "que miraba como siempre un punto lejano" (that, as always, she kept her gaze fixed on a distant point). Then, after returning to reality, to answer a question or to pass a judgment, "la mirada se le perdió de nuevo en lejanías, donde ya no me fue posible alcanzarla" (her glance was again lost in the far-away, where it was no longer possible for me to reach her). This, of course, has no necessary connection with mysticism, but it is a common factor with creative artists. She relates that Gabriela treasured friendships, experiences, and affections. This warmth may well be the mark of a great lover of God, for the salvation of man is through love, but "y también antipatías y rencores"[59] (and also antipathies and rancors) cannot be, for it is contrary to the command of Christ: "A new commandment I give unto you: That you love one another; as I have loved you, that you also love one another."[60]

Other critics have alluded to this ambivalence in Gabriela's personality. Manuel Pedro González observes: "Under that serene, apparently impassible and imperturable exterior palpitated a tremendously passionate soul and an ardent temperament capable of achieving the mystic ecstasy in human or divine love as well as violent dislikes and antipathies."[61]

Julio Saavedra Molina remembers her "sátira mordaz, acentuada por una fila de blancos dientes, que sonreían con desdén, en rima con sus ojos claros" (bitter satire, accentuated by a line of white teeth, which smiled with disdain, in rhyme with her bright eyes). He adds: "Porque Gabriela, cuando se cree ofendida, burlada o menospreciada, sabe también odiar y dar la vuelta, o el vuelto, como en Chile decimos. Lo que por lo demás es archihumano"[62] (For Gabriela, when she believes herself offended, mocked, or despised, also knows how to hate and give the cold shoulder, or "the turn," as we say in Chile. This for the rest of men is quite human). The implication seems to be that the human reaction is not expected of Gabriela Mistral. Yet, the urgency of her need to avert ridicule when she heard of the book *Santa Gabriela Mistral* caused her to cable Benjamín Carrión in Quito and beg him to change the title, "evitándome comentarios malintencionados y burlescos"[63] (preserving me from evil-intentioned and burlesque commentaries).

Luis Amador Sánchez comments: "Desde esta exaltación del sentido carnal del amor, con fluidez, pasa la poetisa chilena a su misticismo que corre por su obra poética, como la sangre en las venas. Dios está en el total panorama de su poesía, como lo están en su paisaje, las fuentes y los ríos"[64] (From this sublimation of the carnal perception of love, the Chilean poetess passes, with fluidity, to her mysticism, which flows through her poetic work as blood courses through the veins. God is in the whole panorama of her poetry, as the fountains and rivers are in her landscape).

Dámaso Alonso pays poetic homage to her and places emphasis on the idea of "song out of sorrow":

Maestrita de un pueblo dormido,
y el amor, amarillo jaguar . . .
Dios te hirió, porque quiso tu canto,
Gabriela Mistral.

Riberas de Chile, oh mujer, tierna roca,
Dios te hería, te hería, como un hosco mar.
Rezumabas de amor y de pena . . . Eso es todo.
Y nosotros te amamos, Gabriela Mistral.[65]

(Little teacher of a town asleep,
and love, a jaguar yellow . . .
God wounded you, because He desired your song,
Gabriela Mistral.

Shores of Chile, O woman, tender rock,
God wounded you, wounded you, like a tempestuous sea.
You oozed love and pain . . . That is all.

And we love you, Gabriela Mistral.)

"Pena y amor" (Pain and love) may imply the idea of purification as a preparation for union with God. Enrique Lihn's elegy seems to indicate as much:

> Con ojos que sus ojos de polvo le cegaron
> todo lo ve en su Dios que lo ve todo.
> . . . . . .
> Silencio ahora guarda feliz, como de niño;
> dirán que está en la Gloria.[66]
>
> (With eyes, for her eyes with dust were blinded,
> she sees all in her God who sees all.
> . . . . . .
> Silence now she keeps, happy, as when a child;
> they will say that she has entered into Glory.)

That Gabriela Mistral now beholds the Glory of God is the firm belief of many. That the Rector of the University of Chile subscribes to this creed is evidenced in the final remark of his funeral oration:

> Hoy al despedir su cuerpo la llamaremos, porque era sabia en la virtud, en el amor y en la belleza: Gabriela Mistral, Doctora angélica.[67]
> (Today, while bidding farewell to her body, we shall call her, because she was wise in virtue, in love, and in beauty: Gabriela Mistral, Angelic Doctor.)

That mysticism[68] can be traced in the works of Gabriela Mistral, no thoughtful reader can deny. An analysis of her poetry and of her "La oración de la maestra" ("Prayer of a Teacher") reveals the potencies of her latent capacity for those extraordinary movements which intervene in the mystical life.

In "La oración de la maestra," she stands before her God in full realization of her unworthiness to assume the title and responsibility which He, the greatest of teachers, assumed here on earth:

> ¡Señor! Tú que enseñaste, perdona que yo enseñe; que lleve el nombre de maestra, que Tú llevaste por la Tierra.[69]
>
> (Lord! You who taught, forgive me for daring to teach; for daring to bear the name of teacher, which You bore here on earth.)

It is her "Domine, non sum dignus" (Lord, I am not worthy). She begs for a singular love for her school that nothing may rob it of her tenderness; she pleads to be delivered from the impure desire for justice that torments her when her pupils wound her; she prays that misunderstanding may not cause her sorrow, nor that forgetfulness on the part of others sadden her. She desires to be more mother than true mothers to those who are not flesh of her flesh. She asks to make of one of her little ones her perfect verse, and that her perfect melody be that in which His image is engraved, for the time when her lips can no longer sing. She longs to see His Gospel practiced in her day, so that for its sake, she may never renounce her constant warfare. She seeks strength, despite her weak femininity, to despise all power that is not legitimate, all possession that is not His Will governing her life.

Then, she changes His title. She no longer calls Him

"Señor" (Lord) but "Amigo" (Friend). She does not call him "Amado" (Beloved), as she begs that He accompany and sustain her when she will have none but Him at her side. She reminds Him that when her doctrine is most chaste and her truth most scorching, the worldly-wise will desert her. Then, He must press her to His Heart—that Heart which had its share of loneliness and abandon. How perfect is the offering of her magisterial office when she exclaims: "Yo no buscaré sino en tu mirada la dulzura de las aprobaciones"[70] (Only in your glance shall I seek the sweetness of approval).

She prays for simplicity and depth; to be delivered from complexity and banality in her daily lesson; she begs for suavity in punishing so that she may remember to love while she is chastising. As a final petition, she asks to be taught the lesson that to teach and to love intensely here on earth is to have but one recompense:

> Y, por fin, recuérdame desde la palidez del lienzo de Velázquez, que enseñar y amar intensamente sobre la Tierra es llegar al último día con el lanzazo de Longinos en el costado ardiente de amor.[71]
>
> (And, finally, from the paleness of the canvas of Velázquez, remind me that to teach and to love intensely here on earth is to arrive on the last day with the sword of Longinus in a side ardent with love.)

The magic of the brush of the great master Velázquez has infused contemplation into the minds of other artists endowed with a profound religious sense. Among these, there towers one who "beneath all his ideas and his doubts feels the presence of God in his life, of a God who is the Christian, one and triune, with the three persons, with the virgin maternity of Mary, with all the content of the Catholic liturgy; a God represented and made visible in the images, above all in the bleeding Spanish Christs that he so loved, and more than them all, in the Christ of Velázquez that moved him to genuine and pious devotion."[72] The towering figure is Miguel de Unamuno who, in his "tragic sense of life and agony of Christianity," has bequeathed to posterity his magnificent meditation on his dead Christ:

¿En qué piensas Tú, muerto, Cristo mío?
¿Por qué ese velo de cerrada noche
de tu abundosa cabellera negra
de nazareno cae sobre tu frente?
. . . . . .
Que eres, Cristo, el único
Hombre que sucumbió de pleno grado,
triunfador de la muerte, que a la vida
por Ti quedó encumbrada.[73]

(What are You thinking about, dead, O my Christ?
Why does that veil of dark night
of your abundant black hair
of a Nazarite fall over your countenance?
. . . . . .
For You are, O Christ, the only
Man who died willingly,
Victor over death, which to life
by You was raised.)

Unamuno, like Gabriela, knows the pangs of a tortured spirit and seeks his consolation in identifying his pain with that of Christ:

De pie y con los brazos bien abiertos
y extendida la diestra a no secarse,
haznos cruzar la vida pedregosa
—repecho de Calvario—sostenidos
del deber por los clavos, y muramos
de pie, cual Tú, y abiertos bien de brazos,
y como Tú, subamos a la gloria
de pie, para que Dios de pie nos hable
y con los brazos extendidos.

(Standing and with arms wide-open
and the right hand extended that it may not dry up,
make us cross the rugged way of life
—the steep hill of Calvary—supported
by the nails of duty, and let us die
standing, like You, and with arms wide-open,
and like You, let us rise to glory
standing, in order that God, standing, may speak to us
and with arms extended.)

His final petition reveals his anxiety to "sobrevivirse" (his yearning for eternity):

Me entre en el claro día que no acaba,
fijos mis ojos de tu blanco cuerpo,
Hijo del Hombre, Humanidad completa,
en la increada luz que nunca muere;
mis ojos fijos en tus ojos, Cristo,
mi mirada anegada en Ti, Señor![74]

(May I enter into the bright day that never ends,
my eyes fixed on your white body,
Son of Man, complete Humanity,

on the uncreated light that never dies;
my eyes fixed on your eyes, O Christ,
my gaze immersed in You, O Lord!)

Thus are Unamuno the philosopher and Mistral the teacher linked together as great poets in the Catholic tradition. In this same tradition, hand in hand with suffering, is Mistral's high esteem for humility in a teacher. So highly did she esteem this virtue that she denounced vanity as a teacher's greatest obstacle to perfection: "La vanidad es el peor vicio de una maestra, porque la que se cree perfecta, se ha cerrado, en verdad, a todos los caminos hacia la perfección"[75] (Vanity is the worst vice in a teacher, because she who believes herself perfect has, in truth, cut herself off from all paths to perfection).

Her poems directed to God, however, are more the outpouring of a tormented soul than the mystic's expression of love. In "Al oído del Cristo" ("In the Ear of Christ"), she speaks to Christ, recalls His agony, and complains about the condition of the people:

Cristo, el de las carnes en gajos abiertas;
Cristo, el de las venas vaciadas en ríos:
estas pobres gentes del siglo están muertas
de una laxitud, de un miedo, de un frío![76]

(Christ, You with your flesh wide-open in ridges;
Christ, You with your veins emptied in rivers:
these poor people of the century are dead
with laxity, with fear, with cold!)

She deplores their lack of love and compassion for His sufferings and pleads for a change in their phlegmatic lassitude. She does not, however, try to compensate for their indifference by her own passionate devotion to Him, as does the mystic author[77] of the sonnet to Christ Crucified:

Muévesme al tu amor en tal manera
que, aunque no hubiera cielo, yo te amara,
y, aunque no hubiera infierno, te temiera.

No me tienes que dar porque te quiera;
que, aunque cuanto espero no esperara,
lo mismo que te quiero te quisiera.[78]

(You draw me to your love in such a manner
that, although there were no heaven, I would love You,
and, although there were no hell, I would fear You.

You need give me no reason for loving You;
for, although all I hope for I could not hope for,
the same as I love You now, would I love You then.)

In "Viernes santo" ("Good Friday"), Gabriela does compassionate Jesus, but again she lacks the ardor of the lover who seeks identification with the Beloved. Although she "hates her bread, her verse, her joy, because Jesus is suffering," the intensity of personal love is wanting. A similar sentiment is expressed in "Canto del justo" ("Song of the Just One"):

¡Yo cantaré cuando
te hayan desclavado![79]

(I shall sing when
they have drawn the nails out of You!)

In her "Credo," she believes in her heart which reclines on the breast of a God "terrible y fuerte" (terrible and strong). The mystic, however, sings of reclining "sobre los dulces brazos del Amado" (on the sweet arms of the Beloved). It is the difference between the "Old Law" and the "New Law," between fear and love:

Quedéme y olvidéme,
el rostro recliné sobre el Amado.
Cesó todo, y dejéme,
dejando mi cuidado
entre las azucenas olvidado.[80]

(There I remained, forgetful,
my face reclining on the Beloved.
All ceased, and I surrendered,
leaving my cares
among the lilies forgotten.)

In "El Dios triste" ("The Sad God"), there is an identification of Divinity with Nature, as the poetess searches for "el rostro de Dios" (the face of God) in the "vejez amarilla de otoño" (the yellow old age of autumn):

Y en esta tarde lenta como una hebra de llanto
por la alameda de oro y de rojez yo siento
un Dios de otoño, un Dios sin ardor y sin canto
¡Y lo conozco triste, lleno de desaliento![81]

(And in this afternoon, lingering like a vein of weeping,
through the poplar grove, gold and red, I sense
a God of autumn, a God without ardor, without song.
And I know him sad, completely exhausted!)

Her "Himno cotidiano" ("Daily Hymn") is a true Christian prayer of petition for joy, for personal betterment, faith, and ardor, but not a cry of desire for love, except for:

> . . . la suma de bondad,
> de actividades y de amor
> que a cada ser se manda dar:
> suma de esencias a la flor
> y de albas nubes a la mar.[82]
>
> (. . . the height of excellence,
> of activities and of love
> which must be given to each being:
> the sum of perfumes to the flower
> and of white clouds to the sea.)

In "Éxtasis" ("Ecstasy"), as in "Al oído del Cristo" and "Viernes Santo," Cora Santandreu sees the mysticism of one who "se dirige a Él (Dios) como pudiera hablarle al Amado" (speaks to Him—God—as she would speak to the Beloved). She continues: "Al referirnos a él, no podemos dejar de evocar la silueta de la Doctora de Avila: Santa Teresa de Jesús, para quien Dios es un ser de carne y hueso, como para nuestra poetisa . . ."[83] (In referring to it, we cannot help but evoke the figure of the Doctor of Avila: Saint Teresa of Jesus, for whom God was a being of flesh and blood, as He is for our poetess . . .). That both women love intensely is true. The difference, however, lies in the object of their love. Saint Teresa speaks to God as her Divine Lover; Gabriela speaks to Him about her human lover. The ecstasy of the mystic is that of being lost in the rapture of love; the ecstasy of Gabriela is the agony of rupture with the man she loves:

Me miró, nos miramos en silencio
mucho tiempo, clavadas,
como en la muerte, las pupilas. Todo
el estupor que blanquea las caras
en la agonía, albeaba nuestros rostros.
¡Tras de ese instante, ya no resta nada![84]

(He looked at me; in silence, we looked at each other,
fixed for a long time, as in death,
were our eyes. All
the stupor that blanches faces
in an agony whitened our faces.
After that instant, nothing now remains!)

The same torment recurs in "Tribulación" ("Tribulation") and in "Nocturno" ("Nocturn"):

Padre Nuestro que estás en los cielos,
¿por qué te has olvidado de mí?
. . . .

Me vendió el que besó mi mejilla;
me negó por la túnica ruin.
. . . .

Ha venido el cansancio infinito
a clavarse en mis ojos al fin:
. . . .[85]

(Our Father who art in heaven,
why have You forsaken me?
. . . .

He who kissed my cheek betrayed me;
he denied me for the ruinous tunic.
. . . . . .

Infinite exhaustion has come
to be fixed in my eyes, at last:
. . . . . .)

In "Los sonetos de la muerte" ("Sonnets on Death") and "Interrogaciones" ("Interrogations"), all the ardor of her love is poured out, not for God, but for the man she loves. Here, she calls God "Amor" (Love) to entice Him to have compassion on her lover who had committed suicide:

Tal el hombre asegura, por error o malicia;
mas yo, que te he gustado, como un vino, Señor,
mientras los otros siguen llamándote Justicia,
¡no te llamaré nunca otra cosa que Amor![86]

(Such does man affirm, through error or malice;
but I, who have tasted You, like a wine, O Lord,
while others keep calling You Justice,
I shall never call You anything but Love!)

If Gabriela Mistral had not been here so preoccupied with her "puñado de huesos" (handful of bones), she might have channelled the warmth, the impulses, the love of her heart through the ineffably sweet experience of knowing Christ in her soul, the experience that carries the initiate in the mystical life into the consciousness of immersion, of self-loss in the Eternal. But Gabriela did not know this experience, for to share the love of God calls for a more searching self-surrender. Love and self-surrender are not the same thing, but they are inseparable things.

Nevertheless, Gabriela Mistral was gifted with a prodigious spiritual potency; she lived an intense interior life. Dulce María Loynaz has perhaps best described the depth of her intensity: "Hablar de Gabriela Mistral es un honor, pero también una aventura que mueve a la defensa, pues no es posible disponerse a hacerlo sin correr los riesgos del que escala una montaña o se adentra en una selva virgen o intenta vadear el Amazonas"[87] (To speak of Gabriela Mistral is an honor, but also an adventure which prompts caution, for it is not possible for one to prepare to do so without running the risks of him who scales a mountain or who penetrates into a virgin forest or who attempts to ford the Amazon).

But the way from intense inwardness to greatness leads through sacrifice. The sacrifice of Gabriela Mistral came in the guise of human love and human death, and these she regarded as an extension of human life into the infinite. Her passion and hunger for love could not be satisfied by the object that awakened them, for that object was ruthlessly snatched from her. Then, she lifted her eyes above the horizon of her particular love to that sphere which extends beyond the visible side of life, to the reverted, invisible side that is called death, and found her fulfillment in universal love. Thus did she become a great woman and a great poet, for penetration into this sphere requires a concentration of all one's senses, a withdrawal which ". . . gives to a work of poetry that primitive swing, that unlimited movement, which is necessary to it; for it must have begun by being too vast in the soul of the poet in order, afterwards, to be great enough in the eyes of other men."[88]

This withdrawal is a psychological phenomenon common to the poetic state and to mystical contemplation. In the mystical experience, as Jacques Maritain explains, the object touched is God, present in and united with the soul of him who contemplates. In the poetic experience, the object touched is the reality of things and the word, the knowledge of which flows from a union of another order with God, the Creator and organizer of nature. Thus, "la poésie est le fruit d'un contact de l'esprit avec la réalité en elle-même ineffable et avec sa source, que nous croyons être Dieu lui-même dans le mouvement d'amour qui le porte à créer des images de sa beauté. Le chant, la poésie sous toutes ses formes, cherchent . . . à libérer une expérience substantielle"[89] (poetry is the fruit of a contact with reality which is in itself ineffable and with its source which we believe to be God Himself in the movement of love which prompts Him to create images of His beauty. Song, poetry in all its forms, seek . . . to liberate a substantial experience). It is consciousness of this truth that caused the poet to exclaim:

> O world invisible, we view thee,
> O world intangible, we touch thee,
> O world unknowable, we know thee,
> Inapprehensible, we clutch thee![90]

In this sense is Gabriela Mistral a mystic, for in the psychological design of her own experience, she dwells in that which Henri Brémond terms "les états mystiques profanes"[91] (profane mystical states). In these states are the poets, artists, and great inventors. While they draw on the same divine source as the true mystics, they do so with different dispositions and according to essentially distinct types of relations to that source:

> Ils sont les uns et les autres des imitateurs de Dieu, mais les uns sont appelés tout particulièrement à augmenter le trésor humain de la beauté et de la science, ils sont

les imitateur du Dieu créateur; les autres sont tout particulièrement appelés à entrer dans le mystère de la Déité elle-même et à faire connaître en ce monde, par quelque image et par quelque ressemblance, la Sainteté de Dieu, à l'imitation de Jésus-Christ, par l'abnégation de soi-même et de tout ce qui est de ce monde. La nature et la grâce ont des ouvriers qualifiés, et qui se portent mutuellement un secours mystérieux, pour l'ascension et la spiritualisation de l'humanité. C'est donc très justement que les uns sont appelés des "créateurs" et les autres des "saints."[92]

(They are all of them imitators of God, but some are particularly called to augment the human treasure of beauty and of science; they are imitators of God the Creator; the others are particularly called to enter into the mystery of the Deity itself and to make known in the world, by some image and by some resemblance, the sanctity of God, through imitation of Jesus Christ, through abnegation of self and of all that is of this world. Nature and grace have qualified workers who mutually render a mysterious assistance for the raising and spiritualization of humanity. It is then quite properly that the former are called "creators" and the latter are called "saints.")

All that has been considered in these pages is by way of introduction and explanation. The thesis must now be verified in terms of the concrete experience of souls who have embarked upon the mystical life and the experience of the soul of Gabriela Mistral, who admitted her defeat:

¡Cielos morados, avergonzados
de mi derrota.

Capitán vivo y envilecido,
nuca pisada, ceño pisado
de mi derrota.
Cuerno cascado de ciervo noble
de mi derrota![93]

(Heavens, purple with shame
of my defeat.
Head, alive and debased,
neck bowed, waist chained
with my defeat.
Horn of noble deer, broken
by my defeat!)

Hence, before examining in detail the personality, religion, and poetry of Gabriela Mistral, we offer the reader a more definite and precise definition of mysticism in its Catholic orthodox connotation, mysticism in other great religions, and mysticism as identified with poetry.

CHAPTER I—FOOTNOTES

1. Juan Gómez Millas, "Oración del Rector de la Universidad de Chile," *Homenaje a Gabriela Mistral, Anales de la Universidad de Chile,* CXV (1957), 8. Since this work is the memorial most frequently used throughout the dissertation, all further references to it will be designated as *Homenaje.*

2. *Loc. cit.*

3. Luke i.48.53.

4. Francis Thompson, "The Hound of Heaven," in *The Works of Francis Thompson,* ed. W. Meynell (New York, 1913), II, 111.

5. *Homenaje,* p. 8.

6. Critics differ in their explanation for Gabriela Mistral's pseudonym. Some claim that "Gabriela" was chosen to honor the Archangel Gabriel, and some claim that it is a tribute to the Italian poet Gabriele D'Annunzio. Some hold that "Mistral" is taken from the violent, cold, and dry northerly wind of southern France, etc., and some hold that it pays tribute to the

Provenzal poet Frédéric Mistral. Two of these critics are quoted here:

Raúl Silva Castro: "Podría, en fin, avanzarse, sin temor de errar demasiado, que la señorita Lucila Godoy Alcayaga en la vida civil, cuando comenzó a usar como seudónimo Gabriela Mistral entendía con ello rendir tributo de admiración a Federico Mistral el autor de *Mireya* (Finally, one could affirm, without fear of grave error, that Miss Lucila Godoy Alcayaga, in civil life, when she began to use Gabriela Mistral as her pseudonym, intended thereby to render tribute of admiration to Frédéric Mistral, author of *Mireya*). See *Producción de Gabriela Mistral de 1912 a 1918* (Santiago, Chile, 1957), p. 10.

Enrique Espinoza: "La mujer con nombre de arcángel y apellido de viento. . . . Este provenía del arcángel Gabriel y del viento Mistral en vez del apellido de quien escribió *Mireya* y del nombre de quien compuso los *Laudi*" (The woman with the name of an archangel and the surname of a wind. . . . These were derived from the Archangel Gabriel and the mistral wind, instead of the surname of him who wrote *Mireya* and the name of him who composed the *Laudi*). See "Gabriela Mistral y el espíritu de la Biblia," *Homenaje*, pp. 99-100.

7. Some biographers give April 6 as the birthday of Gabriela Mistral. According to her birth certificate, she was baptized on April 7, "de un día de edad." This is interpreted by some as meaning "baptized on the same date as her birth," and by others as meaning "baptized on the day after her birth."

8. With Doris Dana's permission, I read on microfilm the unpublished *Lagar II*. The volume includes three significant poems pertaining to her names. The first, "Balada de mi nombre" ("Ballad of My Name"), refers to her baptismal name:

El nombre mío que he perdido
¿dónde vive, dónde prospera?
Nombre de infancia, gota de leche,
rama de mirto tan ligera.
. . . . . .
Llanto mío no conoce
y no la quemó mi salmuera;
cabellos blancos no me ha visto
ni mi boca con acidia
y no me habla si me encuentra.

(Name of mine which I have lost,
Where does it live? Where does it prosper?
Name of infancy, drop of milk,
branch of myrtle so light.
. . . . . .
My weeping it does not know,
and my thirst it has not parched;
my white hairs it has not seen,

nor my mouth with bitterness,
and it does not speak to me if we meet.)

The remaining two, both entitled "Arcángeles" ("Archangels"), confirm Miss Dana's statement that anyone who knew Gabriela Mistral would know that she would never name herself for another poet. She loved the Archangels, Michael, Gabriel, Raphael, and to them she dedicated poems of *Lagar II*. She hails them respectively as "vaina del rayo" (Thunderbolt Scabbard), "mano de Aurora" (Hand of Dawn), "único hombre" (Unparalleled Man). In the concluding four lines of the second of these poems, she skillfully synthesizes the function of each angelical messenger:

El Dragón ya no da la Muerte,
a Tobías la luz fué dada
y las manos de Myriam-María
azoradas entregan la Gracia.

(The Dragon no longer gives Death,
To Tobias light was given,
and the hands of Miriam-Maria,
awed, deliver Grace.)

This is the message which they "cuentan delante del Trono en fuego" (relate before the fiery Throne).

9. ". . . los poetas surgidos después de 1920 ya no están ligados a la generación modernista en forma directa. Estos hombres y mujeres que han producido entre las dos guerras mundiales tienen el sello de una patética desolación y un quebranto moral. Angustia, soledad, son sus notas más frecuentes porque el mundo que se les ofrece no tiene salida posible." Octavio Corvalán, *El Postmodernismo* (New York, 1961), pp. 23-24.

(. . . the poets who appeared after 1920 are no longer directly linked to the Modernist generation. These men and women who produced between the two World Wars bear the stamp of a pathetic desolation and of a crushing morale. Anguish and loneliness are their most frequent characteristics, because the world which is offered to them has no possible way out.)

10. E. Díez Echarri y J. M. Roca Franquesa, *Historia de la literatura española e hispanoamericana* (History of Spanish and Hispanic American Literature) (Madrid, 1960), p. 1349.

11. Gabriela Mistral used these words in reference to herself during the discourse at the banquet given in her honor when, in 1945, she was awarded the Nobel Prize for Literature. See *Les Prix Nobel en 1945* (Nobel Prizes in 1945) (Stockholm, 1947), pp. 61-62.

12. Delmira Agustini, "Lo inefable," *Antología de la poesía española e hispanoamericana* (Anthology of Spanish and Hispanic American Poetry), ed. Federico de Onís (New York, 1961), pp. 916-917.

13. Díez Echarri y Roca Franquesa, p. 1352.

14. *Op. cit.*, p. 1353.
15. Thompson, p. 111.
16. Alfonsina Storni, "La que comprende," *Obra poética completa,* ed. Juan Julián Lastra (Buenos Aires, 1961), p. 232.
17. Storni, "Voy a dormir" ("I Am Going to Sleep"), p. 440.
18. "El mar se ha tragado, en estos últimos años, muchas grandes cosas. Y también criaturas extraordinarias. . . . Una de ellas, la inolvidable Alfonsina Storni." (The sea, in these last years, has swallowed up many wonderful things. And extraordinary creatures also. . . . One of them, the unforgettable Alfonsina Storni.) See Carmen Conde, "Poetisas de lengua española" ("Poetesses of the Spanish Tongue"), *Mundo Hispánico* (The Hispanic World), XIII (1960), 29.
19. Storni, "Epitafio para mi tumba" ("Epitaph for My Tomb"), pp. 292-294.
20. Storni, "Saludo al hombre" (I Greet Man"), p. 290.
21. Díez Echarri y Roca Franquesa, p. 1351.
22. Gabriela Mistral, "Soneto de la muerte" ("Sonnet on Death"), *Poesías completas* (Complete Poetic Works), ed. Margaret Bates with a critical-biographical study by Julio Saavedra Molina and a lyrical remembrance by Dulce María Loynaz (Madrid, 1962), p. 81. All quotations of Gabriela Mistral's poetry, unless otherwise indicated, will be taken from this edition. Further references to the edition will be designated as *Poesías.*
23. Gabriela Mistral, "Como la vió mi espíritu" ("How My Spirit Saw Her"), in Silva Castro, *Producción,* p. 72.
24. "Soneto de la muerte" ("Sonnet on Death"), *Poesías,* p. 81.
25. "Epistolario, Cartas a Eugenio Labarca (1915-1916)" ("Epistolary, Letters to Eugenio Labarca from 1915 to 1916"), *Homenaje,* p. 267.
26. Matilde Ladrón de Guevara, *Gabriela Mistral, rebelde magnífica* (Gabriela Mistral, Magnificent Rebel) (Santiago, Chile, 1957), p. 48.
27. Alfonso Reyes, "Himno a Gabriela" ("Hymn to Gabriela"), *Homenaje,* p. 19.
28. *Loc. cit.*
29. Díez Echarri y Roca Franquesa, p. 1327.
30. That Gabriela Mistral and Amado Nervo were kindred spirits may readily be seen from the evaluation made by Angel Valbuena Briones in "El lugar de Amado Nervo en el Modernismo" ("The Place of Amado Nervo in Modernism"). Here, referring to the portrait of Nervo painted by Julio Ruelas, he states: "La mirada abierta e iluminada nos recuerda la tendencia mística" (The open and radiant glance recalls the mystic tendency). And again: "Hubo siempre en su corazón un anhelo hacia Dios, espantado a veces por el análisis positivista, pero constante compañero. La tristeza del hombre que en medio del camino ha perdido la senda de su religión se asoma en sus versos. ¿Existe el azul?, se pregunta. Un sentimiento poderoso le conduce por interrogantes con enigmas e inquietudes: ¿Dónde está Dios? ¿Por qué no habla? La ironía se esfuma ante esta angustiosa necesidad de comunicarse con la divinidad. . . ." Sus meditaciones cristalizaron en un volumen, *Místicas,* 1904. . . .

(In his heart, there was always a yearning for God, daunted at times by postivistic analysis, but a constant companion. The sadness of a man, who in the midst of the road has lost the way of his religion, appears in his verses. Does the blue exist?, he asks himself. A strong feeling leads him through interrogations with enigmas and inquietudes: Where is God? Why does he not speak? Irony is stumped before this anguished necessity to communicate with Divinity. . . . His meditations crystallized in one volume, *Mystics,* 1904). See *Literatura hispanoamericana* (Hispanic American Literature) (Barcelona, 1965), pp. 215 and 221.

31. "Espistolario" ("Epistolary"), *Homenaje,* p. 273.

32. "Epistolario" ("Epistolary"), *Homenaje,* p. 271.

33. "El ruego" ("The Plea"), *Poesías,* p. 100.

34. "Poema del hijo" ("Poem of the Son"), *Poesías,* p. 106.

35. "Poemas de la madres" ("Poems of Mothers"), *Desolación* (New York, 1922), pp. 178-179. Further references to this edition will be designated as *Desolación.*

36. "La mujer fuerte" ("The Valiant Woman"), *Poesías,* p. 15.

37. "La encina" ("The Oak"), *Poesías,* pp. 54-55.

38. When Gabriela Mistral was awarded the Nobel Prize for Literature, M. Hj. Gullberg, member of the Swedish Academy, pronounced a discourse which briefly traced the passage of the private individual, Lucila Godoy y Alcayaga, to the universal fame of Gabriela Mistral: "De la vallée perdue dans les montagnes désertiques et brulées du Chili monta une voix et loin à l'entour les hommes l'écoutèrent. Une banale tragédie de la vie de tous les jours perdit son caractère privé et entra dans la littérature universelle."

(From the valley lost in the desert and burning mountains of Chile, there rises a voice, and far from its surroundings, men listen to it. A common tragedy of everyday life loses its private character and enters into universal literature.) See "Discours de M. Hj. Gullberg" ("Discourse of M. Hj. Gullberg"), *Les prix Nobel en 1945* (Nobel Prizes in 1945), p. 48.

39. Federico de Onís, "Gabriela Mistral," *Homenaje,* p. 20.

40. "Alone," "Interpretación de Gabriela Mistral," *Homenaje,* p. 15.

41. ". . . Es un error. Ciertos recursos técnicos, más bien bebidos en los místicos castellanos, puede recordar la influencia de la Biblia. Gabriela Mistral viene de Elqui, su valle natal. La aspereza de esta huerta estrecha, quemada por un sol de fuego, de sus cerros desollados y de sus duraznales fragantes, vibra en el grito ronco de su poesía y es su aporte a la lírica chilena, de estos últimos tiempos.

. . . Su verso tiene la ruda antítesis de la piedra y de la fruta . . . el grito lancinante, el alarido de poseída, la desesperación mística."

(" . . . It is an error. Certain technical means, somewhat imbibed in the Castilian mystics, can recall the influence of the Bible. Gabriela Mistral comes from Elqui, her native valley. The asperity of this narrow garden, burnt by a fiery sun, of its steep hills, and of its fragrant peach trees, vibrates in the harsh cry of her poetry, and is her contribution to Chilean lyricism of these latter times.

. . . Her verse bears the rude antithesis of the stone and the fruit . . . the piercing cry, the shout of the possessed one, mystical desperation.") See Mariano Latorre, *La literatura chilena* (Chilean Literature) (Buenos Aires, 1941), p. 171.

42. Benjamín Carrión, *Santa Gabriela Mistral* (Quito, 1956), pp. 21-22.

43. Carrión, p. 25.

44. "Por este libro *(Lagar)*—como por *Tala* y como por algunos poemas de *Desolación*—pasan hálitos teresianos y aún de San Juan de la Cruz y de otros místicos. Y es que, salvo excepciones, lo que toda poesía verdadera hace, es hablar *a* Dios o *de* Dios, unas veces directamente, o, en otras, por medio de imágenes. La mística lo hizo de un modo explícito. Volver a su origen—¡Dios!—es lo que quiere la Poesía, ya sea de un modo o de otro. Por esto, Gabriela tocada tantas veces por la muerte, ha sabido libertarse al fin de sus dolores, encontrando una serenidad última que no es precisamente filosófica, sino más bien religiosa, vencidas profundas crisis del alma."

(Through this book *Wine Press*—as through *Felling of Trees,* and through some poems of *Desolation*—there pass Teresian breaths and even those of Saint John of the Cross and of other mystics. And it is that, except for some exceptions, all which true poetry does, is either talk *to* God or *about* God, sometimes directly or, at other times, through the medium of images. The mystic does so in an explicit manner. Return to its origin—God!—is what poetry desires, be it in one way or another. For this reason, Gabriela Mistral, touched so often by death, finally learned how to liberate herself from her sorrows, finding an ultimate serenity which is not precisely philosophical, but rather, religious, after having conquered the profound crises of her soul.) See Concha Zardoya, "Desde *Desolación* a *Lagar*" ("From Desolation to Wine Press"), *Revista Hispánica Moderna,* XXII (1956), 137-138.

45. "El pensador de Rodin" ("The Thinker of Rodin"), *Poesías,* p. 3.

46. The Dictionary of the Spanish Academy gives two definitions of mysticism:

(1) "Estado extraordinario de perfección religiosa, que consiste esencialmente en cierta unión inefable del alma con Dios por el amor, y que va acompañada accidentalmente de éxtasis y revelaciones."

(2) "Doctrina religiosa o filosófiica que enseña la comunicación inmediata y directa entre el hombre y la divinidad, en la visión intuitiva o en el éxtasis."

(1) Extraordinary state of religious perfection, which consists essentially in a certain ineffable union of the soul with God through love, and which is accompanied accidentally by ecstasy and revelations.

(2) Religious or philosophical doctrine which teaches the immediate and direct communication between man and divinity, in intuitive vision or in ecstasy.)

It also defines mysticism as "estado de la persona que se dedica mucho a Dios o a las cosas espirituales" (state of the person who dedicates himself much to God and to spiritual things), and a mystic as "que se dedica a la vida espiritual" (one who dedicates himself to the spiritual life).

47. Julio Saavedra Molina, "Gabriela Mistral: su vida y su obra" ("Gabriela Mistral: Her Life and Work"), *Poesías,* pp. lxviii-lxix.

48. *Loc. cit.*

49. Cora Santandreu, "Aspectos del estilo en la poesía da Gabriela Mistral" ("Aspects of Style in the Poetry of Gabriela Mistral"), *Homenaje,* p. 129.

50. Américo Castro, as quoted by Cora Santandreu, p. 172.

51. *Loc. cit.*

52. San Juan de la Cruz, "Coplas del alma que pena por ver a Dios" ("Couplets of a Soul That Craves For the Sight of God"), *Poesías completas y otras páginas* (Complete Poetic Works and other Pages), ed. J. M. Blecua, 4th ed. (Madrid, 1961), p. 41. Further references to this edition will be designated as *Poesías.*

53. Juan de la Cruz, "El cántico espiritual" ("Spiritual Canticle"), *Poesías,* p. 35.

54. Sister John Berchmans, O.P., "Gabriela Mistral and the Franciscan Concept of Life," *Renascence,* V (1952), 42: "But Mistral even in her devotion is not moved by this intense desire for union with the Divine Beloved which uniquely marks the genuine mystic."

55. Santandreu, p. 125.

56. Santandreu, p. 175.

57. Espinoza, p. 99.

58. *Ibid.,* p. 100.

59. Dulce María Loynaz, "Gabriela y Lucila," *Poesías,* p. cxxiv.

60. John xiii.34.

61. Manuel Pedro González, "Profile of a Great Woman," *Hispania,* XLI (1958), 429.

62. Saavedra Molina, p. xxxii.

63. Enrique Labrador Ruíz, "Gabriela Mistral," *La Nueva Democracia,* XXXVII (1957), 44.

64. Luis Amador Sánchez, "El existencialismo cristiano de Gabriela" ("Christian Existentialism of Gabriela"), *La Nueva Democracia,* XXXVII (1957), 46.

65. Dámaso Alonso, "Gabriela Mistral," *Homenaje,* p. 103.

66. Enrique Lihn, "Elegía a Gabriela Mistral" ("Elegy for Gabriela Mistral"), *Homenaje,* p. 105.

67. Gómez Millas, p. 9.

68. "One of the greatest hindrances to the study of mystical literature is the looseness with which critics employ the words 'mystical' and 'mysticism.' So wide is the gulf between the precise and formal definition of Catholic practice and tradition and the diverse and vague connotations current in non-specialist writings and in popular speech that the description of any particular writer or work as mystical has no meaning unless its author makes it clear in what sense the adjective is used . . . the adjective

is apt to be applied not only to any devotional manual or ascetic treatise, but to any writing which contains . . . 'intimations of a consciousness wider and deeper than the normal.' " E. Allison Peers, "Mysticism in the Poetry of Lope de Vega," *Estudios dedicados a Menéndez Pidal,* I (Madrid, 1950), 349-358. It is in this "loose" interpretation of the word that mysticism can be traced in the works of Gabriela Mistral.

69. "La oración de la maestra," *Desolación,* p. 173.
70. "La oración de la maestra," *Desolación,* p. 174.
71. "La oración de la maestra," *Desolación,* p. 174.
72. Julián Marías, "Prologue," *The Christ of Velázquez,* trans. Eleanor L. Turnbull (Baltimore, 1951), p. xiii.
73. Miguel de Unamuno, *El Cristo de Velázquez* (Madrid, 1920), pp. 15-16.
74. Unamuno, pp. 163-164.
75. Gabriela Mistral, "El testamento pedagógico," *Educación,* VI (1960), 7.
76. "Al oído del Cristo," *Poesías,* p. 5.
77. Anonymous sonnet of Spanish literature attributed to San Francisco Xavier, San Ignacio de Loyola, Fray Pedro de los Reyes, Fray Miguel de Guevara, and Santa Teresa de Avila.
78. "A Cristo Crucificado," *Ten Centuries of Spanish Poetry,* ed. Eleanor L. Turnbull (New York, 1955), p. 236.
79. "Canto del justo," *Poesías,* p. 19.
80. San Juan de la Cruz, "Noche oscura," *Poesías,* p. 32.
81. "El Dios triste," *Poesías,* p. 37.
82. "El himno cotidiano," *Poesías,* p. 351.
83. Santandreu, p. 171.
84. "Éxtasis," *Poesías,* p. 64.
85. "Nocturno," *Poesías,* pp. 79-80.
86. "Interrogaciones," *Poesías,* p. 85.
87. Loynaz, p. cxv.
88. Edmond Arnould, *Essais de théorie et d'histoire littéraire,* pp. 20-21, in Henri Brémond, *Prayer and Poetry* (London, 1927), p. 99.
89. Jacques and Raïssa Maritain, *Situation de la poésie* (Paris, 1938), p. 47.
90. Francis Thompson, "The Kingdom of God," *Poems,* ed. Terence L. Connolly (New York, 1932), p. 293.
91. Brémond, *Poésie et mystique* (Paris, 1926), p. 105.
92. Maritain, *Situation de la poésie,* pp. 40-41.
93. "Nocturno de la derrota" ("Nocturn of Defeat"), *Poesías,* p. 388.

chapter **II**

DEFINITION OF MYSTICISM

1. The Catholic Orthodox connotation

> Allí me dió su pecho,
> allí me enseñó ciencia muy sabrosa,
> y yo le dí de hecho
> a mí, sin dejar cosa;
> allí le prometí de ser su esposa.[1]

Here, in five short verses, San Juan de la Cruz has given that which may be considered the most complete and the most significant definition of Catholic mysticism. For mysticism is love between God and the enamored soul. The infinite God seeks the soul of finite man. The soul becomes overwhelmingly conscious of God, and is possessed with an ineffable desire for union with Him. Then, having reached the term of its adventure, it passes over into that boundless life where the desirous and the desired are one. Its joyous and awakened love is requited: "There He gave me His breast, / there He taught me most savoury knowledge," the soul sings. It is that experience in which the soul is filled with the Life of God; it savours and knows divine things affectively. Lost in the abyss of Deity, it surrenders to Love: "and I gave myself to Him, / keeping nothing back; / there I promised to be His bride."

Mystical life, therefore, is life with God. It is an interior life hidden from the eyes of men, hence its name mystical, which means "something hidden." It is a special experience of the soul whereby the human being becomes conscious of God and desires to live in secret intercourse with Him. Such an experience is ineffable. It cannot be expressed by the limited operations of the created intelligence. It cannot be confined to the concepts and images of the understanding. Even those who possess it have difficulty in expressing it. San Juan de la Cruz, in his prologue to "El cántico espiritual" ("The Spiritual Canticle"), admits this:

> . . . sería ignorancia pensar que los dichos de amor en inteligencia mística, . . . con alguna manera de palabras se pueden bien explicar; porque el Espíritu del Señor que ayuda nuestra flaqueza, . . . pide por nosotros con gemidos inefables lo que nosotros no podemos bien entender ni comprender para lo manifestar. . . . porque ésta es la causa por que con figuras, comparaciones y semejanzas, antes rebosan algo de lo que sienten, y de la abundancia del espíritu vierten secretos y misterios que con razones lo declaran.[2]
>
> (. . . it would be ignorance to think that the favors of love, mystically understood, . . . can be well-explained by any manner of words; because the Spirit of the Lord who helps our weakness, . . . pleads for us with ineffable groanings for that which we cannot well understand or comprehend in order to express it. . . . for this is the reason why with figures, comparisons, and similes they permit something of that which they feel to overflow and, from the abundance of the spirit, utter secrets and mysteries, rather than declare them with reason.)

The categories of reason are too narrow to grasp it; language is too inadequate to express it; bodies have swooned and have been caught up in rapture and ecstasy, and hearts have broken under the impact of this tremendous Love. He who is happiness by His Essence,[3] desires the love of man, and this desire is the craving of every human heart for a good that is in reality for Him.

Mysticism is essentially a movement of that inmost sanctuary of personal being, the synthesis of its love and will. The mystic is one whose awareness of God absorbs and eclipses all other centers of interest. In love with the Absolute, he presses forward at all costs and through all dangers toward union with the Object Beloved.

Having accepted the call of the Beloved, the soul enters upon the mystic journey with its threefold way. This is a stripping process, which is described as the passage of the soul from desire to purgation, to illumination, to union with its Beloved in spiritual nuptials. The doctrine of these mystical states supplies the material for mystical writings. Canon Auguste Saudreau claims that Clement of Alexandria had divided the spiritual life into three phases; Dionysius the Areopagite treats it in the same way; the life of purgation, of illumination, and of perfection appear again and again under his pen. Through him, this division, already so well-grounded, has become classic.[4]

In the purgative way, the soul passes from the life of the senses to the life of the spirit, an undertaking which demands effort and constancy and a deep unquestioning faith. This is the route of "la noche oscura del alma" (the dark night of the soul). Because its end, the object of all its desires, God, remains to the finite being here below incomprehensible, the soul encounters anguish, temptation, difficulties, and sufferings of every kind. This is the narrow gate and the straight way leading to the Beloved, whom the soul feels she has lost: "¿A dónde te escondiste, / Amado, y me dejaste con gemido?"[5] (Where have you hidden yourself, Beloved, and left me with my sighing?).

In the illuminative way, the soul receives some glimpses of the glory of God. After suffering and anguish, splendid horizons open to her who has remained faithful; to her who has permitted God to seize her and to sanctify her to the full measure and power of the grace to which He destines her, for God gives His grace and love according to the desire and love of the soul. For this cause, she must never fail to engrave upon her spirit the heavenly beauty of the Beloved. By this means will she move the Beloved to cast a look upon her: "If therefore I have found favor in Thy sight, show me Thy face, that I may know Thee, and may find grace before Thy eyes."[6] By this means does she render the Beloved powerless in His omnipotence, because He can no longer resist the languishing love of the enamored soul.

The third is the way of union, in which the soul arrives victorious at the state of spiritual marriage which she has so much desired. This state is more than betrothal. It is a complete transforming union with the Beloved. Here, there is a mutual exchange of love in which the soul becomes deified. It is the highest state of union with God that a soul can enjoy on earth. Just as the consummation of the marriage bond makes of two, one in one flesh, so does spiritual marriage between God and the soul unite two natures in one spirit. Two loves, seeking each other with such purity and such ardor, meet in the perfect and mutual gift of spiritual marriage. A new relationship is formed. The soul has reached the end of her journey, the center of herself, the Seventh Mansion where He dwells. This union, besides being complete, is also definitive, for the soul remains all the time in its center with her God.

An attempt at description of this state is an attempt to describe the ineffable. Yet, through the inspiration of the

Holy Spirit, from the pens of great mystics, the ineffable has flowed, making intelligible and radiant that which naturally is unintelligible and dark to the human understanding, for the experience "must be clothed with flesh, to create an organism which can come down and live among men."[7] Thus does Santa Teresa make an attempt at description:

> Ya he dicho que aunque se ponen estas comparaciones, porque no hay otra más a propósito, que se entienda que aquí no hay memoria de cuerpo más que si el alma no estuviese en él, sino sólo espíritu, y en el matrimonio espiritual, muy menos, porque pasa esta secreta unión en el centro muy interior del alma, que debe ser adonde está el mesmo Dios, y, a mi parecer, no ha menester puerta, por donde entre: digo que no es menester puerta, porque en todo lo que se ha dicho hasta aquí parece que va por medio de los sentidos y potencias, y este aparecimiento de la Humanidad del Señor ansí debía ser; mas lo que pasa en la unión del matrimonio espiritual es muy diferente. Aparécese el Señor en este centro del alma sin visión imaginaria, sino intelectual, aunque más delicada que las dichas, como se apareció a los Apósteles, sin entrar por la puerta, cuando les dijo: "Paz vobis." Es un secreto tan grande y una merced tan subida lo que comunica Dios allí a el alma en un instanto, y el grandísimo deleite que siente el alma, que no sé a qué lo comparar, sino a que quiere el Señor manifestarle por aquel momento la gloria que hay en el Cielo, . . . porque de tal manera ha querido juntarse con la criatura, que ansí como los que ya no se pueden apartar Él de ella.[8]

(I have already said that although these comparisons are set forth, because there are no other fitting ones, let it be understood that here there is no more awareness of the body than if the soul were not in it, but were spirit only, and much less in spiritual marriage, because this secret union takes place in the deepest center of the soul which must be where God Himself dwells, and to my way of thinking, a door through which He may enter is not necessary: I say that a door is not necessary, because in everything that has been said up to now, it seems that He passes through the medium of the senses and faculties, and this appearance of the Humanity of the Lord should be so; but that which passes in the union of spiritual marriage is very different. The Lord appears in this center of the soul, not through an imaginary vision, but through an intellectual one, although more subtle than that already mentioned, as He appeared to the Apostles, without entering through the door, when He said to them: "Peace be to you." It is a secret so great and a favor so sublime that which God communicates there to the soul in an instant, and the very great joy that the soul feels, that I do not know to what to compare it, except that the Lord wishes in that moment to manifest to the soul the glory that is in heaven, . . . for He has desired to unite Himself with His creature in such a manner that they have thus become like those who cannot be separated one from the other.)

Love, then, is the most distinctive note of true mysticism, the note that marks it off from every other kind of transcendental theory and practice. It is the banner of Saintship, the touch of God. All great lovers of God have felt this embrace as they penetrated regions closed to reason and understanding. This region is the summit of the mystical mountain sketched by San Juan de la Cruz. It is a new world, a luxuriant garden into which the Bride enters and where God holds her a willing captive in the bonds of His love.

St. Catherine of Siena records in her dialogue that God Himself looks with joy upon the beauty of a soul clothed with the nuptial garment of love: ". . . they are another Myself, inasmuch as they have lost and denied their own will, and are clothed with Mine, are conformed to Mine."[9] Blessed Henry Suso, another illustrious Dominican, describes the soul in this state: ". . . they are then deprived of their own being and transformed into another form, another glory, and another power . . . the Divine Nature and the Divine Essence."[10]

These are examples of true mystics, as are Santa Teresa and San Juan de la Cruz, the Carmelite saints, who have come out of Spain's nursery of mystics and mystical theologians, more numerous and more illustrious perhaps than any other national group of the kind in the history of the western Church, for as David Rubio affirms: ". . . it is mysticism, not stoicism, which is the essence of the Spanish soul. If the existence of the soul is acknowledged and mysticism clearly understood, Spain ceases to be an enigma."[11]

Rafael Altamira, however, poses the question: "¿Senequismo, ascetismo o misticismo?" ("Senecanism, asceticism, mysticism"). His answer leans toward the position that one of the most deep-seated and characteristic aspects of the Spanish character is stoicism. Of the two facets of Christianity, asceticism and mysticism, it is the former which predominates over the latter:

> Por otra parte es cierto que nuestro pueblo bajo . . . cuenta, entre sus ideas más arraigadas y características, . . . la de la resignación con su suerte, por mala que sea; su estoicismo respecto del dolor y la desgracia . . . y su creencia en que todo eso es inevitable, porque el mundo

será siempre como ha sido hasta aquí. ¡Cuántas veces he oído, a pobres labradores que no sabían leer ni escribir, estas elocuentes palabras: "¡Hay que padecer!" Ahora bien, esas ideas son las más salientes y típicas de Séneca. . . . lo verosímil es que nuestra masa popular las haya obtenido por intermedio de las predicaciones religiosas. . . . Todo el problema histórico consistiría, pues, en averiguar, ahondando en la psicología popular, si el sentido que ésta da a las referidas ideas está más próximo al senequismo que al cristianismo, o al contrario. . . . Viniendo al campo cristiano, que es el nuestro fundamental, se ha solido decir que de las dos posiciones principales que lo caracterizan, el ascetismo y el misticismo, es aquélla la que predomina en nosotros, aunque la segunda ofrezca algunos de los casos más perfectos y hondos que conoce la Humanidad. Como para llegar al misticismo hay que pasar antes por el ascetismo, la consecuencia es que siempre esta posición será más frecuente y extensa que la otra; y como es reconocido—la misma Santa Teresa lo deja entender algunas veces—que no son vulgares y abundantes las facultades que permiten llegar a ella, es indudable que su cifra será escasa siempre.[12]

(On the other hand, it is certain that our lowly people . . . reckon, among their most deep-rooted and characteristic ideas, . . . that of resignation with their lot, however bad it may be; their stoicism with regard to sorrow and misfortune . . . and their belief that all that is inevitable, because the world will always be as it has been up to now. How often have I heard, from poor laborers who do not know how to read or write, these eloquent words: "One has to suffer!" Now, those ideas are the

> most salient and typical of Seneca. . . . the probable thing is that our masses have obtained them through the intermediary of religious preachings. . . . The whole historical problem would consist, then, in verifying, by penetrating into the psychology of the people, whether the meaning that this gives to the aforesaid ideas be closer to the philosophy of Seneca than to Christianity, or vice versa. . . . Coming to the Christian idea, which is our fundamental one, it has been customary to say that of the two principal positions which characterize it, asceticism and mysticism, it is the former which predominates in us, although the second may offer some of the most perfect and most profound cases which Humanity knows. Since to arrive at mysticism it is necessary first to pass through asceticism, the consequence is that this position will always be more frequent and extensive than the other; and as it is known—Saint Teresa herself sometimes makes it understood—that since the faculties which permit one to arrive at it are neither common nor abundant, it is doubtless that their number will always be small.)

But Rubio insists that mysticism is the true philosophy of Spain and expounds his position:

> Is it strange, then, that in the soul of such a race there should exist such a powerful tendency toward mysticism? In no other Christian nation has it penetrated so deeply into the heart or so profoundly shaped literature. Mysticism does not appear in Spain in the form of a poem, as in Italy; nor in the form of theology, as in France; nor does it show itself in revolutionary experiments, pantheistic and biblical dreams, as in England, Germany, or Switzerland. The action of Spanish mysticism is in-

finitely more extensive; it has penetrated every corner of life and left nothing untouched. It has influenced not only the intelligence but also the customs of the people. We find mysticism in the lecture hall and the cloister, in literature, the arts, and in philosophy. El Greco's figures are consumed by a mystic flame. This is the true philosophy of Spain, the most profound element of her religion and of her genius.[13]

E. Allison Peers is of the same opinion: "Ningún viajero consciente puede pasar unas semanas en España sin darse cuenta de que el misticismo es algo innato en su pueblo. . . . en el alma del pueblo español discurren subterráneas corrientes de misticismo. . . . lo profundamente arraigado que está el misticismo en el alma española"[14] (No conscious traveler can pass several weeks in Spain without realizing that mysticism is something innate in its people. . . . in the soul of the Spanish people, subterraneous currents of mysticism flow. . . . how profoundly rooted is mysticism in the Spanish soul).

Out of the mystic soul of Spain, there have come a Dominic of Guzmán, a Vincent Ferrer, an Ignatius of Loyola, all burning with the love of God and setting the world on fire with it, for their contemplation goes hand in hand with activity: "Contemplare et aliis tradere contemplata"[15] ("To contemplate and to bring to others the things contemplated"). One of its most notable features is that of self-sacrifice for one's neighbor.

Among the Spanish mystics who soar aloft on wings of Divine Love to heights known to few are Teresa and John, the one perhaps the simplest, the most unstudied, and yet, the most accurate narrator of personal experiences in the various degrees of the spiritual life; the other, the keen psychologist, the clear, scientific mind who stands as the authentic expositor of mystical theology in something of the prominent position given to St. Thomas Aquinas in the realm of philosophy. Thus do the two saints, allies united in deep mutual reverence and spiritual friendship during the fifteen years of the sixteenth century in which their lives ran parallel, differ greatly in natural gifts and temperament, but resemble each other closely in their ardent desire for union with God.

Santa Teresa, a woman in every trait of her character, affectionate, impulsive, motherly, practical, loyal, and gay, with an immense capacity for love and sacrifice, had a virile courage and resolve and an intellectual clarity of vision directed to a single purpose. The qualities of her idiomatic simplicity and sensibility have helped to make her a literary classic. Nowhere is this more in evidence than when she describes her adventures in *Las fundaciones* ("The Foundations"), or gives vivid pen-pictures of some of her nuns or acquaintances.

In the history of Catholic mysticism, she is a figure of epoch-making significance, for hers, together with that of San Juan, is a doctrine and a system of ascetical and mystical teaching which has come to be known as the Carmelite school of spirituality. Theirs was the task of setting forth more clearly and more completely the degrees of the mystical life lived by the individual who seeks the perfect following of Christ. Hers is one of the most celebrated books on mystical theology in existence. The mystical figure of the mansion, *Las moradas,* was revealed to her in a vision which God granted her in response to her wish of obtaining some insight into the beauty of a soul in grace. Here, in spite of her protest "I am a stupid creature and don't know what I am saying," she sets down the experiences of her questing soul as they occur to her.

The figure is used to describe the soul's progress from the First Mansion to the Seventh, where His Majesty dwells, and its transformation from an imperfect and sinful creature into the Bride of the Spiritual Marriage. Here, there is a complete change in the soul; here, there is unspeakable and perfect peace. No higher state is conceivable, save that of the Beatific Vision in the life to come:

> Aquí es de otra manera; quiere ya nuestro buen Dios quitar las escamas de los ojos, y que vea y entienda algo de la merced que le hace, aunque es por una manera estraña y metida en aquella Morada por visión intelectual; por cierta manera de representación de la verdad, se le muestra la santísima Trinidad, todas tres personas, con una inflamación que primero viene a su espíritu, a manera de una nube de grandísima claridad, y estas personas distintas, y por una noticia admirable, que se da a el alma entiende con grandísima verdad ser todas tres personas una sustancia y un poder y un saber y un solo Dios; de manera que lo que tenemos por fe allí lo entiende el alma, podemos decir, por vista, aunque no es vista con los ojos del cuerpo ni del alma, porque no es visión imaginaria. Aquí se le comunican todas tres personas, y le hablan, y le dan a entender aquellas palabras que dice el Evangelio que dijo el Señor: que venía Él y el Padre y el Espíritu Santo a morar con el alma, que le ama y guarda sus mandamientos.[16]
>
> (Here, it is different; our good God now desires to remove the scales from the eyes of the soul, so that the soul may see and understand something of the favor which He is granting it, although it is through a strange manner; it is drawn into that Mansion by an intellectual vision, where by a certain manner of representation of the truth, all three Persons of the Most Holy Trinity are revealed to it, with a kindling of the spirit which first comes as a

cloud of greatest brightness, and these three distinct Persons, through a wonderful kind of knowledge which is given to the soul, are understood with the greatest clarity to be one Substance, and one Power, and one Knowledge, and one God alone; in such a way that what we hold through faith, there the soul understands, we may say, through sight, although it is not through the eyes of the body, nor those of the soul, because it is an imaginary vision. Here, all three Persons communicate Themselves to the soul, speak to it, and enable it to understand those words which the Gospel attributes to the Lord as saying: that He and the Father and the Holy Spirit would come to dwell with the soul that loves Him and keeps His commandments.)

In San Juan de la Cruz, the highest and the most inflamed mystical poet, there is but one outstanding characteristic, easily traced in both his life and his works: He fell so completely and hopelessly in love with God that all he did and spoke and wrote became an assiduous, passionate search after union with his "Amado" (Beloved). In his hours of enraptured creation, the Holy Spirit, the Sanctifier, inflamed his heart, liberated and expanded his powers to sustain a vision, a radiant revelation which produced mystical writings transcending all literary criticism. The "llama de amor viva" (living flame of love), brightened his intellect and enriched his tongue to sing a canticle in which all his capacities of theologian, philosopher, poet, man of the Renaissance, careful observer of surroundings, and experimenter of the secrets of mysticism are used.

Menéndez Pelayo, whose profound research in Spanish literature is testimony of his knowledge of the culture and production of the Spanish genius, was aware of this passage of the Spirit of God over the works of San Juan, and confessed that the very thought of touching them filled him with a religious terror:

> . . . por allí ha pasado el espíritu de Dios, hermoseándolo y santificándolo todo . . . ; confieso que me infunde religioso terror al tocarlo . . . ; no parece de este mundo, ni es posible medirla con criterios literarios, y eso que es más ardiente de pasión que ninguna poesía profana, y tan elegante y exquisita en la forma, y tan plástica y figurativa como los más sabrosos frutos del Renacimiento.[17]
>
> (. . . over them, the Spirit of God has passed, beautifying and sanctifying all . . . ; I confess that it fills me with religious terror to touch them . . . ; they do not seem of this world, nor is it possible to measure them with literary criteria, and they are more ardent in passion than any profane poetry, and so elegant and exquisite in form, and as plastic and figurative as the most savory fruits of the Renaissance.)

The admirable mystery of such works may be felt but cannot be explained. The perfect tribute to them is silent adoration when fitly read with the reverence of a receptive soul, for the reader becomes aware that the author, in truth, accepted the challenge of His Beloved: "Diliges Dominum Deum tuum ex toto corde tuo, et ex tota anima tua, et ex totis viribus tuis"[18] (Love the Lord your God with all your heart, and with all your soul, and with all your strength). The culmination of this love is poured out in "Llama de amor viva" (Living Flame of Love), that "all-astounded exclamation and fire, fire that illumines while it burns in it":[19]

¡Oh cauterio suave!
¡Oh regalada llaga!
¡Oh mano blanda! ¡Oh toque delicado,
que a vida eterna sabe,
y toda deuda paga!
Matando, muerte en vida le has trocado.[20]

(Oh, mild burn!
Oh, delightful wound!
Oh, soft hand! Oh, delicate touch,
which savors of eternal life,
and pays every debt!
Slaying, you have changed death into life.)

It is the end of the lover's quest, the omega of his existence. In the most vibrant and the most dynamic love story ever told, Love begets a Beloved. It is the Divine romance, ever ancient, ever new, between Love and its fruit, between the Creator and His creature, between God and man. And "this sense of a double movement, a self-giving on the Divine side answering to the self-giving on the human side, is found in all mysticism. Though some creeds have proved more helpful to the mystic than others, he is found fully developed in every great religion."[21]

The subsequent section of this chapter aims to show that man by nature tends toward mysticism. Beginning with Plotinus in the third century—for he is one of the world's greatest mystical writers—the section develops the Indian, Buddhist, and Unanimist doctrine of union with the Absolute. The reason for this selection is that, at one time or another, Gabriela Mistral's quest for God led her through these devious paths.

2. Mysticism in other great religions

> Man, by a natural condition, seeks the Absolute: It is impossible for any created good to constitute man's happiness. For happiness is the perfect good, which lulls the appetite altogether; else it would not be the last end, if something yet remained to be desired. Now the object of the will, i.e., of man's appetite, is the universal good; just as the object of the intellect is the universal true. Hence it is evident that naught can lull man's will, save the universal good. This is to be found not in any creature, but in God alone; because every creature has goodness by participation. Wherefore God alone can satisfy the will of man, according to the words of Ps. cii.5: Who satisfieth thy desire with good things. Therefore God alone constitutes man's happiness.[22]

It is to be noted that Thomas Aquinas here describes a natural appetite found in every rational creature. It is an appetite that is not confined to Catholic or Protestant, to Hebrew or Buddhist. Through the course of the years, great lovers of God have expressed this truth. Francis de Sales compares it to a river pursuing its natural course: "Les fleuves coulent incessament, et, comme dit le Sage, 'ils retournent au lieu duquel ils sont issus' (Eccl. i.7). La mer, qui est le lieu de leur naissance, est aussi le lieu de leur dernier repos: tout leur mouvement ne tend qu'à les unir avec leur origine"[23] (Rivers flow incessantly, and as the wise man says, "they return to the place from which they came." The sea, which is the place of their birth, is also the place of their last repose: all their movements tend only to unite them with their origin). Augustine cries out: "You have made us for Yourself, and our hearts are not at rest until they rest in You."[24] The royal psalmist expresses a similar sentiment: "What have I in heaven? And besides Thee what do I desire upon earth? / Thou art the God of my heart, and the God that is my portion forever."[25]

From this natural type of man's condition while on earth, there is no escape, but there are as many ways from man to the Absolute as there are variations in the spirit of man. "What is essential is . . . this adoring and all-possessing consciousness of the rich and complete divine life over against the self's life, and of the possible achievement of a level of being, a sublimation of the self, wherein we are perfectly united with it."[26] This is the common factor which unites the ways that lead to the Absolute, and this common factor may be discerned in Plotinus, in Kabir, in Rabindranath Tagore, in the Buddhist, and the Unanimist, who are here discussed.

Plotinus, founder and incomparably the greatest philosopher of the Neoplatonist school, which was primarily metaphysical but with theological emphasis tending toward mysticism, was a man of deep contemplative religion. Although a pagan, he has influenced Christian theology perhaps more than any other thinker.[27] His unusual power to inspire, to raise men's minds to the eternal, and to encourage a moral virility is derived from his doctrine of "The One," a source and term of all being that transcends all being as it transcends all knowledge. The doctrine, already elaborated and detached from its Old Testament origin, is discoverable in the writings of both Plotinus and Philo.

Plotinus's doctrine of "The One" is supplemented by the notion of the "ego," or the self as a philosophic principle. Porphyry, his pupil and biographer, relates that it was "by meditation and by the method that Plato teaches in the *Banquet* that Plotinus lifted himself . . . to the first and all-transcendent divinity."[28]

The method of Plotinus consists of a twofold purgation of the mind, one qualitative, the other quantitative. The first requires a successive transposing of the object of one's thought to a plane progressively more immaterial and spiritual, more completely disengaged from the sense realm, more closely allied to the intelligible. There are three levels of knowing that correspond to three levels of life: physical beauty, moral beauty, intellectual beauty. The second purgation demands a progressive detachment from the singular, from all the individualities that may characterize this or that object loved, in a separation from the changing and incidental in order to attach oneself to an object that is immovable, essential, fixed.

Plotinus's view of all creation moves in a giant cyclic rhythm, an endless process of going and returning: the source whence came the human soul and its final term is the same transcendent and unknowable One: "Such was the pattern on which . . . St. Thomas Aquinas constructed his *Summa Theologica*. It was the scheme that many a medieval mystic attempted to reproduce within him, in order to achieve his itinerary to God. It was an idea that came like a flame through the most devious channels of chance phrases . . . to fire the theological genius of such diverse minds as those of Scotus Eriugena, Hugh of St. Victor, Meister Eckhart. The Middle Ages itself performed a masterly exegesis on Plotinian material, . . ."[29]

It is said that Plotinus lived like a saint ascetically, but without the severe discipline of the Christian monks, and that his rapt meditations several times brought him, so he believed, to the beatific vision of the mystics, which he attempts to describe in sincere language in "the flight of the alone to the Alone." "It is thus that this divine man, whose thoughts were always turned to the Supreme God and the unseen world, merited the privilege of beholding several times the immediate presence of the Godhead, who has neither sensible nor intelligible form, since he is exalted above intelligence and being itself."[30]

Kabir, who lived in the latter part of the fifteenth century and who is claimed by both Hindus and Moslems, is one of the most remarkable figures in the religious history of India. He taught a religion of love. A mystic poet of a high order, he preached, in the medieval period of stress and tension, the equality before God of all men, whether of high caste or of low. He was a ruthless critic of orthodox exclusivism who aimed at an emotional integration of the soul with God. This simple union *(sahaja-yoga)* could be achieved by an aspirant, regardless of caste, creed, or sex, through ardent, personal devotion: "How shall I find words for the beauty of my Beloved? For He is merged in all beauty. His color is in all the pictures of the world, and it bewitches the body and the mind."[31] The songs of Kabir, which are written in popular, unsophisticated Hindi, continue to move the masses of Hindus and Moslems in northern India, even to this day.

The great Indian poet and author, Nobel Prize winner in 1913, Rabindranath Tagore (1861-1941), man of Bengali literature and thought, plunged into the "Great Unknown" to find his one consuming desire, his "Beloved." His abundant writings, permeated by a sense of the beauty of the universe, by a love of children and simplicity, and by a consciousness of God, did much to interpret for the West the more serious reflections of the people of Bengal. To the classical and folk-poetry traditions he has joined the eager curiosity of the most modern mind Bengal has known, a mind with a very wide acquaintance with physical science.

The beauty of his religious poetry has made him world famous, for in literature he has been the representative man of his time, in touch with the fullness of his intellectual heritage. From his earliest years, Rabindranath grew up in the one house where all the surging tides of the Indian Renaissance might flow round his daily life. Indeed, so fortunate was he in his home that his biography disproves the Bengali proverb that the goddesses of Learning and Good Fortune, Saraswati and Lakshmi, will not live together, for "here every movement found echoes, and the political and literary and religious disturbances rippled against these banks. His brothers were eager and full of genius. He was encouraged to write verse almost as soon as he could walk; he was a member of secret societies that studied politics in what was felt by their members to be a very bold and revolutionary freedom. Music and drama were the air he breathed."[32]

Here, too, he experienced the ecstasy with which he first saw fresh mornings and rich sunsets and the Ganges, the life-blood pulsing through his prose and verse. Here, he enjoyed the deepest and the most joyous communion with Nature: "Whatever my eyes fell upon found a response within me."[33] He understood no dogma save the love and joy which are in the universe; and out of this love and joy, there emerge the two great activities of his work: the earlier worship of beauty and the worship of God. In the latter, ". . . the artist is subdued by the man of God; the naked spirit is humble in the presence of God and speaks in tones of utter simplicity. This indeed is the keystone of his spiritual philosophy or intuition: he will see God within himself and also permeating everything in the Universe, big or small . . ."[34]

His *Gitanjali* or *Song Offerings,* one of his key books, an epitome and microcosm of his later works, seems to re-echo the lover's plaints in the songs of San Juan de la Cruz:

> Where dost thou stand behind them all, my lover, hiding thyself in the shadow?

> The rain has held back for days and days, my God, in my arid heart.
> I have not seen his face, nor have I listened to his voice; only I have heard his gentle footsteps from the road before my house.
> I shall ever try to drive all evils away from my heart and keep my love in flower, knowing that thou hast thy seat in the inmost shrine of my heart.[35]

These songs have been the faithful transcript of his soul, the magnificent harvest of his gleanings in the fields of Nature and of spirit:

> Pluck this little flower and take it, delay not! I fear lest it droop and drop into the dust.
> I am only waiting for Love to give myself up at last into his hands.[36]

The Buddhist approach to the Absolute is through meditation; it is the core and the very heartbeat of the religion. Enlightenment, or the state of Nirvana, is the ultimate aim of this meditation. On the way to Nirvana, the meditation serves to promote spiritual development, to diminish the impact of suffering, to calm the mind, and to reveal the true facts of existence. There is a deep sense of the perishable nature of all that exists, and a desire not to become again. Hence, there is a promise that one will eventually abide in the god rather than be reborn; that one will arrive at a state from which there is no more coming back to be: "Oh would that I who hourly waste might change / For that which n'er decays . . ."[37] Such doctrine can be found in the classical expression of the Bhagavad-Gita:

> Whoever serve Me—as I show Myself—
> Constantly true, in full devotion fixed,
> These hold I very holy. But who serve—
> Worshipping Me, the One, the Invisible,
> The Unrevealed, Unnamed, Unthinkable,
> Uttermost, All-pervading, Highest, Sure—
> Who thus adore Me, mastering their sense,
> Of one set of mind to all, glad in all good,
> These blessed souls come unto Me.[38]

By devotion to a God, therefore, and by trust in Him, one can find hope, peace, meaning, love in this life and in the life to come.

Thus, the Buddhist who believes that every sentient being will achieve release from the round of rebirth, can be rightly classified as mystical, for since this is so, it is only a matter of time before any particular being achieves Buddhahood. This belief, however, has none of the urgency of decision and commitment characteristic of Catholic mysticism. If one chooses to take seriously the Buddha's teaching in this life, well and good. If not, there are many more millenniums and many more lives during which one can learn and follow the truth.

In countries other than India, Buddhist practices are expressed differently. Tao-ngan, a Chinese author, relates that ". . . the place of the practitioner of Yoga is the mysterious hall in which are assembled those who are attuned to the truth. It is the secret chamber of the immortals who prepare themselves to ascend to Heaven. Hard to climb is this expanse of Non-production, because it is so sublime; hard to cross is this rampart of Non-action, because it is so immense. The absolute truth is like the ocean; each day you may bowl out some water, and yet, you can never exhaust it. This absolute truth contains the infinite, it is calm, it seems to exist, but cannot be expressed in words."[39]

The Unanimist who finds in other men—more in the whole web of life—that mysterious living essence which is a mode of God's existence, and which he loves, seeks, and recognizes everywhere, is also a mystic.

The title of mystic and mysticism cannot be refused to any person or religion mentioned above, because in each case, the aim is union between God and the soul. This is the highest achievement of human consciousness and the ultimate object of mysticism. But, when anyone speaking of mysticism proposes an object that is less than God, he is not using the word in its strict connotation, and is disregarding the essential quality of mysticism.

That literary critics have disregarded this essential quality of mysticism is evidenced not only in the case of Gabriela Mistral but also in such poets as Sor Juana Inés de la Cruz, Amado Nervo, and Lope de Vega.

In the case of the first, Gerard Cox Flynn wrote an article in which he discusses the signposts a mystic leaves in his writings:

> In the first place, mystical literature is based on experience. The mystic doesn't write about what ought to be or might have been, but about things that he heard and touched and saw, . . . The first signpost of mystical literature is habitual experience. A second characteristic is the recurrence of certain metaphors and images which the French critic Gaston Etchegoyen called a "terminologie traditionelle." Another trait of mystical literature is its paradoxicalness, which arises from the disproportion between the Lover and the Object of his love or comos, like the exclamations above, from the hiatus between

> intuitive experience and our discursive language. The last is the most difficult to describe . . . which comes from the sensible signs of Love that always accompany it: "Insouciance, Confiance, Souffrances, Nostalgie" ("Unconcern, Confidence, Sufferings, Nostalgia"). . . . where are these signposts in the prose and poetry of Sor Juana Inés de la Cruz? Apparently, nowhere.[40]

Flynn concludes that the writings of Sor Juana do not show the signposts of mystical literature, for there is strong autobiographical evidence against the habitual experience. "Occasionally she uses words that belong to the 'terminologie,' but their use is wooden; and the paradoxes that exist in her verses belong to the intellectual conceits of the seventeenth century rather than to the language of the Lover trying vainly to describe the experience with the Beloved. There is never the rapture, the ineffability of the 'confiance.' "[41]

Roderick A. Molina discusses mysticism and Franciscan influence in Amado Nervo and affirms:

> We must not seek in Amado Nervo the subjective, psychological, nor ascetical qualities of the profound mystics of the Spanish school of the sixteenth century, although his works give clear proofs that he was acquainted with it. But the wings of his verse lacked the power of that spiritual impulse that was needed to lift him up to close union with God and to lose himself in God, as it were, in that very intimate union with God that St. John of the Cross and St. Teresa of Avila have described in letters of fire. In the depth of Nervo's inspiration we find no principle of thought, but rather a principle of love; his poetry offers us, especially in his times of serenity, a world of affections rather than a

world of ideas. He was attracted to St. Teresa of Avila and from her he learned that ardent, vehement effusion of his love and his longing that the world of his day might come to understand from the Gospel the universal law of love and brotherhood.[42]

He points out that Nervo's affection for religious themes is projected so frequently and so intimately in all his work that it is the reason for literary critics' classification of him among the number of the mystical poets—those privileged beings who aspired to union with God through love and who expressed their sublime thoughts in poetic form. "It must be admitted, however, that the spiritual path of the poet is not so clearly marked nor so precisely outlined as that of his literary development."[43]

E. Allison Peers states that "of the major poets of the Golden Age, it is probably Lope de Vega, after San Juan de la Cruz and Luis de León, whose lyrics are most generally referred to as mystical." He examines the "Rimas Sacras," the "Soliloquois amorosos de un alma a Dios," and the "Romancero espiritual para recrearse el alma con Dios" ("Sacred Rhymes," "Amorous Soliloquies of a Soul to God," "Spiritual Ballad for the Soul to Recreate Herself in God"), and finds that the dominant theme is repentance. He admits:

Within this framework there would be ample place for the mystical, for it is precisely the realization of the greatness of that which is *(Id quod est),* and of the nothingness of man (My God, what am I and what art Thou?), a theme often developed by San Juan de la Cruz, that inspires the mystic's initial attempts at self-adjustment . . . suggestive of the Purgative Way but gives no hint of anything beyond. . . . In his most spiritual moments,

> Lope de Vega might be termed a mystic *"in posse."* His aspirations, it is true, are not to union, like San Juan de la Cruz's, nor to vision, like Luis de León's, but mainly to service and to worthier living. . . . One can recognize the true lover in the hyperboles, the rhetorical questions, the whispers of endearment, and the fond pleadings. And love lends him wings, but though he mounts on them, he cannot sustain his gaze, and again like St. Augustine, he is left with only a loving memory and a yearning for what he has savoured but is not yet able to feed upon.[44]

Allison Peers concludes that ". . . he was about as unmystical a religious poet as his age produced."[45]

3. Poetry and Mysticism

> To divert the poetic experience or the mystical experience towards oneself is to offend the heart of God and of things and cause all real substance to vanish in illusion. But when the poet renounces the vain search after magical powers and is willing to submit "to that orientation of his entire being towards a reality which surpasses exterior reality," from which precisely, according to Albert Béguin, recent poetry has received its distinctive character, he enters into true mysteries and advances in the fruitful and nondeceptive line of his own discoveries.
>
> Indeed it is difficult with the experience so described to know whether it is the most mystical of poetic graces, or the most poetic of mystical graces.[46]

Every true poet goes, by his own experience of those depths where all is spirit and life, from the visible to the invisible, from images of the real to the reality without images. From this imageless reality, he returns with words, sounds, colors, and forms. Then he faces the "problem that has baffled poets in all languages: how to say the unsayable."[47] In a desperate attempt to utter the ineffable, to translate the beauty of the poetic world into the beauty of this, he is forced to speak in symbols, to employ images and metaphors, knowing indeed that they are unequal to the task, but believing that there is an inner unity between the image and material worlds, which makes the things of reality a reflection, though but a faint one, of the things of imagery:

> To see a world in a grain of sand
> And a heaven in a wild flower,
> Hold infinity in the palm of your hand
> And eternity in an hour.[48]

The poet must break through the rigid forms of an idiom incapable of expressing lofty poetic conceptions and soar on wings of genius to "regions where the self is renounced in favor of a presence which it perceives within itself—the efficacious action of the image."[49] There he must enshrine his thoughts in a magnificent and sublime language of his own creation. As Rainer Maria Rilke so beautifully put it:

> For gazing, look, has a limit.
> And the on-gazeder world
> wants to mature in love.
>
> Work of sight is achieved,
> now for some heart-work
> on all those images, prisoned within you;
> for you overcame them, but do not know them as yet.[50]

Therefore, does the language of the poet abound in symbol-clothing, paradoxes, hyperboles, device of parallelism. His metaphors ring harmoniously even upon the ears of those to whom his poetry is obscure. It is the charm of his language and the purity and exactness of his choice of words which delight such a reader. The poet is a lover of Nature who mounts from the loveliness of earth to the loveliness of the poetic realm where visible nature is submerged in the invisible. This task, to create and explore these moments, Juan Ramón Jiménez set for himself each day in solitude and meditation, for to him, as to all great poets, "poetry is an attempt to approximate the absolute by means of symbols. Universality is personal—the essence of each one elevated to the absolute. . . . Poetry in its conception should be sacred, winged, and full of grace, and the proper realm of poetry is mystery and enchantment."[51]

Much of this mystery and enchantment leads the critic to confuse poetic graces with mystical graces. To produce this "sacredness, wingedness, fullness of grace," the author must be a poet, an artist, and a musician. It is the trinity which leads Francis Thompson to suspect the existence of the Blessed Trinity:

> If the Trinity were not revealed, I should nevertheless be induced to suspect the existence of such a master-key by the trinities through which expounds itself the spirit of man. Such a trinity is the trinity of beauty: Poetry, Art, Music. Although its office is to create beauty, I call it the trinity of beauty, because it is the property of earthly as of the heavenly beauty to create everything to its own image and likeness. Painting is the eye of passion, Poetry is the voice of passion, Music is the throb-

> bing of her heart. . . . Earthly beauty is but heavenly beauty taking to itself flesh.[52]

This "flesh," in the poet's world, is his song which, before it is formulated, is composed in the depths of his soul, and demands expression. It is the term of his experience, for "while the poet progresses toward the Word, the mystic tends toward Silence."[53] It is that which Jorge Guillén calls the "victorious expression": "Something of our emotions escapes us, something that is irreconcilable to logical symbols rationally articulated. At this barrier set up by the inability to equate the soul and the word, many pause. Though deeply moved, they do not know what to say. But in spite of all these difficulties, the poet—dissatisfied, perhaps, but still the supreme sayer—delivers to us at last his victorious expression."[54] It is "la langue royale, faite pour la poésie"[55] (the royal language, made for poetry), of Jean Cassou. It is the paradox, "roots that fly,"[56] of Juan Ramón Jiménez. The poet cannot, without ceasing to be a poet, go beyond this "victorious expression." The mystic surpasses the articulated word, for while

> . . . the poet identifies himself with the forces of the manifest universe, the mystic traverses them and tries to unite with the immutable and unlimited power of the absolute behind them.
>
> Although it very often happens that the mystic feels the need of describing his experience, the fact remains that for him the expression is not a means of completing the experience, it is in no way necessary to its conclusion and perfection; it is only a result of superabundance, a generous attempt at communication.[57]

This generous attempt at communication is the essence of all mystical writings in all the great religions of the world. It is the "espíritu de llama" (spirit of flame) of all the saintly writers who have burst into song, creating masterpieces of mysticism and poetry which betray the criticism of Karl J. Shapiro and belie his judgment:

> Poetic knowledge, on the other hand, loves the world more frankly than it loves God, and this creates a natural barrier between poets and holier men. Some poets, to be sure, are men of God, and some men of God are poets, but in general, churches are weak in esthetics and the glory of this life, while most religious poets, so-called, are weak in talent. The reason is not far to seek: the closer one approaches the mystical experience the more the world falls away, the closer the substance of the world comes to annihilation. The mystical is the opposite of the creative process: to the mystic a poem is just as much a "false reality" as any other phenomenon.[58]

But the mystical life is supereminently active. It must move and cause to gush forth under that divinely gracious and mysterious influence which moves men by capturing their hearts and flooding them with joy. It transforms men as it seems to transform the objects which occupy their attention: a work of art, a landscape. The "false reality" is rather a monument of sacred exegesis, love, and beauty. It is from the mystic that we can learn to understand the poet. As Henri Brémond clarifies: "Au lieu d'éclairer, comme ils semblent vouloir faire, l'expérience mystique par l'expérience poétique, c'est à la première que je demande de me révéler la vraie nature de la seconde: ce n'est pas l'expérience de Shelley qui m'aide à mieux connaître l'expérience de Jean de la Croix, mais, inversement, celle-ci, qui me rend un peu moins obscur le mystère de celle-là"[59] (Instead of clarifying, as it seems customary to do, the mystical experience by the poetic experience, it is of the first that I ask to reveal to me the true nature of the second: it is not the experience of Shelley which enables me to better understand the experience of Saint John of the Cross, but inversely, the latter which renders the mystery of the former a little less obscure for me).

Such is the case when one enters into the mysterious realm of poetry and identifies it with mysticism, which according to its etymology, implies a relation to mystery. Such an identification with poetry and a lack of any common or clear understanding of what is meant when the term mystic is applied to men or women have caused a failure in sympathetic critics to see that the mystic way, the method by which Gabriela Mistral strives to achieve her goal, is at many points very different from the mystic way of Catholicism and that of other religions.

The data provided in the three sections of this chapter are the norms by which Gabriela Mistral may or may not be measured as a mystic. The following chapters, by examining in detail her multifaceted personality, her complex religion, and the great motifs of her poetry, offer a comparison between her and mystics of all great religions. These facts, set up against the norms, can definitively answer the questions: Was Gabriela Mistral a Catholic mystic? Was she a mystic in the religions which she later adopted? Have her personality and her deep interior life prompted the label of mysticism? Can the religion in her poetry be classified as mysticism?

CHAPTER II—FOOTNOTES

1. San Juan de la Cruz, "El cántico espiritual," *Poesías,* p. 35.
2. San Juan de la Cruz, "Prólogo," *Poesías,* p. 63.
3. St. Thomas Aquinas, *Summa Theologica,* I, trans. Fathers of the English Dominican Province (New York, 1947), p. 596.
4. Canon Auguste Saudreau, *The Life of Union with God,* trans. E. J. Strickland (London, 1926), p. 50.
5. San Juan de la Cruz, "El cántico espiritual," *Poesías,* p. 32.
6. Exodus xxxiii.13.
7. Terence L. Connolly, S.J., *Coventry Patmore, Mystical Poems of Nuptial Love* (Boston, 1938), p. vii.
8. Santa Teresa de Avila, *Las moradas (Interior Castle), Clásicos castellanos,* I (Madrid, 1962), 226-227.
9. St. Catherine of Siena, *The Dialogue of the Seraphic Virgin,* trans. A. Thorold (London, 1896), p. 20.
10. Blessed Henry Suso, *Little Book of Eternal Wisdom and Little Book of Truth,* trans. James M. Clark (New York, 1953), p. 186.
11. David Rubio, O.S.A., *The Mystic Soul of Spain* (New York, 1946), p. 4.
12. Rafael Altamira, *Los elementos de la civilización y del carácter españoles,* 2nd. ed. (Buenos Aires, 1950), pp. 233-234.
13. Rubio, pp. 41-42.
14. E. Allison Peers, *El misticismo español* (Buenos Aires, 1947), pp. 13 and 55.
15. Motto of the Order of St. Dominic.
16. Santa Teresa de Avila, *Las moradas,* p. 221.
17. M. Menéndez y Pelayo, in *San Juan de la Cruz, el cántico espiritual* ("St. John of the Cross, Spiritual Canticle"), ed. M. Martínez Burgos (Madrid, 1936), p. ix.
18. Mark xii.30.
19. Jorge Guillén, *Language and Poetry* (Cambridge, Mass., 1961), p. 86.
20. San Juan de la Cruz, "Llama de amor viva," *Poesías,* p. 40.
21. Evelyn Underhill, *The Essentials of Mysticism,* 2nd ed. (New York, 1960), p. 4.
22. *Summa Theologica,* pp. 595-596.
23. Saint François de Sales, *Traité de l'amour de Dieu,* I ("Treatise on the Love of God") (Paris, 1925), 121.
24. Augustine, *The Confessions,* ed. J. H. Lelen (New York, 1952), p. 21.
25. Psalm lxxii.25-26.
26. Underhill, pp. 5-6.
27. "Plotinus is by far the greatest figure of this age of transition. His Christian contemporary, Origen, was a learned Biblical scholar and a theologian of remarkable independence; but as a thinker, though he de-

serves to be treated with great respect, he was not to be compared with Plotinus. One of the great figures in the history of thought, Vacherot, calls the *Enneads* 'the vastest, richest, and perhaps the most powerful synthesis in the whole history of philosophy.' Whittaker calls Plotinus 'the greatest individual thinker between Aristotle and Descartes'; Drews, 'the greatest metaphysician of antiquity.' 'No other thinker,' says Benn, 'has ever accomplished a revolution so immediate, so comprehensive, and of such prolonged duration.' Euchen speaks of the 'weltheherrschenden Geist des Plotin' ('the world dominating spirit of Plotinus'), and says that he, though a pagan, has influenced Christian theology more than any other thinker—a judgment which does not seem absurd to those who have traced the ideas of Plotinus in the Cappadocian Fathers, in Augustine, in Erigens, in Eckhart, and in the whole series of Christian Platonists to our own day." Reverend W. R. Inge, C.V.O., *Plotinus* (Oxford, 1929), pp. 21-22.

28. *The Essential Plotinus,* trans. Elmer O'Brien (New York, 1964), p. 16.

29. *The Essential Plotinus,* p. 20.

30. Inge, p. 24.

31. Underhill, p. 5.

32. Edward John Thompson, *Rabindranath Tagore, His Life and Work* (Calcutta, 1921), p. 7.

33. Thompson, p. 16.

34. Krishna Kripalani, *Rabindranath Tagore, A Biography* (New York, 1962), pp. 181-182.

35. Rabindranath Tagore, *Gitanjali* (New York, 1916), pp. 4, 30.

36. *Ibid.,* p. 32.

37. Edward Conze, *Buddhist Meditation* (London, 1959), p. 12.

38. *Bhagavad-Gita, The Song Celestial,* trans. Edwin Arnold, in David G. Bradley, *A Guide to the World's Religions* (Englewood Cliffs, 1963), p. 99.

39. Conze, pp. 12-13.

40. G. C. Flynn, "The Alleged Mysticism of Sor Juana Inés de la Cruz," *Hispanic Review,* XXVIII (1960), 235-238.

41. Flynn, p. 244.

42. Roderick A. Molina, O.F.M., "Amado Nervo: His Mysticism and Franciscan Influence," *The Americas,* VI (1949), 195.

43. Molina, pp. 178-179.

44. E. Allison Peers, "Mysticism in the Poetry of Lope de Vega," *Estudios dedicados a Menéndez Pidal,* I (Madrid, 1950), 352-353.

45. *Ibid.,* p. 358.

46. Jacques and Raïssa Maritain, *The Situation of Poetry,* trans. Marshall Suther (New York, 1955), pp. 29-30.

47. Howard T. Young, *The Victorious Expression* (Madison, 1964), p. xxi.

48. William Blake, "Auguries of Innocence," *Selected Poetry and Prose,* ed. Northrop Frye (New York, 1953), p. 90.

49. Maritain, p. 31.

50. "Wendung," *Selected Works,* trans. J. B. Leishman, II (London, 1960), 305-306.
51. Young, pp. 79-80.
52. Francis Thompson, "Nature's Immortality," *Works,* III, 83.
53. Maritain, p. 34.
54. Guillén, p. 151.
55. Jean Cassou, *Trois poètes: Rilke, Milosz, Machado* ("Three Poets: Rilke, Milosz, Machado") (Paris, 1954), p. 93.
56. Young, p. 79.
57. Maritain, p. 34.
58. *Beyond Criticism* (Lincoln, Nebraska, 1953), p. 10.
59. Henri Brémond, *Prière et poésie,* pp. 86-87.

chapter **III**

PERSONALITY OF GABRIELA MISTRAL

1. The years before "Los sonetos de la muerte"[1]

En presencia de Gabriela nadie podía estar espiritualmente inactivo; era preciso compartir su perplejidad, sufrir o aceptar su problemática, seguirla, discutir o pelear con ella. Acompañaban siempre a Gabriela por esa fuerza y mensaje que emanaba de su persona, numerosos hombres y mujeres. En todas partes donde estuvo ejerció una especie de Ministerio moral de América que no tenía otro poder y otra sanción que la de su limpia y justiciera sinceridad.

"Llegará recogido el cabello, lento el paso, el andar meciéndose en un dulce y grave ritmo," decía Pedro Prado. Y agregaba que Gabriela como ninguna mujer tenía "la boca rasgada por el dolor" y se le reconocía en todas partes "por la nobleza que despierta." "Por donde pasa ablanda los duros terrones y hace germinar las semillas ocultas que aguardan."[2]

(In Gabriela's presence, no one could remain spiritually inactive; it was necessary to share her perplexity, suffer, or accept her problematical position, follow her, dispute, or fight with her. Through that strength and message which emanated from her person, numerous men and women always accompanied Gabriela. Every place she was, she exercised a kind of moral ministry of America, which had no other authority and no other sanction than that of her pure and just sincerity.

"She will arrive with her hair pulled back, her step slow, her walk swaying in a sweet and grave rhythm," Pedro Prado would say. And he added that Gabriela, like no other woman, had "a mouth drooped with care," and she was known everywhere "by the nobility which she inspires." "Wherever she passes, she softens the hard terrains and she makes the hidden seeds which they guard germinate.")

To undertake an analysis of the personality of the woman here described is a difficult and perilous task. To attempt to fathom the depth and breadth of her inwardness would require the same risks as those so expertly presented by Dulce María Loynaz, the risks of scaling a mountain, of penetrating a virgin forest, of fording the Amazon.[3]

In an attempt to sound the profound personality of Gabriela Mistral, Hellén Ferro experiments with a Freudian thesis:

> Aquí debemos introducir una tesis un tanto freudiana (al fin de cuentas Freud influyó a toda la época de Gabriela y aunque se han exagerado y mistificado sus teorías, nadie puede negarlo importancia): . . . y es la gran camarada de los hombres, a quienes trata sin esfuerzo de igual a igual, sin dejar por esto de ser exquisitamente femenina, con su suavidad bonachona e irónica capaz del enojo de una walkiria llegado el momento. . . . Las derivaciones freudianas pueden ser múltiples y esperemos que si alguien las intenta—o las ha intentado ya, como es probable—no exagere la nota patológica y cargue sobre la complexión psicológica. Si la Mistral no tenía

tortuosidades y desequilibrios interiores era capaz de una intraversión total—siempre afable exteriormente—, dominada por su voluntad, en su vida de relación. La voluntad es uno de los rasgos más salientes de su personalidad. Su psicología, su mentalidad, era densa y difícil de desentrañar. Recibía a todos, con todos era abierta, franca y amigable, pero se confiaba en muy pocos, por lo menos en cuanto a su vida íntima se refiere. . . . Aunque con los años se volvió un tanto narcisista, siempre primó en ella la generosidad—más que la bondad—, una generosidad voluntaria, . . .

Perdida y desolada—pero no destruída, y hay un matiz psicológico en el título de su primer libro, que no es lamento sino asombro de que lo que ha pasado pueda pasar—Gabriela se repone. . . . Tal vez el amor se haya mezclado alguna vez, pero en el balance siempre primó la amistad que fue una de las virtudes de Gabriela, la que estimaba más. Y que gustaba más, por menos matizada, la amistad del hombre que la imaginativa y volátil amistad de las mujeres.[4]

(Here, we ought to introduce a thesis, somewhat Freudian [After all, Freud did influence all of Gabriela's epoch, and although his theories have been exaggerated and shrouded in mystery, no one can deny them importance]: . . . and she is the great comrade of men, whom she treats, without effort, as equals, without ceasing thereby to be exquisitely feminine, with her good-natured and ironic suavity, capable of the annoyance of a Valkyrie, when the moment arrives. . . . The Freudian deductions can be multiple, and let us hope that, if anyone attempts them—or has already attempted them, as is probable—he will not exaggerate the pathological note and stress

> the psychological aspect. If Mistral did not have interior tensions and disorders, she was capable of complete introversion—always affable exteriorly—dominated by her will, in her rapport with others. Her will is one of the most salient traits of her personality. Her psychology, her mentality were deep and difficult to fathom. She would receive all; she was open with all, frank, and friendly, but she confided in very few, at least in that which referred to her intimate life. . . . Although with the years she became somewhat narcissistic, generosity in her was always predominant—more than kindliness—a voluntary generosity, . . .
>
> Lost and desolate—but not destroyed, and there is a psychological note in the title of her first book which is not a lament but astonishment at the thought that what happened could happen—Gabriela recovers. Perhaps love was intermingled at times, but in the balance, friendship was always primary; friendship which was one of Gabriela's virtues, the one she esteemed the most. And because it is less fickle, she preferred the friendship of men to the imaginative and volatile friendship of women.)

Her exteriorness reveals that she was a complete person, a person through whose manifold and varied gifts, she pursued and reached her destination, "un hermoso reino, más vasto y más seguro que el de muchos monarcas cuyos nombres pasaron a la Historia"[5] (a beautiful kingdom, more vast and more secure than that of the many monarchs whose names have passed on in History). Little wonder, then, that upon her arrival she uttered the victor's cry, "Triumph!"[6] Innately reflective and withdrawn, she turned her glance inward but learned how to look outward. Distracted beyond the physical world, she moved in silence: "No hagáis ruido en torno a ella; proque anda en batalla de silencio"[7] (Don't make any noise around her; for she walks in a battle of silence).

Even the simplest personality is a complex structure of a certain type of temperament and disposition. A research into the complexity of that of Gabriela Mistral cannot exhaust the possibilities inborn in her individuality. Yet, a study of her biography, emotional disturbances, and spiritual crises may afford some understanding and interpretation of this impassioned "magnificent rebel": "En sus grandes instantes era una rebelde magnífica, capaz de entregar su seguridad y su vida misma, siempre y cuando la causa o la persona a quien defendía lo merecieran"[8] (In her great moments she was a magnificent rebel, capable of surrendering her security, her very life, always and whenever the cause or the person whom she was defending merited it).

The rustic Lucila Godoy y Alcayaga was of humble origin. Her father, Gerónimo Godoy Villanueva, native of the village of Monte Grande, near Vicuña, capital of Elqui, was a primary school teacher who was fond of composing verses. He would improvise them for his little Lucila and sing her to sleep with songs which lamented his lot and pleaded for her better fortunes. His weak and vacillating character manifested propensities toward falling in love and imbibing regional wines. To these were added wanderlust and a frequenting of fiestas with his friends. When he married Lucila's mother, she was a widow with one daughter. He soon lost all attraction for his lowly spouse and surrendered to more interesting loves outside the sphere of his dull household. Lucila was three years old when he departed. She missed the kindred poetic warmth her father possessed. Her mother, however, accepted her plight as an ordinary turn in the course of events, for "la conducta del jefe de la familia era en el valle un hábito varonil"[9] (the conduct of the head of the family was, in the valley, a male habit).

The child Lucila experienced her first sorrow. She was, unwittingly perhaps, embarking on her long series of rejections. The vivid and deep impression made on her sensitive spirit was to remain, for a child is never too young to be affected by what happens to him. He is often too young to understand, but he is never too young to feel intensely, though he has no capacity to express in speech the emotions which stamp his budding mind. Hellén Ferro alludes to this sorrow as one which ". . . puede tener la explicación freudiana a que aludimos"[10] (. . . may have the Freudian explanation to which we allude).

Lucila's mother, Petronila Alcayaga de Molina, was also a Chilean by birth.[11] That she tenderly loved and cared for the child is evidenced by Lucila's devotion to her, and by the sorrow she experienced on hearing the news of her death in 1929. It was this sorrow which, in 1938, she poured out in that section of *Tala,* "Muerte de mi madre" (*Felling of Trees,* "Death of My Mother").

For Emelina Molina Alcayaga, her half sister, Lucila has left no legacy. Emelina, child of her mother by a former marriage and fifteen years older than Lucila, was her teacher and guide during her childhood. Yet, there is no indication of the fact that she had endeared herself to Lucila.[12] By imitation or by vocation, Lucila became Emelina's assistant, thereby beginning her career as a school teacher.

Lucila's second sorrow was a traumatic experience that haunted her throughout her life. She had been commissioned to guide the blind Doña Adelaida Olivares who directed the primary school. It was also her commission to distribute school supplies to her classmates. Since Lucila suffered from a morose timidity, her companions took advantage of her introversion and helped themselves to large quantities of the supplies. When she found herself in deficit and was asked to give an explanation, she could not. The directress summoned the student body, and placing Lucila before her pupils, she publicly denounced her as a thief and a liar. That evening, as she was leaving the building, she found that a group of merciless children were waiting for her. They chased and stoned her until, bleeding and terrified, she reached her home.

Lucila never forgot the incident. Years later, while visiting her native Vicuña, she stopped to watch a funeral procession, wondering who had died. When asked if she remembered the old, blind school teacher, she gave the stony, stoic reply: "Yo nunca olvido" (I never forget). Díaz Arrieta notes: "Lucila no olvidaba los sucesos dolorosos; era su primera y profunda amargura"[13] (Lucila never forgot sorrowful events; it was her first, profound bitterness).

Matilde Ladrón de Guevara, her friend and confidante, also comments on this incident: "De su infancia, la perseguía una escena que le provocó un trauma. Muchas veces me lo repitió, terriblemente dolida. Fue la vez que, por razones posiblemente nimias, una profesora de Vicuña la echó de la escuela y la apedrearon en la plaza de la ciudad. En eso me parecía Gabriela una mujer ofuscada"[14] ("An incident which provoked in her a traumatic experience haunted her from childhood. Profoundly afflicted, she repeated it to me many times. It was the time when a teacher of Vicuña, probably through miserliness, dismissed her from school and she was stoned in the public square of the city. In this, it seemed to me that Gabriela was an obfuscated woman"). Doris Dana, moreover, affirmed that perhaps no other incident of her childhood had such a far-reaching repercussion on the formation of her character.

Her third frustration came when she was denied admission into Normal School. She had become infatuated with the style and romantic ideas of the Colombian writer, Vargas Vila, who, suffering from pathological delusions of grandeur, called himself "el divino." His was a violent talent. Lucila burned in its fire,[15] and in its fire she destroyed the opportunity for her formal teacher training. Her application had been accepted. When she presented herself, she was detained at the door with no further explanation than that the Council had decided to revoke her matriculation. One critic explains: "Quiere regularizar sus estudios en la Normal serenense, pero el capellán de ésta, don Manuel Ignacio Munizaga, más soldado que pastor de Cristo, se opone a su ingreso por considerar sus escritos 'algo socialistas y un tanto paganos.' "[16] (She wished to regularize her studies in the Normal School of la Serena, but the Chaplain of the school, Manuel Ignacio Munizaga, more soldier than pastor of Christ, opposed her admission because he considered her writings somewhat socialistic and pagan). Another relates: "Era el derrumbamiento sin esperanza. No le quedaba sino estudiar sola y luchar por su cuenta, formándose en la batalla, día a día, hasta triunfar; pero la curva de los labios caídos, que ya muestran los retratos de entonces no se le borraría jamás"[17] (It was a hopeless downfall. There was nothing left for her except to study alone and struggle on her own, forming herself in the battle, day by day, until she triumphed; but the curve of her fallen lips, which portraits of that time were already showing, would never be erased).

Lucila Godoy y Alcayaga, once denounced as a thief and a liar, was now being classified as an undesirable candidate for the teaching profession. She was regarded as a colleague of Vargas Vila, a harmful influence in perverting Latin American youth. Thus, the trauma of her earlier days and the frustration of her youth, with all their intensity, involved not only the external experiences, but also and especially, the dovetailing of external events and inner psychic organization. Her first feeling of rejection, now aggravated and intensified, needed some surcease from pain, and this, Lucila found through the medium of her paternal grandmother of Hebrew origin. This origin is confirmed by no other hypothesis than that which genealogists hold, based on the fact that she was the only woman in La Serena who possessed a Bible and dedicated much time to reading it:[18]

> El domingo la señora Alcayaga la mandaba a ver a su "abuela loca." La abuela la sentaba a leerle los Salmos de David. Lucila dirá más tarde que el Santo Rey fué su primer amor. En todo caso contrapesaba y reducía a cenizas las flores fatuas del maldito colombiano. La desenfrenada vehemencia de su temperamento, su ansia de expresiones excesivas y su corazón insaciable hallaban su alimento en las metáforas ardientes de la Escritura: repetía los apóstrofes de los profetas, las quejas de Job increpando cara a cara a la divinidad, los gritos de pasión que exhala el "Cantar de los Cantares."[19]
>
> (On Sunday, Mrs. Alcayaga would send her to see her "crazy grandmother." The grandmother would seat her to read the Psalms of David. Lucila will later say that the Holy King was her first love. In any case, he offset and reduced to ashes the fatuous flowers of the cursed Colombian. The unrestrained vehemence of her temperament, her eagerness for excessive expressions, and her insatiable heart found their nourishment in the ardent metaphors of the Scriptures: she would repeat the apostrophes of the prophets, the complaints of Job, rebuking

the Divinity, face to face, the cries of passion which the "Song of Songs" exhales.)

For Vargas Vila's ill-famed, revolutionary romanticism, she substituted David's inspired, transforming classicism. And, when the hour of her tragic love arrived, the substitution found ready expression from her broken heart. To her may be applied the words spoken of Fray Luis de León.

> It has been said of Luis de León that he had a Hebrew soul. Perhaps it would be truer to say that he was essentially a poet. His devotion to Hebrew was due largely to the fact that he recognized in the writings of the Old Testament the world's greatest poetry, culminating, as it seemed to him, in the "Song of Songs." Sublimity, as Coleridge remarked, is Hebrew by birth. The Scriptures, said Luis de León, contain not only the science of moral and supernatural doctrine, but the seeds of natural philosophy and of all other arts and sciences.[20]

To her may be attributed the words spoken by Luis de León: ". . . llevando siempre, como en estrella de guía, puestos los ojos en la luz de la Escriptura Sagrada, y siguiendo las pisadas de los doctores y sanctos antiguos"[21] (. . . bearing always, as a guiding star, eyes fixed on the light of Sacred Scripture, and following the footsteps of the old doctors and saints).

Beginning with the year 1905, Lucila Godoy went from one pedagogical position to another. At first she was an assistant in the Primary School of La Compañía, neighboring village of La Serena, and from thence, to the Liceo de Niñas de la Serena. At this time, some of her published prose and poetry were already gaining for her considerable fame. Margot Arce de Vázquez states that by 1912 she was well settled in

Santiago, her pedagogical work recognized not only in her own country but even beyond its borders. She lived on the outskirts of the Capital, visited at all hours by writers, artists, workers, ladies of Santiago's aristocracy, and students.[22]

She continued, however, to suffer from a complex: "Se creía fea—siempre padeció ese 'complejo,' conviene no olvidarlo. . . . se juzgaba sin gracia ni atractivos, o lamentaba en silencio y buscaba la soledad"[23] (She believed that she was ugly—she always suffered from this "complex"; it is well not to forget it. . . . she judged herself to be without grace or charm, or she lamented in silence and sought solitude). Linked with this complex, there was in her character a natural inclination toward melancholy: "No lo sé; hay algo en mi ser que engendra la amargura, hay una mano secreta que filtra hiel en mi corazón, aún cuando la alegría me rodee"[24] (I don't know what it is; there is something in my being that engenders bitterness; there is a secret hand that filters ice in my heart, even when happiness surrounds me).

This introversion was steadily increasing when, for the first time, she saw Romelio Ureta, a railroad employee, seven years her senior. This sight proved to be "el nacimiento de un amor inmortal y la poesía suele venir por extraños rieles"[25] (the birth of an immortal love, and poetry usually comes through strange ingots). To this immortal love, Lucila has testified. Jerónimo Lagos recorded the testimony in the article which appeared in *El Diario Ilustrado,* December 1, 1957:

> Nos amábamos de verdad. Un mal día rompimos. Yo tenía entonces un carácter irascible: tan fuerte hablábamos uno y otro en la pieza en que discutíamos, que mi madre se impuso y lo despidió. Pasó el tiempo y los míos creyeron que yo estaba muy tranquila. Transcur-

rieron cinco años en los que, cuando nos divisábamos, huíamos el uno del otro.

Durante el último tiempo se dió a una vida de relajación y de mujeres; gastaba en eso mucho dinero. Su novia, por otra parte, que era muy elegante y cuya familia gastaba mucho, lo explotaba sin compasión. Gastaba, pues, más de lo que ganaba y tuvo que robar.[26]

(We truly loved each other. One bad day, we broke up. At that time, I had an irascible character; so vehemently did we speak, in the room where we were quarreling, that my mother interfered and dismissed him. Time passed and my loved ones thought that I was very peaceful. Five years passed during which, when we descried each other, we fled from each other.

During his last days, he gave himself up to a life of laxity and of women; in that, he spent much money. His sweetheart, on the other hand, who was very elegant and whose family spent a great deal, exploited him without compassion. He, therefore, spent more than he earned and had to steal.)

Here, Lucila tried to relieve the agony and the misery of her jealousy by pouring them into verse. Through the outpouring, she gave to posterity the ballad:

Él pasó con otra;
yo lo vi pasar.
Siempre dulce el viento
y el camino en paz.
¡Y estos ojos míseros
lo vieron pasar!

(He passed by with another;
I saw him pass by.
Always sweet the wind
and the road in peace.
And these miserable eyes
saw him pass by!)

She watched them enviously: "Él va amando a otra," "Él besó a la otra," "Él irá con otra / por la eternidad," and wondered: "¡Y no untó mi sangre / la extensión del mar!"[27] (He goes loving another, He kissed the other, He will go with another / for eternity. And my blood did not smear the vast expanse of the sea!). The torture of that final quarrel she spilled out in "Éxtasis" ("Ecstasy"):

Me miró, nos miramos en silencio
mucho tiempo, clavadas,
como en la muerte, las pupilas. Todo
el estupor que blanquea las caras
en la agonía, albeaba nuestros rostros.
¡Tras de ese instante, ya no resta nada![28]

(He looked at me, we looked at each other in silence
for a long time, fixed,
as in death, our eyes. All
the stupor which blanches faces
in agony whitened our faces.
After that instant, nothing now remains!)

From her conversation with Jerónimo Lagos, it is revealed that two weeks before his suicide, Lucila saw Romelio Ureta again. He confessed to her: "¡Si mi vida de hoy es un asco!" (Indeed, my life today is a despicable thing!). Lucila continues: "Quince días después se dió un balazo. En la cartera interior del paletó guardaba una de dos tarjetas que yo le había escrito"[29] (Fifteen days later, he shot himself. In the inside pocket of his overcoat, he had one of the two cards which I had written to him).

The intensity of the impact of this suicide on the personality of Lucila Godoy, the desolation and the devastation of her spirit, may be gleaned from the tempestuous torrents that cascade from the ardent lines of *Desolación,* and especially, from "Los sonetos de la muerte" ("Sonnets on Death"). The reader of these vehement verses is tempted to wonder why she, like another Alfonsina Storni who could no longer support life's contradictions and deceits, did not put an end to her misery, or why Romelio Ureta, like the husband of Delmira Agustini, did not murder Lucila before his own suicide. The fact remains that Lucila Godoy suffered neither fate. She remained "una pobre mujer que tiene su cara llena de lágrimas" (a poor woman who has her face full of tears). She remained to sing her song born of sorrow. Turning to the "Man of Sorrows," she pleads with Him to sustain her in her grief. Then comes her despair, as she imagines His eyes filling with icy coldness:

En esta hora, amarga como un sorbo de mares,
    Tú sostenme, Señor.
. . . . . .

¡Mira! De cuantos ojos veía abiertos sobre
    mis sendas tempraneras,
solo los tuyos quedan. Pero se van llenando
    de un cuajo de neveras . . .[30]

(In this hour, bitter like a draught of seas,
    You sustain me, Lord.
. . . . . .

Look! Of all the eyes I used to see opened upon
my early paths,
only yours remain. But they are filling
with the freezing of ice . . .)

The unfortunate Alfonsina did not have recourse even to this frigid God. Hers was the pitiable state of one ". . . sin el asidero de una creencia religiosa que la permitiese resistir las borrascas de su turbulento espíritu, . . ."[31] (without the support of a religious belief that would permit her to resist the tempest of her turbulent spirit). As for Romelio Ureta, he knew that the woman he had rejected was chaste: "¡Mi vida! No se interese Ud. por ella. Se indignaría"[32] (My life! Don't interest yourself in it. You would become indignant).

In her profound sorrow and bitterness, Lucila Godoy withdrew more and more within herself. She continued to teach and to pour her love upon her pupils, to shepherd the children of other mothers. She was attempting to adjust the driving forces of her nature and of her temperament. It was the beginning of the sublimation of her past disappointments, her conflicts, and frustrations. Hers was a social sublimation, mingled with a religious fervor, that seemed to satisfy the previous craving for love, for motherhood, and for children.[33]

Out of this sublimation, there came her delightful "Canciones de cuna" ("Cradle Songs"). In each of these cradle songs, it is always "mi niño," "mi hijo" (my child, my son) whom she fondles and cradles. When she sings to her child, all evils, all cruelties in the world cease to exist:

Cuando yo te estoy cantando,
en la tierra acaba el mal:
. . . .

Cuando yo te estoy cantando,
se me acaba la crueldad:[34]

(When I am singing to you,
evil ceases on earth:

. . . . . .

When I am singing to you,
cruelty ceases for me:)

It is always the fruit of her womb whom she cherishes and holds close to her:

Velloncito de mi carne,
que en mi entraña yo tejí,
velloncito friolento,
¡duérmete apegado a mí!

Yo que todo lo he perdido
ahora tiemblo de dormir.
No resbales de mi brazo:
¡duérmete apegado a mí![35]

(Little fleece of my flesh,
which deep within me I wove,
little fleece so sensitive to cold,
sleep close to me!

. . . . . .

I who all have lost
now tremble with sleep.
Do not slip from my arm:
sleep holding on to me!)

It is she who carries the child within her womb; it is she who suffers the pangs of childbirth:

> Me mire la Tierra y me bendiga, pues ya estoy fecunda y sagrada, como las palmas y los surcos.[36]
>
> Toda la noche he padecido, toda la noche se ha estremecido mi carne por entregar su don. Hay el sudor de la muerte sobre mis sienes; pero no es la muerte, ¡es la vida!
>
> Y te llamo ahora Dulzura Infinita a Ti, Señor, para que lo desprendas blandamente.
>
> ¡Nazca ya, y mi grito de dolor suba en el amanecer, trenzado con el canto de los pájaros![37]
>
> (Let the Earth look at me and bless me, for now I am fecund and sacred, like the palms and the furrows.
>
> All night I have suffered; all night my flesh has trembled to bring forth its gift. The sweat of death is on my forehead; but it is not death, it is life!
>
> And I call You now Infinite Sweetness, O Lord, so that You will deliver him gently.
>
> Let him be born, and let my cry of pain ring out at dawn, mingled with the song of the birds!)

Her "Poemas del éxtasis" ("Poems of Ecstasy") reveal her tremendous capacity and craving for love:

> Me has dicho que me amas, y estoy llorando. Me has dicho que pasarás conmigo entre tus brazos por los valles del mundo.
>
> Mañana me sentaré en el lecho y pediré que me llamen,

para oír mi nombre y creer. Y volveré a estallar en llanto. ¡Me has apuñalado con la dicha![38]

(You have told me that you love me, and I am weeping. You have told me that you will pass along the valleys of the world with me in your arms.

Tomorrow, I shall sit up in bed and beg them to call me, just to hear my name and believe. And I shall burst into tears again. You have pierced me with happiness!)

In all of these driving forces, she tries to understand what God is:

Háblame ahora de Dios, y te he de comprender.

Dios es este reposo de tu larga mirada en mi mirada, este comprenderse sin el ruido intruso de las palabras.

Es esta perfección de la rosa madura, antes de que caiga el primer pétalo.

Y es esta certidumbre divina de que la muerte es mentira.

Sí, ahora comprendo a Dios.[39]

(Speak to me now of God, for I must understand you.

God is this repose of your long gaze fixed in mine, this understanding of each other without the noisy intrusion of words.

He is this perfection of a rose in bloom before the first petal falls.

And He is this divine certitude that death is a lie.

Yes, now I understand what God is.)

It was heart-pourings such as these that found their way into the local newspapers and periodicals and caused her talent to be admired by the Directress of the *Liceo de Niñas de los Andes* (Lyceum for Andean Girls), who, in 1912, invited Lucila to teach in her school. Lucila accepted, and in 1914 was still there, discharging the duties of Professor and Inspector General, when she entered her "Sonetos de la muerte" in the *Juegos Florales* (Floral Games) held in Santiago. To these sonnets she signed the name to which her talent has given universal fame, Gabriela Mistral.

As was mentioned in the introductory chapter, page 17, the sonnets were chosen. The author was to appear at the festival, on December 22, to read the verses in public and to receive the highest distinction and award bestowed by the municipality of Santiago: the *Flor Natural* (National Flower) and a gold medal. But the author did not appear in public. Perhaps it was her old timidity; perhaps, modesty or reserve; or perhaps, an inferiority complex led her to believe that she possessed neither the dignity nor the apparel for such a public appearance. Whatever the motive, Lucila petitioned another to read her poems and to accept in her stead the crowning gifts of the queen of the floral games. From an obscure post in the popular gallery she watched the performance and later related in a sonnet "como había visto a la Reina de los Juegos"[40] (how she had seen the Queen of the Games). Before this occasion, the poetess was little known, despite the fact that she had already published some of her writings at home and abroad.

Raúl Silva Castro opines that these sonnets were written in 1909, immediately after the suicide of Romelio Ureta, and that the author guarded them secretly until the time of the floral games in 1914.[41] This supposition would seem likely even if the date 1909 had not appeared with the sonnets, for the ardor of five intervening years would have simmered into less volcanic lines than "que hemos de soñar sobre la misma almohada"; "¡No le puedo gritar, no le puedo seguir!"; "Retórnalo a mis brazos o le siegas en flor" (that we have to dream upon the same pillow; I cannot cry to him, I cannot follow him!; Return him to my arms or gather him as a flower). The red-hot lava of these words would seem to indicate that they erupted from a heart newly wrenched, and that the gratified vengeance would have burst into a less provocative song than:

Me alejaré cantando mis venganzas hermosas,
¡porque a ese hondor recóndito la mano de ninguna
bajará a disputarme tu puñado de huesos![42]

(I shall withdraw singing my sweet vengeances,
because to that recondite depth, the hand of no one
shall come down to dispute with me your handful of bones!)

2. The years after "Los sonetos de la muerte"

After the public acclaim of 1914, Gabriela receded into the introvert shell of Lucila and there remained until

> . . . tras diez o doce años de una pasión única por extraña y unilateral, pues la sufrió ella sola, en su interior, y con intensidad y rasgos desusados, Lucila vuelve a su normalidad psíquica y asume un papel de primera fila en la educación, y después, en el periodismo. En efecto, los poemas publicados, junto con su unción docente, valían para ella una rápida carrera administrativa, pujada por encima de las costumbres, en la que pasó a directora de liceo en las ciudades de Punta Arenas (1918-1920),

Temuco (1920) y Santiago (1921). Protegióla en estas circunstancias muy particularmente el político don Pedro Aguirre Cerda, a quien ella, en agradecimiento, dedicó su libro *Desolación*. . . . Y vino en seguida el homenaje extranjero, que culminó en la invitación del Gobierno de México, por iniciativa del ministro Vasconcelos, para colaborar en la reforma educacional de ese país, adonde partió en junio de 1922, habiendo sido, además, comisionada por el Gobierno de Chile.[43]

(. . . after ten or twelve years of a passion, exceptional for its strangeness and one-sidedness, for she suffered it alone, interiorly, and with intense and unusual characteristics, Lucila returns to her psychic normality and assumes a first-rate role in education and, later, in journalism. Actually, the published poems, together with her teaching success, merited for her a rapid administrative career, arrived at more quickly than usual, in which she became administrator of the lyceum in the cities of Punta Arenas (1918-1920), Temuco (1920), and Santiago (1921). The politician, don Pedro Aguirre Cerda, to whom in gratitude she dedicated her book *Desolación*, protected her in these circumstances in a very special manner. . . . And at once there came the foreign homage, which culminated with the invitation of the Mexican Government, through the proposal of the minister Vasconcelos, to collaborate in the educational reform of that country, to which she went in June of 1922, having been commissioned, besides, by the Chilean Government.)

In 1921, however, before she left for Mexico, Federico de Onís of Columbia University had chosen Gabriela Mistral for the theme of a conference which he gave to a group of American teachers of Spanish. So impressed were they with the depth and beauty of the poetry of this extraordinary woman that, when they learned that the poems had never been published in book form, they decided to undertake the task. Her New York admirers, therefore, invited her to collect them and begged her permission to publish them. Thus was born her first volume, *Desolación,* Hispanic Institute, 1922.

In 1923, her book, *Lecturas para mujeres,* a compilation of prose and verse of various authors, was published in Mexico.[44] In 1924, she traveled through the United States and Europe. In Madrid, she published a small book, *Ternura* ("Tenderness"), composed of poems from *Desolación* and a few unedited ones. In 1925, she returned to Chile, where she received a triumphal victor's welcome from the Chilean people, while the Government named her the Chilean representative in the Institute of Intellectual Cooperation of the League of Nations. This appointment brought about, in 1926, her second departure from Chile. In Europe, in 1929, she received the news of her mother's death.

In 1930 and 1931, she again visited the United States, the Antilles, and Central America. Here she acted as visiting professor in several colleges and universities, especially in that of Puerto Rico. Everywhere she was enthusiastically hailed and acclaimed. Men revered her; women regarded her as a symbol of their emancipation.

From 1932 on, she belonged to Chile's Consular corps and represented her country in Naples, Madrid, Lisbon, Brazil, Uruguay, and Argentina. In 1938, she returned to Chile and completed there the publication of *Tala* ("Felling"), her third book of verses. After a brief stay, she again resumed her travels.

Somewhere in her life, she had suffered another humiliating experience, the rejection of a second lover. The details of this romance are not well known: "Mientras ella vivió no lo dije a nadie; la más elemental delicadeza movía a ello, bien que no me había comprometido al silencio. Pero ya ahora me parece que no hay razón para ocultarlo; antes bien, entiendo yo que si Gabriela Mistral pertenece a la posteridad, la posteridad tiene derecho a conocer cuanto se relacione con su criatura. . . . le oí decir, con el consiguiente asombro, que el novio aquel que le fuera doblemente arrebatado no había sido en verdad su único amor. Muchos años después, cuando Lucila era ya Gabriela, y su libro famoso en el mundo, surgió otro hombre en su vida, al que amó intensamente y también desdichadamento"[45] (While she lived, I told it to no one; the most elemental delicacy prompted it, although she had not bound me to silence. But now, it seems to me that there is no reason to conceal it; on the contrary, I feel that if Gabriela Mistral belongs to posterity, posterity has a right to know all that relates to its creature. . . . I heard her say, with consequent astonishment, that that sweetheart with whom she was doubly enraptured, was not in truth her only love. Many years later, when Lucila had become Gabriela and her book famous in the world, another man appeared in her life, one whom she loved intensely and also unfortunately).

What is known, for she herself revealed it to Matilde Ladrón de Guevara, is that to him she dedicated "Dios lo quiere"[46] ("God wants it"), a poem revealing passion and tenderness smothered by jealousy. Here, portraying love as a cunning, demanding god, she warns her beloved that the earth will become as a stepmother to him, if his soul betrays hers. She threatens that snakes will spring up from the earth, that Christ and Christian charity will be stifled within her, if his soul betrays hers. She menaces that hunger and thirst will seize him, for God will not let him drink unless she trembles in the water, and that the kiss he may give another will echo in her ears, while the clouds paint on her house the image of the other whom he loves. She bids him go like a thief to the bowels of the earth to kiss her, but reminds him that when he lifts her face, he will find hers tear-filled before him. She commands him, whether he hates or sings or loves, to clamor for her alone. Then, finally, there is a reminder of her indomitable, "Yo nunca olvido!" (I never forget):

Si te vas y mueres lejos,
tendrás la mano ahuecada
diez años bajo la tierra
para recibir mis lágrimas,
sintiendo cómo te tiemblan
las carnes atribuladas,
¡hasta que te espolvoreen
mis huesos sobre la cara![47]

(If you go and die faraway,
you will hold your hand hollowed
for ten years under the earth
in order to receive my tears,
feeling how my afflicted flesh
trembles for you,
until my bones sprinkle
your face with dust!)

In 1942 and 1943, she again suffered the shattering experience of losing loved ones by self-inflicted death. The first was that of her dear friends, Stefan Zweig and his young wife.[48] The second was that of her adopted nephew, Juan Miguel.[49]

Juan Miguel was the son of an imaginary or adopted brother; "semifabuloso" (semifabulous) Dulce María Loynaz calls him.[50] This "brother" bequeathed his child to Gabriela when he was but an infant. The joy with which she received the fulfillment of her consuming desire can be estimated only by the measure of her craving for motherhood. She called him "Yin-Yin." She raised and educated him and lavished upon him all the love of which her great heart was capable. Then, on the night of August 14, 1943, he was poisoned with arsenic. To this day, no one knows whether it was suicide or murder. Gabriela feared the former, but to the end, refused to admit it.[51]

"Yin-Yin" was then about seventeen years of age. The spiritual crisis Gabriela suffered from this tragedy, she herself describes in a letter to friends, dated November 17, 1943:

> ¡Ay, pero tengo que volver a mi vieja herejía y creer en el karma de las vidas pasadas a fin de entender qué delito mío fenomenal, subsidísimo, me han castigado con noche de agonía de mi Juan Miguel en un hospital, tan espantosa a pesar del estoicismo increíble con que soportó las brasas del arsénico en su pobrecito cuerpo querido! Tengo que "echar atrás mi cristianismo" y dar oído a los muchos brasileros que me han repetido en letanía esto:—No viene de ahora ni de aquí sino de una orilla oscura que Ud. no sabe, este golpe, este azotazo y esta ceniza.[52]

> (Ah, but I must return to my old heresy and believe in the Karma of past lives in order to understand what phenomenal crime of mine, most subsidiary, has punished me with a night of agony of my Juan Miguel in a hospital, so dreadful, in spite of the incredible stoicism with which he withstood the burning of arsenic in his little beloved body! I have to cast my Christianity behind me and give ear to the many Brazilians who have re-

peated, in litany, this to me:—It doesn't come from the here and now, but from an obscure shore about which you know nothing, this blow, this severe lashing, and these ashes.)

So distraught was Gabriela over this culminating sorrow that she could find no relief, no explanation for the criminal deed except, in some way, to blame herself for it. This she could do by resorting to karma, a doctrine that every deed, good or bad, receives due retribution. In Hindu thought, it has been combined with the doctrine of transmigration, making it possible to explain any apparently undeserved pleasure or pain as a result of deeds performed in a previous existence. It has remained an essential part of the Indian religions that accept the doctrine of transmigration of souls. Both the Jains and the Buddhists took it for granted. The Jains worked it out consistently by making the extinction of karma essential to the attainment of salvation. The Buddhists interpreted karma strictly in terms of ethical cause and effect. In all sects the doctrine remains a powerful ethical argument, hence its name, a Sanskrit noun, from the root "kri," to do, meaning "deed" or "action."

Thus, when Gabriela cries out that she must return to her old heresy and cast away her Christianity, she refers to her more than twenty years when she believed in Buddhism and practiced Yoga: "Yo fui budista durante más de veinte años"[53] (I was a Buddhist for more than twenty years). In moments of severe frustration, when she again finds her path to happiness blocked, the feeling of tension increases to a breaking point, and she attempts to find an alternate route to her goal. "Yin-Yin" had been the realization of her dream, the rewarding "karma" for all her heartbreaks. On the fatal night, he had begged and received her permission to attend his first and last *fiesta*.

Again, Gabriela relieved her sorrow by pouring it into verse. This she called "Luto" ("Mourning"), and when in 1954, she published her fourth and last book of poems, the mournful lines of "Luto" were incorporated into *Lagar (Wine Press)*. Perhaps she so named it because, toward the end of her life, she was remembering Him who trod the wine press alone. Perhaps she was identifying herself with the One who was thought "a leper, and as one struck by God and afflicted."[54]

In "Luto," how painfully and tenderly she remembers "el voleo de tus voces, las saetas de tus pasos y unos cabellos . . ." (the volley of your words, the darts of your steps and a few hairs . . .). It still seems strange to her that she can no longer "apartar tus naranjas ni comer tu pan sobrado . . . abrir y cerrar por mano mía tu casa" (part your oranges or eat your leftover bread . . . open and close your house with my hand). She is still with him, "parada y fija en tu trance" (suspended and fixed in your peril), although she can neither hear the call of eternity nor see the face of Him who calls: "la llamada aún no se oye ni el Llamador da su rostro" (Still the call is not heard, nor does the Caller show His face). Suddenly, she ends her anniversary lament on a tone of optimism:

> ¡Pero tal vez esto sea,
> ¡ay! amor mío, la dádiva
> del Rostro eterno y sin gestos
> y del reino sin contorno![55]
>
> (But perhaps this may be,
> Oh, my love, the gift
> of the eternal Face without expression
> and of the kingdom without environs!)

In "El costado desnudo" ("The Naked Side"), she remembers all her past sorrows, and in her bent grief, seems to presage her approaching death: "Y a cada día camino lenta, lenta . . ." (And each day I walk slowly, slowly . . .), hoping thereby to arrive

Hacia ese mediodía
y esa eternidad sin gesto,[56]

(Toward that noon
and that eternity without gesture,)

She could no longer sit at table without remembering. There her bread was ashamed, her fruit without light, her glasses empty, the entire table offended, for their master was exiled, and strangers were seated in his place:

A la mesa se han sentado,
sin señal, los forasteros,
válidos de casa huérfana
y patrona de ojos ciegos;
y al que es dueño de esta noche
y esta mesa no le tengo,
no le oigo, no le sirvo,
no le doy su mango ardiendo.[57]

(At the table there have been seated,
without distinction, strangers,
availing themselves of a house orphaned
and protector of blind eyes;
and him who is master of this house
and of this table, I no longer have,
I do not hear him, I do not serve him,
I do not give him his over-ripened mango.)

Two years after the death of "Yin-Yin," December, 1945, Gabriela was in her hotel room in Petrópolis, Brazil, when she heard the radio news of her crowning glory: she had received the Nobel Prize for Literature. She herself relates: "Estaba sola en Petrópolis, en mi cuarto de hotel, escuchando en la radio las noticias de Palestina. Después de breve pausa en la emisora, se hizo el anuncio que me aturdió y que no esperaba. Caí de rodillas frente al crucifijo que siempre me acompaña y bañada en lágrimas oré: '¡Jesucristo, haz merecedora de tan alto lauro a esta tu humilde hija!' "[58] (I was alone in Perópolis, in my hotel room, listening to the news of Palestine on the radio. After a short pause in the broadcast, the announcement was made which amazed me and which I was not expecting. I fell to my knees before the crucifix which always accompanies me, and bathed in tears, I prayed: "Jesus Christ, make your humble daughter worthy of such a high honor!").

In her humility, she gave the credit for her glory to the Swedish translator: ". . . si no fuera por la traducción maestra que hizo de mi obra el escritor sueco, puliendo mi ténica, y con ello, mejorando mis poemas, tal vez jamás me habrían favorecido con el gran premio"[59] (. . . if it had not been for the master translation which the Swedish writer made of my work, polishing my technique and, with it, improving the poems, perhaps they would never have favored me with the great prize). Julio Saavedra Molina, however, states that she heard the news without surprise, ". . . porque Gabriela sabía que Chile le había pedido para ella desde años antes"[60] (. . . because Gabriela knew that Chile had petitioned it for her years before).

Gabriela Mistral had left the rejected Lucila Godoy far behind her. In compensation for the rejection of her father, the accusation of her teacher, the denial of admission to formal teacher-training, the desertions of the men she loved, the suicides of her loved ones, she was accepted, heralded, and acclaimed by the whole world.[61]

3. Psychology of her personality

Gabriela Mistral had a tremendous capacity for love and, consequently, a tremendous capacity to suffer. In her veins there coursed a confluence of Spanish, Hebrew, and Indian blood.[62] Hence, the specific pattern of behavior integration which constituted her multifaceted personality. All her critics agree that there was more than one side to the gigantic person of Gabriela Mistral. She was capable of exercising a magnetic attraction on some individuals and of repelling others with her disdain. Even her pupils experienced this contrariety and seeming paradox that manifested themselves openly in her association with them: "Entre las alumnas despierta sentimientos opuestos: unas la admiran sin condiciones; las más, sumidas en lo temporal, mantiénense alejadas"[63] (In her pupils she awakens opposite feelings: some admire her unconditionally; the others, submerged in the temporal, keep themselves at a distance).

Some, like Saavedra Molina, believe that this is a natural effect, the consequence of a rich interior life, to be "silenciosa, fría y hasta taciturna y huraña en su contorno" (silent, cold, and almost taciturn and unsociable in her environment), for she lived alone in her interior world and wrote "como quien habla en la soledad"[64] (as one who speaks in solitude). "Alone" explains: "Porque en el fondo, el hombre sólo ama su reflejo sobre los seres y las cosas, una especie de doble etéreo proyectado sobre lo que llamamos 'mundo interior.' "[65] (Because, fundamentally, man loves only his reflection on beings and things, a kind of heavenly fold projected on that which we call the "interior world.")

If Gabriela Mistral sought to find in her exterior world that which she carried in her interior world, it is not surprising that she so often lost awareness of her surroundings, fixed her gaze on some invisible world, and seemed suddenly to part company with those who were engaged in conversation with her. For, she was a superior being, maladjusted in a society built up around the average man and his needs. By virtue of her superior abilities, she was more keenly aware of shortcomings and injustices which she observed, and therefore, was subjected to more emotional storms. Hers was a sensitive and imaginative genius, quick to discern a lack of rapport with another. A lack of mutual understanding would sometimes bring about opposition and petty persecutions. This, coupled with her life of sorrows, could easily bring about misunderstanding and even ridicule on the part of the unsympathetic.

Life under such conditions is not conducive to the development of a stable and well-adjusted personality. Even when her genius was recognized, all her actions and iodiosyncrasies became, in the glare of publicity, common knowledge. Any of her behavioral deviations, too slight to attract attention in a less outstanding individual, were discussed and evaluated and elaborated until they assumed, in the myopic vision of some, proportions of neurotic or psychotic symptoms. Among those symptoms, the most frequently discussed are the carelessness of her personal appearance, her indomitable will, her irascible temperament, her haughty bearing, and her abstracted, distant air which gave her an aura of loneliness and mystery.

If Gabriela had lived in a century when trances and visions were not so unusual, perhaps her critics would have attributed her behavior to this phenomenon. Her haughty bearing could not be otherwise, for she absorbed within herself, within that majestic figure: the Iberian race, full of energy and powerful vitality and an insatiable need of believing firmly in and consecrating itself to its ideals, heroic, fervent, obdurate; the Hebrew race, with its impassioned David, stoic Job, lamenting Jeremiah, and pompous Solomon; the Indian race, admixture of Inca with its glorious heritage of magnificence and splendor and Araucanian with its unconquerable courage and the tenacity of a Caupolicán and a Lautaro, who won the admiration of Ercilla and caused him to burst into song, the only song of epic quality sung on American soil.

Gabriela was aware of this heritage. That is why, when she was wounded, her burning passions and impetuous blood spilled from a triple fountain. That is why metempsychosis was such a powerful factor in her personality, why she confessed: "A veces sé que he vivido otras vidas"[66] (Sometimes I know that I have lived other lives). That is why when one of her colleagues tried to describe her, he found it necessary to resort to a line from the Chilean anthem, "majestuosa la blanca montaña"[67] (majestic the white mountain). And that is why, in this awareness, Gabriela felt unworthy and humbled, and was forced to admit: "Soy modesta hasta la humildad y altiva hasta el orgullo"[68] (I am modest unto humility and haughty unto pride). This is what Dulce María Loynaz captures in her lyrical reminiscence of the poetess: "Su sonrisa era un don inesperado en ella, habitualmente grave, ensimismada, casi hierática. Las pasiones de más de una raza atormentada—por de pronto, la india, la judía—la resollaban en el verso y hasta en la misma palabra cotidiana. Esta carga de vidas y de muertes ajenas alcanzaba a veces resonancias extrahumanas para un oído fino, y era entonces como un jadeo de antiguas bestias extinguidas por la maldad del hombre"[69] (Her smile was an unexpected gift in her, habitually grave, withdrawn within herself, almost hieratic. The passions of more than one tormented race—provisionally, the Indian, the Jewish—breathed in her verse and even in her very daily speech. This weight of lives and deaths of others reached at times a superhuman resonance for an acute ear, like the panting of ancient animals extinguished by the cruelty of man).

Such are the characteristics or driving forces that compelled the rustic Lucila Godoy to make the amazing journey from the desk of the school mistress to the throne of poetry,[70] where the whole world pays homage to Gabriela Mistral. On this throne, she received from the hands of Hj Gullberg, member of the Swedish Academy, in the name of her Royal Majesty Queen of Sweden, the Nobel Prize for Literature.

After her reception in Stockholm, she visited England, France, and Italy. The University of Florence bestowed on her an honorary doctoral degree, and Pope Pius XII received her in private audience.

Upon her return to the United States, she represented Chile as Consul in Los Angeles. Columbia University and the University of California both awarded her honorary degrees. When she was stricken with diabetes, she was invited by President Alemán to convalesce in Veracruz. Here, the Mexican Government presented her with a beautiful house and garden. In Naples, in 1951, she received the National Award for Chilean Literature. In 1953, she was in Cuba, taking part in the centennial celebration given in honor of José Martí to whom she had dedicated articles and conferences: "La lengua de Martí," "El hombre José Martí," "El trópico y José Martí." ("The Language of Martí," "José Martí, the Man," "The Tropics and José Martí"). From Cuba, she moved to New York as Chilean delegate to the United Nations. In Columbia University, she participated in their colloquia on the freedom of culture.

In 1954, the state of her health was such that she was forced to resign her post in the United Nations and retire to her home in Roslyn Harbor where, in the company of her devoted friend and secretary, Doris Dana, she lived until a few days before her death. It was in Hempstead Hospital, Long Island, January 10, 1957, that she died of cancer of the pancreas. Into that hospital, she brought with her a record which seemed to proclaim as a final boast:

> Yo nací de una carne tajada
> en el seco riñón de Israel,
> Macabea que da Macabeos,
> miel de avispa que pasa a hidromiel,
> yo he cantado cosiendo mis cerros
> por cogerte en el grito los pies.[71]
>
> (I was born of a flesh cleaved
> out of the dry center of Israel,
> Macabees who produce Macabees,
> wasp honey that becomes hydromel,
> and I have sung, keeping close to my hills,
> to grasp your feet in the cry.)

(Reference is made here to the Chilean character in its strong and stubborn aspect.)

The record, "Kol Nidre," is a solemn song whose complex chant came from the singing school of the monastery of St. Gall in Switzerland, at some time before the eleventh century. It is an abrogation of all vows made to the Almighty, from one day of Atonement to the next day of Atonement. In the resounding splendor of Hebrew, filled with that religious ardor which in the Jewish people serves for both patriotism and religion, Gabriela's spirit was uplifted: ". . . como su entrada al hospital de Hempstead con el disco de Kol Nidre, esa melodía que la acompañó casi toda la vida, . . . Tal vez alguien pueda decir entonces lo que el general Yadin expreso a propósito de los 'Himnos de acción de gracias,' que él duda de que ninguna otra lengua a no ser el hebreo original, pudiera transmitir la profunda emoción y la belleza espiritual de estos versos"[72] (. . . like her entrance into Hempstead Hospital with the record of Kol Nidre, that melody which accompanied her almost all her life, . . . Perhaps someone may then say that which General Yadin expressed in reference to the "Hymns of Thanksgiving," that he doubts if any other language, except the original Hebrew, could transmit the profound emotion and the spiritual beauty of these verses).

Eduardo Barrios, too, in his tribute to her, calls her "un alma de Israel, convertida al cristianismo" (a soul of Israel converted to Christianity) and gives his reason: "Porque Gabriela Mistral es David, Job y Salomón en Mateo, Pablo y Juan. Antes de evocar su 'Mujer fuerte' y su 'Ruth' la moabita 'bajo el sol caldeo,' nos dijo en occidente su más genuino ardor 'Al oído del Cristo.' Su aliento bíblico nos llega siempre aromado en el aliento del Nazareno. Su corazón está henchido por la sangre piadosa del Hijo"[73] (Because Gabriela Mistral is David, Job, and Solomon in Matthew, Paul, and John. Before evoking her "Valiant Woman" and her "Ruth," the Moabite "under the Chaldean sun," she tells us, in occident, her most genuine ardor "In the Ear of Christ." Her biblical breath always reaches us fragrant with the breath of the Nazarene. Her heart is filled with the merciful blood of the Son).

Her swan song was not a "Nocturno de la derrota" ("Nocturn of the Defeated One"), nor was it a "Nocturno de la consummación" (Nocturn of Consummation"), for when her remains reached Chile, on January 19, they were installed in the *Salón de Honor* (Hall of Honor) of the University of Chile where more than two hundred thousand people passed by her coffin in silent tribute to their *maestra rural* (Rural Schoolmistress) who had returned home, who had gone to her kingdom, "donde todas íbamos a ser reinas"[74] (where we were all going to be queens). On January 22, she was temporarily interred in the Cemetery of Santiago, awaiting the construction of the mausoleum which would tabernacle the precious relics. Today, the Andean village of Montegrande boasts of the definitive resting place of her whose heart embraced the children of the world. From her book now, they may repeat the words which she dedicated to the masters to whom she was indebted:

¡Os amo, os amo, bocas de los poetas idos,
que deshechas en polvo me seguís consolando,
y que al llegar la noche estáis conmigo hablando,
junto a la dulce lámpara, con dulzor de gemidos!

De la página abierta aparto la mirada,
¡oh muertos!, y mi ensueño va tejiéndoos semblantes:
las pupilas febriles, los labios anhelantes
que lentos se deshacen en la tierra apretada.[75]

(I love you, I love you, mouths of poets gone,
which, crumbled to dust follow me consoling,
and, when the night arrives, you are with me speaking,
close to the comfortable lamp, with gentleness of sighs.

From the open page, I withdraw my gaze,
Oh, dead ones! and my fantasy goes weaving likenesses:
feverish eyes, eager lips
which slowly crumble in the compressed earth.)

Poets never die, and when poetry spills from the broken heart of an impassioned woman, it bears the impress of eternity. Just as Gabriela Mistral perpetuates in her works the masters who inspired her and the loves which shaped her, so does she, in turn, live on in them, for they "finger all the stops of the spirit, and we hear . . . the still sad music of humanity . . . the regal air, the prophetic ardors, the apocalyptic vision."[76] Her masters and her loves we know, for she has told us who they are: "Mis amores en el arte para regir la vida son: la Biblia, el Dante, Tagore y los rusos. Mis grandes amores son: la fe, la tierra, la poesía"[77] (My loves in art to govern my life are: the Bible, Dante, Tagore, and the Russians. My big loves are: faith, the earth, poetry). Gabriela Mistral conquered because Lucila Godoy suffered: ". . . by torture life tries the elected victors of her untriumphed triumphs, and of cypress is the commemoration on their brows. Sadness, the king-maker, *morituri te salutant* (we who are about to die, salute you)! No man ever attained supreme knowledge unless his heart had been torn up by the roots."[78]

Gabriela could sing her song because Lucila had been torn up by the roots to wrest the scorching song from the throat of Gabriela:

> Yo tengo una palabra en la garganta
> y no la suelto, y no me libro de ella
> aunque me empuje su empellón de sangre.
> Si la saltase, quema el pasto vivo,
> sangra al cordero, hace caer al pájaro.[79]

> (I have a word in my throat,
> and I do not set it free, and I do not free myself of it
> although its surge of blood impels me.

If I should set it free, it would burn the green pasture,
bleed the lamb, make the bird fall.)

And Gabriela learned her lesson well. She understood that only through such wrestling would her song be worth singing:

> Los que cual Cristo hicieron la Vía-Dolorosa,
> apretaron el verso contra su roja herida,
> y es lienzo de Verónica la estrofa dolorida;
> ¡todo libro es purpúreo como sangrienta rosa![80]
>
> (They who like Christ made the Way of the Cross,
> pressed their verse against their red wound,
> and the sorrowful stanza is the veil of Veronica;
> every book is purple like a bloodstained rose!)

CHAPTER III—FOOTNOTES

1. That these sonnets mark the turning point in Gabriela Mistral's life is a fact generally accepted by most of her critics: "En la obra lírica de Gabriela Mistral, los 'Sonetos de la muerte' ocupan lugar céntrico, ya que en opinión de casi todos sus críticos, son piezas extraordinariamente reveladoras de quien las escribió. Esto en lo que se refiere a la apreciación estética; por lo que toca a la historia de Gabriela Mistral, los 'Sonetos de la muerte' marcan la hora de la revelación de la nueva poetisa, revelación pública, con singular publicidad periodística."

(In the lyrical work of Gabriela Mistral, the "Sonnets on Death" occupy a central position, since in the opinion of almost all her critics, they are extraordinarily revealing pieces of the one who wrote them. This refers to the esthetic evaluation; in regard to that which touches the story of Gabriela Mistral, the "Sonnets on Death" mark the hour of the revelation of the new poetess, public revelation, with singular journalistic publicity.) See Raúl Silva Castro, "Notas sobre los 'Sonetos de la muerte' de Gabriela Mistral" ("Notes on the 'Sonnets on Death' of Gabriela Mistral"), *Hispanic Review,* XXXIII January, 1965), 57.

2. Mariano Picón Salas, "Crítica de *Santa Gabriela* por Benjamín Carrión" ("Criticism of *Saint Gabriela* by Benjamín Carrión"), *Homenaje,* p. 301.

3. Quoted in Chapter I of this dissertation, p. 47.

4. Hellén Ferro, "Gabriela Mistral," *Historia de la poesía hispanoamericana* ("History of Spanish American Poetry") (New York, 1964), pp. 337-338.

5. Loynaz, pp. cxxxviii-cxxxix.

6. "Creo que tú también lo supiste, pero luego; al menos en el instante de tu tránsito, y de ahí que tus labios pronunciaron esa palabra 'triunfo' que a todos ha parecido tan extraña." (I believe that you also knew, but later; at least in the instant of your passing away, and hence your lips pronounced that word "triumph" which seemed so strange to all.) In Loynaz, p. cxxxix.

7. "En otra página, la más hermosa, sin duda, que sobre ella se ha escrito, dijo Pedro Prado a los artistas de México, cuando Gabriela Mistral partió de Chile rumbo a esas costas, estas palabras." (On another page, the most beautiful, without a doubt, which was ever written about her, Pedro Prado said these words to the artists of Mexico, when Gabriela Mistral left Chile, en route for those shores.) In Hernán Díaz Arrieta, *Gabriela Mistral* (Santiago, Chile, 1946), p. 45.

8. Ladrón de Gueavara, p. 11.

9. Hernán Díaz Arrieta, *Gabriela Mistral—Antología* (Santiago, Chile, 1945), p. i.

10. Ferro, p. 337.

11. "Su madre y su padre eran chilenos, de cepa españnola crecida en Indias, posiblemente un tanto vasca, mezclada con sangre indígena procedente de alguna súbdita de los incas." (Her mother and her father were Chileans, of Spanish origin, raised in the Americas, possibly somewhat Basque, mixed with Indian blood proceeding from some strain of the Incas.) In Saavedra Molina, *Poesías,* p. xvi.

12. Doris Dana told me that Lucila had for Emelina a profound respect which was not the "cariño" (affection) which she felt for her mother.

13. Díaz Arrieta, *Antología,* p. ii.

14. Ladrón de Guevara, p. 29.

15. "Casi en los mismos términos en que nombra Dante a Virgilio, ensalza Gabriela adolescente a su Maestro: 'Y hace dos años que el arte me fue revelado por la persona de un libro, de un libro adorable de Aquél que es mi Maestro y al que profeso una admiración fanática, un culto ciego, inmenso, como todas mis pasiones: Vargas Villa. . . . Yo beso el diamante del genio aunque esté encubierto de lodo.' "

(In almost the same terms with which Dante names Virgil, the adolescent Gabriela extols her teacher: "And it is now two years since art was revealed to me through the person of a book, of an adorable book of Him who is my teacher and to whom I profess a fanatic admiration, a blind cult, immense, like all my passions: Vargas Vila. . . . I kiss the diamond of his genuis, although it may be covered with mud.") In Díaz Arrieta, *Gabriela Mistral,* pp. 49-50.

16. José Santos González Vera, "Comienzos de Gabriela Mistral" ("Beginnings of Gabriela Mistral"), *Homenaje,* p. 23.

17. Díaz Arrieta, *Antología,* p. iii.

18. Since these racist speculations are impossible to document, we offer the reader the qualifications made by Julio Saavedra Molina, *Poesías,* pp. xvi-xvii: (1) In reference to p. 131, n. 11: "Tal 'vasconidad' no se basa en documentos, sino en la frágil presunción que sugieren las letras de sus apellidos." (2) "La susposición de ascendientes judíos tiene menos consistencia todavía; no se apoya en documentos ni en tradición alguna, sino en la afición de la poetisa por la Biblia, rara entre católicos; su imitación de temas del gran libro, y su antojo de sentirse judía, como si la voluntad bastase para hacer la historia. Por esto ella ha dicho en su libro *Tala:* 'Yo nací de una carne tajada / en el seco riñón de Israel . . .' (pág. 21), y también: 'Gabriela es una mestiza de vasco . . .' (pág. 271)." He elaborates in a footnote: "Nadie niega que cualquier descendiente de españoles puede tener sangre de la razas que habitaron la Península. Lo imposible es saber de cuáles y en qué proporción. Bastan elementos de etnología y biología para comprenderlo. Las teorías anatómicas y psicológicas de racistas como Gobineau, V. de Lapouge, H. S. Chamberlain, etc., perdieron el crédito. Don Américo Castro ha enseñado en la Universidad de Chile que iberos, godos, moros y judíos habían escalado hasta la nobleza y el alto clero; y ha explicado el cómo y porqué de la expulsión en 1492, no de todos los judíos, sino de los racistas, y por los no racistas."

(1) Such "Basque heritage" is not based on documents, but on the fragile presumption which the letters of their surnames suggest. (2) The supposition of Jewish ancestors has still less solidity; it rests neither on documents nor on any tradition, but in the fondness which the poet had for the Bible, rare among Catholics; her imitation of themes of the great book, and her fancy to consider herself Jewish, as if wishing, were sufficient to make history. For this reason, she has said in her book *Felling:* "I was born of flesh cut from the dry center of Israel . . ." (p. 21), and also: "Gabriela is a Basque mestiza . . ." (p. 271). He elaborates in a footnote: "No one denies that any descendant of Spaniards can have blood of the races that inhabited the peninsula. The important thing is to know which and in what proportion. Ethnological and biological elements are sufficient to understand this. The anatomical and psychological theories of racists like Gobineau, V. de Lapouge, H. S. Chamberlain, etc., lost merit. Americo Castro taught in the University of Chile that Iberians, Goths, Moors, and Jews lived in very close union in the thirteenth and fourteenth centuries, in which the Jews had ascended to the nobility and hierarchy among the clergy; and he has explained the how and the why of the expulsion of 1492, not of all the Jews, but of the racists, and of those without racial discrimination.")

19. Díaz Arrieta, *Antología,* p. iv.

20. Aubrey Fitzgerald Bell, *Luis de León: A Study of the Spanish Renaissance* (Oxford, 1925), p. 226.

21. Luis de León, *De los nombres de Cristo* ("Of the Names of Christ"), *Clásicos Castellanos,* XXVIII (Madrid, 1914), p. 195.

22. Margot Arce De Vázquez, *Gabriela Mistral, the Poet and her Work,* trans. Helene Masslo Anderson (New York, 1964), p. 3.

23. Díaz Arrieta, *Antología,* p. v.

24. "Reflexionando sobre esa melancolía precoz, decía ella misma, por entonces estas palabras." (Reflecting on that precocious melancholy, she herself would then say these words.) In Díaz Arrieta, *Gabriela Mistral,* p. 49.

25. Díaz Arrieta, *Antología,* p. vi.

26. Jerónimo Lagos, in Díaz Arrieta, *Antología,* p. vii.

27. "Balada," *Poesías,* pp. 75-76.

28. "Éxtasis," *Poesías,* p. 64.

29. *Antología,* pp. vi-vii.

30. "Tribulación" ("Affliction"), *Poesías,* pp. 77-78.

31. Díaz Echarri y Roca Franquesa, p. 1350.

32. Díaz Arrieta, *Antología,* p. vii.

33. "There are two forms of sublimation, the social and the religious, according as the form of activity has to do with other human beings or with God. It is to be noted that there sometimes exists an analogy between the form of sublimation which is chosen and the past disappointment or form of unsatisfactory behavior. It is therefore likely that the craving which dominated the older drive is partially active in the later sublimation. It may lend to it a peculiar charm and determine that this particular form of sublimation may be chosen rather than another." See Thomas Verner Moore, *The Driving Forces of Human Nature and their Adjustment* (New York, 1948), p. 317.

34. "Suavidades" ("Suavities"), *Poesías,* p. 161.

35. "Apegado a mí" ("Attached to me"), *Poesías,* p. 163.

36. "La sagrada ley" ("The Sacred Law"), *Desolación,* 4th ed. (Buenos Aires, 1945), p. 130.

37. "El amanecer" ("Dawn"), *Desolación,* p. 129.

38. "Estoy llorando" ("I am weeping"), *Desoloción,* p. 142.

39. "Dios" ("God"), *Desolación,* pp. 142-143.

40. Saavedra Molina, p. xix.

41. "En la reproducción que hizo la revista *Zig-Zag* de los 'Sonetos de la muerte,' en la edición de 6 de marzo de 1915, aparecen estos poemas con la fecha 1909 al pie (ver núm. 26). Nos atrevemos a señalar que nadie hasta ahora se ha detenido en esta singularidad, y por eso reproducimos también esos versos que bien pudieron ser omitidos por obvios. Tenemos la sospecha de que los 'Sonetos,' efectivamente compuestos in 1909, quedaron guardados por la autora en atención al matiz íntimo y confidencial que sin duda revisten, a pesar de las muchas oportunidades de publicación que se le ofrecían por aquellos años, y enviados a los Juegos Florales sólo a fines de 1914, cuando ya la tragedia personal podía considerarla Gabriela Mistral como tema de construcción poética. Sea lo que fuere, allí queda esa impresión con una fecha que puede creer anómala sólo quien ignore que Romelio Ureta, a cuyo recuerdo fueron dedicados los 'Sonetos,' se había quitado la vida precisamente en 1909." See *Producción de Gabriela Mistral* de 1912 a 1918, p. 11.

(In the reproduction of the "Sonnets on Death" which the periodical

Zig-Zag made, in the edition of the 6th of March of 1915, these poems appear with the date 1909 beneath—see no. 26. We dare to point out that no one until now has observed this singularity, and for this reason, we also reproduce those verses which could well be omitted as obvious. We have the suspicion that the "Sonnets," actually composed in 1909, were kept by the author because of the intimate and confidential character which they undoubtedly cloaked, in spite of the many opportunities for publication which were offered to her during those years, and were sent to the Floral Games only at the close of 1914, when Gabriela Mistral could consider her personal tragedy as a theme of poetic construction. Be it what it may, there that printing remains with a date which can be considered anomalous only by him who does not know that Romelio Ureta, to whose memory the "Sonnets" were dedicated, had taken his own life precisely in 1909.)

42. "Los sonetos de la muerte," *Poesías,* pp. 81-83.

43. Saavedra Molina, pp. xxiv-xxv.

44. "En 1923, por encargo de la Secretaría de Educación, publica *Lecturas para mujeres,* selección de trozos de la literatura mundial, para el servicio de las escuelas mexicanas. Escribe para esta recopilación un prólogo—que es toda una exposición de las doctrinas de la artista—y en el que termina expresando su gratitud para México, con esta humildad y sencillez, propia de su grandeza: 'Ha sido para la pequeña maestra chilena una honra servir por un tiempo a un gobierno extranjero que se ha hecho respetable en el Continente por una labor constructiva de educación tan enorme que sólo tiene paralelo digno en la del gran Sarmiento. . . . Será en mi siempre un sereno orgullo haber recibido de la mano del licenciado señor Vasconcelos el don de una Escuela en México y la ocasión de escribir para las mujeres de mi sangre en el único período de descanso que ha tenido mi vida.' "

"A una escuela se bautiza con su nombre y se tiene la delicadeza de alzar su efigie en el patio principal. Ella, que de la Escuela, de las Madres y de los Niños, hizo una nueva y santa trilogía, no podía recibir mejor ofrenda."

"En reciente artículo, el escritor Roberto Núñez y Domínguez, recuerda el banquete que los intelectuales mexicanos, a instancia de *Revista de Revistas,* le ofrecieron en Xochimilco y las emocionadas palabras de agradecimiento que pronunció: 'Este será uno de los días más inolvidables de mi vida. . . . Nunca pensé después de desearlo tanto, que mi amargo destino me había de conceder un goce tan inefable como el verme rodeada hoy en esta meseta de anáhuac, por todos los bardos con quienes convivía de antaño en pensamiento y emoción, a pesar de la ausencia y la distancia.' " See Guillermo Lagos Carmona, *Gabriela Mistral en México* (México, 1945), pp. xii-xiii.

(In 1923, commissioned by the office of the Secretary of Education, she publishes *Readings for Women,* a selection of world literature pieces, for the benefit of Mexican schools. For this compilation, she writes a prologue —which is entirely an exposition of the doctrines of the artist—and in which she ends by expressing her gratitude to Mexico with that simplicity and humility proper to her greatness: "It has been an honor for the little Chilean school mistress to serve for a time a foreign government which has made itself respectable on the Continent for a constructive work of education so enormous that it has a parallel worthy only of the great Sarmiento. . . . In me, there will always be a serene pride for having received from the hands of the licentiate Sir Vasconcelos the gift of a School in Mexico and the opportunity to write for the women of my blood during the only peaceful period my life has had."

One school is baptized in her name, and they have the delicacy to erect her effigy in the principal square. She who made a new and holy trilogy of the School, of Mothers, and of Children, could not receive a better tribute.

In a recent article, Roberto Núñez Domínguez, the writer, recalls the banquet which the Mexican intellectuals, at the request of *Review of Reviews,* held in her honor in Xochimilco and the emotion-filled words of gratitude which she pronounced: "This shall be one of the most unforgettable days of my life. . . . Never did I think, after desiring it so much, that my bitter destiny would have to concede me a pleasure so ineffable as to see me surrounded today on this plateau of Anáhuac, with all the bards with whom I used to live long ago, in thought and emotion, in spite of absence and distance.")

45. Loynaz, pp. cxxxvi-cxxxvii.

46. Ladrón de Guevara, p. 30.

47. "Dios lo quiere" (God wishes it), *Poesías,* pp. 70-71.

48. Stefan Zweig, a distinguished man of letters, and his wife, Elizabeth Charlotte Zweig, died by their own hands at Petropolis, Brazil, on February 23, 1942.

49. "Los anales policíacos registraron el caso como suicidio, y el mundo entero se estremeció al conocer el triste fin del niño amado por Gabriela: otro suicidio en su vida, otro perder de igual manera la criatura de su corazón." See Loynaz, p. cxxxiv. (The police records registered the case as suicide, and the entire world shuddered on learning of the sad end of the child loved by Gabriela: another suicide in her life, another loss, in the same manner, of the creature of her heart.)

50. Doris Dana explained that Gabriela's wandering father had many amorous adventures and consequent illegitimate children. The father of "Yin-Yin" was one of these.

51. The night that "Yin-Yin" died, he was attending a party with school companions. Some of these had already been indoctrinated with the principles of Nazism. Since "Yin-Yin" was mysteriously poisoned that night, Gabriela feared that, as a result of some argument, his schoolmates had deliberately murdered him. She refused to believe that he could put an end to a life such as his, for, ". . . Era Yin-Yin, en el decir de la poetisa, dócile de índole, despejado de habla, sensible, inteligente; era también vivo y alegre como un cervatillo. . . . Sustuvo siempre hasta el final . . ., que el niño aquel le había sido asesinado, aunque nunca nos dio explica-

ción cumplida de tan inconcebible crimen." See Loynaz, pp. cxxxiii-cxxxiv. (Yin-Yin was, in the words of the poetess, docile by nature, clever of speech, sensitive, intelligent; he was also lively and happy as a little deer. . . . She always maintained, to the very end, . . . that that child had been murdered, although she never gave us a full explanation of such an inconceivable crime.)

52. Carta que dirigió a unas amigas," Río de Janeiro, 17 de noviembre de 1943. In Ladrón de Guevara, p. 42. (A letter which she addressed to some friends, Río de Janeiro, November 17, 1943.)

53. Ladrón de Guevara, p. 45.

54. Isaias liii.4.

55. "Aniversario" (Anniversary), *Poesías,* p. 705.

56. "El costado desnudo" (The Naked Side), *Poesías,* p. 710.

57. "Mesa ofendida" ("Offended Table"), *Poesías,* pp. 714-716.

58. See Ladrón de Guevara, p. 34. Today, Gabriela Mistral is one of five Hispanic writers who have been awarded the Nobel Prize for Literature. The first two, José de Echegaray, 1904, and Jacinto Benavento, 1922, received the award for their dramatic works. The next two, Gabriela Mistral, 1945, and Juan Ramón Jiménez, 1956, received the award for their poetry. The last, Miguel Angel Asturias, 1967, received the award for his novels. See Jorge Mañach, "Gabriela y Juan Ramón: la poesía nobelable," *Cuadernos,* XC (1960), 57-61. See also C.A. "Significación de un triunfo" ("Significance of a Triumph"), *Boletín Informativo,* I (1945), 73. Henry Grattan Doyle, "Gabriela Mistral: Nobel Prize-Winner," *Hispania,* XXIX (1946), 69. Arturo Torres Ríoseco, "Gabriela Mistral, el premio Nobel y su significado" ("Gabrelia Mistral, the Nobel Prize and its Significance"), *Revista de América,* V (1946), 127-128, and "Gabriela Mistral, Nobel Prize Winner at Home," *Hispania,* XXIX (1946), 72-73.

59. Ladrón de Guevara, p. 34.

60. "Gabriela Mistral: su vida y su obra"("Gabriela Mistral: Her Life and Her Work"), *Poesías,* p. xxix.

61. See Gastón von dem Büssche, "Visión de una poesía" ("Vision of a Poetry"), *Homenaje,* CXV (1957), 176-194. Hernán Valdovinos, "Falleció Gabriela Mistral y el mundo llora la cantora de América, ganadora del premio Nobel" ("Gabriela Mistral Died and the World Weeps for the Singer of America, Winner of the Nobel Prize"), *Diario de Nueva York,* January 11, 1957, pp. 1, 21.

62. See p. 132, n. 18.

63. González Vera, p. 24.

64. Saavedra Molina, pp. xxxi-xxxii.

65. Días Arrieta, *Antología,* p. xvi.

66. Ladrón de Guevara, p. 46.

67. Arce de Vázquez, p. 4.

68. Figueroa, *La divina Gabriela* ("The Divine Gabriela"), frontispiece.

69. Loynaz, pp. cxix-cxx.

70. "Madame Gabriela Mistral! Vous avez fait un bien long voyage pour être reçue par un discours si court. En l'espace de quelques minutes, j'ai

raconté, comme un conte, aux compatriotes de Selma Lagerlöf, la remarquable pérégrination que vous avez accomplie pour passer de la chaise de maîtresse d'école au trône de la poésie. C'est en rendant homage à la riche littérature hibero-américaine que nous nous adresons aujourd'hui tout specialment à sa reine, la poétesse de la *Desolación,* qui est devenue la grande cantatrice de la miséricorde et de la maternité. Je vous prie, Madame, de bien vouloir recevoir des mains de sa Majesté Royale le prix Nobel de littérature que l'Académie Suédoise vous a attribué." See *Les Prix Nobel en 1945* ("The Nobel Prizes in 1945"), p. 50.

(Madame Gabriela Mistral! You have made a very long voyage to be received by a discourse so short. In the space of a few moments, I have related, as a tale, to the compatriots of Selma Lagerlöf, the remarkable journeying which you have accomplished in passing from the chair of a school mistress to the throne of poetry. It is in rendering homage to the rich Ibero-American literature that we address ourselves today, in a very special manner, to its queen, the poetess of *Desolación,* who has become the great singer of compassion and of motherhood. I beg you, Madame, to graciously receive from the hands of her Royal Majesty the Nobel Prize for Literature which the Swedish Academy bestows on you.)

71. "Nocturno de la derrota" ("Nocturn of the Defeated One"), *Poesías,* p. 387.

72. Enrique Espinoza, "Gabriela Mistral y el espíritu de la Biblia" ("Gabriela Mistral and the Spirit of the Bible"), *Homenaje,* p. 101.

73. Eduardo Barrios, "El primer libro de Gabriela Mistral" ("The First Book of Gabriela Mistral"), *Homenaje,* p. 27.

74. "Todas íbamos a ser reinas," *Poesías,* p. 520.

75. "Mis libros" ("My Books"), *Poesías,* p. 35.

76. J. J. Daly, S.J., *The Hound of Heaven,* p. 14.

77. Magda Arce, "Presencia de Gabriela Mistral" ("Presence of Gabriela Mistral"), *Homenaje,* p. 34.

78. Francis Thompson, "Moestitiae encomium" (Eulogy for the Sorrowful), *Works,* III, 113.

79. "Una palabra" ("A Word"), *Poesías,* p. 721.

80. "Mis libros" ("My Books"), *Poesías,* p. 35.

chapter IV

RELIGION IN GABRIELA MISTRAL

1. Spiritual crisis

Yo no he sido tu Pablo absoluto
que creyó para nunca descreer,
una brasa violenta tendida
de la frente con rayo a los pies.
Bien le quise el tremendo destino,
pero no merecí su rojez.[1]

(I have not been your absolute Paul
who believed to never disbelieve,
a violent live coal suspended
from forehead, with lightning, to feet.
Ardently I wished for the tremendous destiny,
but I did not merit its redness.)

This is the confession of a woman who, on the very day of her entrance into this world, promised through her Godparents not only to renounce Satan and all his pomps, but also to believe in Jesus Christ and the truths which He has revealed through the Catholic Church. For, it is recorded in the parish records of the Church of the Immaculate Conception, Vicuña, that Lucila Godoy y Alcayaga was baptized a Roman Catholic.[2]

The confession is the beginning of the poem, "Nocturno de la derrota" ("Nocturn of the Defeated One"), published in

Tala (Felling), 1938, in the section dedicated to "Muerte de mi madre" ("Death of My Mother"). Before this time, Lucila Godoy had been a Buddhist for more than twenty years. Margot Arce de Vázquez reveals that, in 1912, she was practicing yoga: "Her time was devoted to studies and readings in theosophy and to the practice of yoga; she carried on a correspondence with Annie Besant[3] and Amado Nervo, the Mexican poet who was also interested in these pursuits."[4]

Yoga, akin to the English word "yoke," means to discipline or hold in check one's passions and physical nature and to yoke or link one's own atman with the paramatman and thus cease to be reborn. Atman means "breath," as in "atmosphere," and also, "essential life" or "soul." Each living being has an atman which is conceived to be a portion of a cosmic atman, the atman which is beyond (para) the world. The paramatman, the cosmic spirit or breath, is all that truly exists, all else being but a temporary manifestation of it. An individual's atman is temporarily separated from this worldly soul. The term "yoga" also came to be, like the word "dharma," almost synonymous with religion. Thus the yoga that a Hindu follows is his path (marga) to salvation, just as his dharma is what he must do to fulfill his religious vocation.

During a personal conversation, Doris Dana stated: "I lived with Gabriela for ten years, the last ten years of her life. During that time she never went to Mass and she never went to Confession. Her religion was a very personal relationship between God and her soul. She wanted no intermediaries, no clergy, no dogmatic or liturgical paths."[5]

Matilde Ladrón de Guevara relates that one Sunday, when she invited Gabriela to go to Mass with her, Gabriela made a startling revelation:

Yo no voy a misa. Soy cristiana y creyente, pero tengo

una concepción muy personal sobre la religión. No se debe hablar de esto. Sólo sé decirle que no soy dogmática y que le rezo a Dios muy a mi manera. El cristianismo tiene ventajas espirituales. La fe es algo más grande que ellos mismos, que nosotros mismos. Vivimos de esperanzas y deseos y quisiéramos estar de acuerdo ante Dios, pero . . . Pero a mí me gustan todas las hechicerías y no las liturgias.

Porque me enfrían las pompas. No obstante, si se trata de hablar más, podemos agregar que el sello judío no se borra fácilmente ni se borrará del espíritu occidental. La fe es maravillosa, envidiable. Serena y acepta; cobra y restituye.

Yo fui budista durante más de veinte años; creía en el Karma de los orientales, como otros creen en las Moiras de la Mitología. Fui una buena budista, pero evolucioné, así lo creo.

Soy católica, pero también retorna mi viejo fatalismo. La metempsicosis . . . es algo poderoso en mi personalidad. A veces sé que he vivido otras vidas; a veces ignoro todo, pero creo en las reencarnaciones.[6]

(I do not go to Mass. I am a Christian and a believer, but I have a very personal conception of religion. One should not speak of it. I only know how to say that I am not dogmatic and that I pray to God very much in my own way. Christianity has spiritual advantages. Faith is something greater than they are, greater than we are. We live by hopes and desires, and we would like to be righteous before God, but . . . But as for me, I like all the witchcrafts and not the liturgies.

Because pomp leaves me cold. Nevertheless, if it is a

question of speaking more, we may add that the Jewish stamp is not easily erased, nor will it be erased, from the western spirit. Faith is marvelous, enviable. It calms and accepts; receives and restores.

I was a Buddhist for more than twenty years; I believed in the Karma of the Orientals, as others believe in the Fates of mythology. I was a good Buddhist, but I evolved, so I believe.

I am a Catholic, but my old fatalism also returns. Metempsychosis . . . is something powerful in my personality. Sometimes I know that I have lived other lives; sometimes I am ignorant of all, but I do believe in the reincarnations.)

Matilde listened to her friend, then admitted: "No quise seguirla por el laberinto de sus ideas teológicas . . ." (I did not wish to follow her through the labyrinth of her theological ideas). And, in the labyrinthine ways of those theological ideas, Matilde also received a glimpse of Christianity. When she asked Gabriela how she received the news of the Nobel Prize, the answer she heard bore neither the stamp of yoga, nor the seal of Judaism, nor the impress of fatalism, but was marked with the Sign of the Cross: "Caí de rodillas frente al crucifijo que siempre me acompaña y bañada en lágrimas oré: '¡Jesucristo, haz merecedora de tan alto laura a esta tu humilde hija!' "[7] (I fell to my knees before the crucifix which always accompanies me, and bathed in tears, I prayed: "Jesus Christ, make your humble daughter worthy of such a high honor!")

The main implication in the labyrinth of the theological ideas of Gabriela Mistral is that she was searching for God. She was keenly aware of the existence and of the importance of her soul:

Para mí, la religiosidad es la saturación que ha hecho en la mente la idea del alma, el recuerdo de cada instante, de cada hora de esta presencia del alma en nosotros y el convencimiento total de que el fin de la vida entera no es otro que el desarrollo del espíritu humano hasta su última maravillosa posibilidad . . . Respecto del cuerpo, religiosidad es vivir sacudiendo su dominio y una vez domado, hacerlo el puro instrumento siervo, que debe trabajar para el espíritu, que es su única razón de ser. . . . Estupenda frivolidad es el materialismo, y se cree, sin embargo, hijo de la observación y la ciencia. Quiero repetir la definición que di sobre la religiosidad. Dije que era el recuerdo constante de la presencia del alma.[8]

(For me, religiosity is the saturation which the idea of the soul has made in the mind, the remembrance of each instant of each hour of this presence of the soul in us, and the complete conviction that the end of our entire life is nothing more than the development of the human spirit unto its ultimate marvelous possibility. . . . With respect to the body, religiosity is to live beating down its dominion, and once dominated, making it a pure instrument of service, which should work for the spirit, for it is its only reason for being. . . . Materialism is stupendous frivolity, and nevertheless, it believes itself the child of observation and science. I wish to repeat the definition I gave of religiosity. I said that it was the constant remembrance of the presence of the soul.)

In this awareness, she sought to find for herself the occult nature of all religions, the primeval nature when not yet affected by theologians and evolution. She may, in this respect, be termed a Theosophist, but she was never totally one. She was never totally anything, for she was an avowed eclectic, accepting from various doctrines those aspects which best fulfilled her particular needs.

Hers was the quest of a committed soul, a quest which expresses in one way or another the basic attitude in the famous dictum of St. Augustine: "You have made us for Yourself, O Lord, and our hearts are not at rest, until they rest in You."[9] St. Francis de Sales calls it a thirst in the human heart: "Nos coeurs ont une soif qui ne peut être étanchée par les contentements de la vie mortelle, contentements desquels les plus estimés et pourchassés, s'ils sont modérés, ils ne nous désaltèrent pas, et s'ils sont extrèmes, ils nous étouffent"[10] (Our hearts have a thirst which cannot be quenched by the gratifications of mortal life; gratifications, the most esteemed and sought-after of which, if they are moderated, do not satisfy us, and if they are extreme, they suffocate us). Hers is the duty of inquiry with the whole of her destiny at stake, but with ample room for delusion in the notions acquired along the way.

Pascal would have placed Gabriela in the second of his three classifications of all men, on the basis of the attitude which each man takes with regard to his last end: "There are, as he came to see it, three kinds of persons: those who serve God, having found Him; those who are busy seeking Him, without having found Him; and finally, those who live without seeking Him, and without having found Him."[11] These last he considered insensate persons, men in chains, all of them condemned to death. The first and the second come to live under the Shadow of the Almighty, invisible and vague to the second, but constantly present on the human scene.

What, then, is the reason for the spiritual crisis through which Gabriela Mistral passed? She was baptized a Roman Catholic; she possessed an ardent nature with a tremendous capacity for love and a sincere mind intolerant of deceit and falsehood. Hers was an excellent racial heritage, with its mingling of hardy north-Hispanic blood, of indomitable Araucanian, and of Hebrew with its powerful tendency toward mysticism.[12] Why, then, the poignant concern, the search for clarity, the misery of despair with all that is involved in such a life or death as hers was? She never lost her faith in God, but often lost faith in how to find, love, and serve Him. She never, according to Doris Dana, considered herself outside the Catholic Church, yet she freed herself from its dogmas, its liturgy, and its clergy. Some degree of her Catholic religious tradition permeates her Buddhist days and peers through the veil of her Judaism. Her Hebrew-Christian tradition does not proceed from any theological speculation, but from the reality of God. Because of this genuine religious context of her culture, God appears on every page of her writings, in every line of her lectures, during all the days of her life.

For her, God does exist. For her, the opening words of the Book of Genesis, "In the beginning God . . . ," became the motto of all her relevant thinking. The burden of questioning the reality of the Creator never rests upon her shoulders, for she knows; she needs no proof that the true way originates in Him who is the Alpha and the Omega of all things, the only One, therefore, who can give meaning to the world of nature and of men. Only He can help map out her path because He is the Lord. Her problem rests only in her search for Him.

2. Gabriela Mistral, product of Latin-American Catholicism

To delve here into the history of colonial and independent Latin-American republics and its consequent Church-State relationship would result in a distracting divergence. For such an historical probe, excellent volumes have been written.[13]

These provide proof of the fact that one cannot read very far into the national story of anyone of the Latin-American republics without running head-on into the perennial Latin-American phenomenon, the Church-State controversy, generally of great violence and virulence, which took root in the colonial days with its *Real Patronato* and *Regia pase*[14] and continued to shoot forth its branches through the years of independence and dictatorship. However, an analysis of the circumstances in which the Church must carry on its apostolic mission[15] in the Latin-American republics may contribute to a better understanding of Gabriela's fluctuating from one creed to another.

The analysis must begin by describing what is meant by Latin-American Catholicism, for through the centuries, the Church has accomplished her divine mission of carrying the teachings of Christ to all nations and adapting those teachings in whatever way necessary to particular cultures and societies, consonant always with the essentials. This adaptation will lead to as much diversity as there are diversities in different cultures, nationalities, or societies. It is the glory of the Church, however, that basically it remains one, no matter how great the varieties resulting from racial or national differences. Catholic writers on religious behavior and on the sociology of religion make certain distinctions regarding kinds of Catholicism. These distinctions may help toward the understanding of the complex nature of Latin-American Catholicism, since it is not only different from the Catholicism in the United States, but it has varieties within itself.[16]

Besides, there is an underlying dual nature to Latin-American Catholicism.[17] On the one hand, it is obvious that Catholicism has struck deep roots in the culture of the continent. On the other hand, there is an amazing superficiality that is even more obvious than the profundity of the Catholic customs. Together with the deepest piety and devotion to the Blessed Virgin, there is no real regard for the Mass and the Sacraments. An almost fanatical concern for the Sacrament of Baptism is joined to a profoundly cynical view of the Sacrament of Matrimony. Despite the tradition of Catholicism, it reflects no real grasp of fundamental Catholic principles.

Hence, while Gabriela Mistral did not assist at Mass or receive the Sacraments, she did not consider herself outside the fold of the Catholic Church. Ester de Cáceres wrote of her:

> Su religión de infancia fué la católica. Doris puede mostrarle a usted una emocionante foto de Primera Comunión. La formación fué muy pobre como era en estos países en ese tiempo: formación que no nos defendía luego contra el embate del liberalismo. En el caso de Gabriela, esa formación pobre dejó la grieta por donde entró el Budismo. Había en América del Sur una novelería por el Budismo, un empuje teosófico, determinado por la necesidad de espiritualidad y de fe en seres en quienes el escepticismo y el positivismo habían dejado una nostalgia y una aridez insoportables. Ella me dijo que había vuelto a la Fe, gracias a la influencia de Bergson; luego Maritain.[18]

> (From infancy, her religion was the Catholic one. Doris can show you a touching photo of her First Communion. Her formation was very poor, as it was in these countries at that time: a formation which did not protect us then against the onslaughts of liberalism. In the case of Gabriela, that poor formation left the opening through which Buddhism entered. There was in South America a novelty for Buddhism, a Theosophic thrust, determined by the necessity for spirituality and for faith in beings in

whom skepticism and positivism had left a nostalgia and an aridity that were insupportable. She told me that she had returned to the Faith, thanks to the influence of Bergson, then Maritain.)

She preserved, however, according to Jacques Maritain, "soif de liberté intérieure . . . dans des voies libres de toute formule dogmatique, . . ."[19] (a thirst for interior liberty . . . along the paths free from dogmatic formula).

The influence of Freemasonry and lay liberalism in the form of violent anti-clericalism continued to plague the effort of the Church to modernize herself and find solutions to her many problems. The impact of this turbulence on the history of the Church may be ascertained through her members. In 1953, an Interamerican Catholic Action Week, organized in Lima, Peru, and held in the seaport town of Chimbote, revealed what Latin-Americans themselves say and think about their own Catholicism. From the twenty Latin-American republics, representing some one hundred fifty million Catholics, came three hundred lay men and women with their ecclesiastical moderators to study the state of Latin-American Catholicism, basing the study on three general questions: (1) What may be said of the sincerity of the faith of the Latin-Americans? (2) What is their knowledge of the doctrines of the Church? (3) Are his individual, his family, and his professional lives conformable to the teaching and the spirit of the Gospel?[20]

The delegates further proposed the question: Why this widespread lack of religious instruction? In the first place, there is a lack of clergy and other means of giving the proper amount of instruction. Secondly, it is a question of the kind of religious instruction given. The caliber of religious teaching is much lower than that which is current in the other intellectual disciplines. Often it is out of touch with modern conditions and unrelated to the problems of the students' daily lives. The inertia of tradition has replaced the vital force that should inspire the teachings of the Catholic Church. Jaime Fonseca refers to this religious ignorance as an "open flank to Proselytism, Spiritism, and Communism."[21]

Latin America's drastic shortage of priests and vocations has been labeled by its bishops and the Holy See as that continent's number one religious problem. It has the smallest proportion of priests to faithful of any of the world's major areas, for each priest must serve from three thousand to thirty thousand, with the average being about five thousand. With about a third of the world's Catholics, Latin-America has less than a tenth of its priests.[22]

Bannon and Dunne record that in Latin-America, midway through the twentieth century, Catholicism, though still nominally the professed religion of the vast majority of the Latins, suffers from a number of defects. Some of these are internal to the Catholic body itself; others are attributable to external causes. In the first category and at the top of the list is indifferentism. There is often widespread evidence of a lack of vigor and healthy enthusiasm in religious practice. In many countries the Church has long since lost the active support and regular participation of the male population. Only a small proportion partakes of the sacramental life of the Church or lives up to even the minimum obligations. However, in some of the countries there is a quickening of the religious spirit among the men in late decades.[23]

Into an environment such as this, Lucila Godoy was born. That her family held the Sacrament of Baptism in high regard is evidenced from the fact that she was carried to the Church of the Immaculate Conception, Vicuña, on the day of her birth. There, her Godparents made the solemn promise to raise their spiritual child as a daughter of the Church, instructing her, if her parents failed to do so, in the truths of the Catholic religion.

Now, from the moment of birth, a child's hope of gaining a steadfast religion depends primarily on the attitude of his parents toward God and on the example and teaching they give him. During the present century, psychologists have come to know much about the psyche of childhood. Trained to understand the inner meaning of children's play, fantasy, and dreams, they can see that, at every stage of development, they have spontaneous spiritual impulses and spiritual needs.[24]

The infant Lucila returned to her village home of Monte Grande, where she was to begin her physical, mental, and spiritual development with three companions: her father, her mother, and her half sister, Emelina. Soon she began to feel their inner attitudes, especially those which affected herself, for a child, unless he is mentally very dull, can at a very early age participate in the conscious and unconscious emotional life of his parents. Lucila Godoy was far from being a dull child. She was an introvert and, as such, had an inborn reserve toward outer reality and seemed detached from it. Her first reaction to a new experience was one of withdrawal, lest it should overwhelm her. Yet, she was in constant touch with the land and with nature's beings all about her. She spent long hours talking to the birds and to the animals. She studied the sun, the stars, the moon, the clouds, the constantly changing waters of the river. In her solitary musings, she began to develop the gift for poetry which she inherited from her father. From him, too, she received those stirrings of religious feelings, for Jerónimo Godoy was a former theological student. But he, true to his heritage, was also a vagabond: "Para un chileno, descendiente de los más andariegos conquistadores, y habitante de unos valles y escondrijos, pintorescos, pero situados en la periferia del mundo civilizado, viajar, avecinarse al centro, es cosa que le fascina y que prefiere por encima de todo. No es un perfecto chileno el que no se esfuerza por 'correr tierras,' . . . Pero el chileno es también criatura que está siempre quejosa de su suerte, de su país, de la vida o de cualquier cosa; . . ."[25] (For a Chilean, descendant of the most roving conquistadors and inhabitant of some valleys and hidden spots, picturesque but situated on the periphery of the civilized world, to travel, to approach one's element, is something which fascinates him and which he prefers above all things. He is not a perfect Chilean who does not exert himself "to travel abroad," . . . But the Chilean is also a creature who is always complaining of his lot, of his country, of his life, or of anything whatsoever; . . .).

Lucila was but three years old when her father's wanderlust overpowered his love and admiration for his little daughter, and she was forever deprived of his paternal counsel and spiritual guidance. No longer was she to hear his lullaby, invoking the Angel Guardian to lull her to sleep with a promise that, in the morning, they would pray together:

Angel de la Guarda, cuídame a este lirio,
Que mañana al alba rezará conmigo.
Duérmete, niñita, duérmete por Dios,
Que si no te duermes me enojo con vos.[26]

(Oh Guardian Angel, take care of this lily for me,
Who tomorrow, at dawn, will pray with me.
Sleep, little child, sleep for the sake of God,
For if you don't sleep, I'll be annoyed with you.)

Left entirely under the care of her mother, Doña Petronila Alcayaga, from whom she inherited her physical beauty and artistic temperament, and her half sister, Emelina Molina

Alcayaga, from whom she received leanings toward and training in the teaching profession, Lucilla's spiritual formation suffered a stunning blow and frustration which continued, in one form or another, throughout her life. She never, however, lost sight of her ultimate goal, God. Neither did she ever abandon religion altogether. No matter what the precipitating cause of her loss of the Catholic faith may be, the initial difficulty can be found in the circumstances of her childhood, circumstances which stamped her mind and heart with vivid and deep impressions.

To list Doña Petronila and her daughter Emelina among the estimated seventy per cent of Latin-America's Catholics who do not know the fundamentals of their religion is to presume too much. To affirm that they did not think of the parish Mass as the center around which all the religious life of a parish gravitates, that they did not recognize that Mass-attendance is the ordinary means of learning more about their Faith and the means to strengthen that Faith, is to oversimplify the reason for Lucila's loss of Faith. Her biographers have not related that she accompanied her mother and sister to church on Sunday, but only that, on Sunday, she would visit her paternal grandmother who would seat her to read the Bible.

The strain of Judaism which these readings nurtured and strengthened was constantly alternating or co-existing with that of Christianity. Both fostered in her that which made her turn spontaneously to God. Both guided her natural religious impulses into channels which led her to a keen spiritual awareness and firmly implanted in her deep-rooted moral ideas. Without a doubt, her mother and sister showed, by teaching and example, the need for respect, obedience, honesty, truthfulness, and unselfishness. But the image of God which she formed was essentially determined by that which she sensed in their religious life. One has only to study the picture of Emelina and her pupils, taken in 1895 and reprinted in the copy of the *Anales de la Universidad de Chile,* 1957, to wonder just what Gabriela meant when, in later years, she referred to "mi santa hermana Emelina"[27] (my saintly sister Emelina). Emelina sits with a proud and haughty bearing, apparently lording it over her students, while the six-year-old Lucila stands behind her, rigid, tense, and strained. Did "Santa Emelina" ever discern that behind her little sister's detachment and perfection, there was housed a dormant volcano?[28]

When Lucila wanted to know about God, she began to ask questions. The answers she received could be measured only by the length and depth of those which were passed on to her mother and sister. Whatever those answers were, they did not strike deep roots in the sensitive spirit of Lucila Godoy. If they had, she would not have cast off her Catholicism so easily when sorrow and tragedy shattered her life. She would not have embraced Buddhism for all the years when she tried to find the answer to her torment. If she had received the proper instruction, she would have echoed the words of that ardent apostle who had been convinced ". . . that neither death nor life, nor angels, nor principalities, nor powers, nor things present, nor things to come, nor might, nor height, nor depth, nor any other creature shall be able to separate us from the love of God which is in Christ Jesus our Lord."[29]

Another indication of Lucila's lack of proper religious instruction is her admission, after she returned to Catholicism: "Yo no voy a misa. Soy cristiana y creyente, pero tengo una concepción muy personal sobre la religión."[30] (I do not go to Mass. I am a Christian and a believer, but I have a very personal concept of religion). She did not accept the missing of Mass as the index of her Catholicism. She did not accept the obligation as a precept of the Church, because she wrongly considered the Mass a single, isolated act of religion. For the official, public act of worship and sacrifice, she substituted her own way of talking to God: ". . . que no soy dogmática y que le rezo a Dios, es decir, le hablo a Dios muy a mi manera" (that I am not dogmatic and that I pray to God, that is to say, I speak to God very much in my own way). Her adherence to "folk Catholicism" is revealed in the final declaration: ". . . Pero a mí me gustan todas las hechicerías y no las liturgias. Porque me enfrían las pompas"[31] (But as for me, I like all the witchcrafts and not the liturgies. Because pomp leaves me cold). Such affirmations reflect no real grasp of fundamental Catholic principles and teachings.[32] Yet, when Doris Dana was asked when Gabriela actually returned to the Church, she answered: "Why, she never considered herself out of it. Therefore, there was no return."[33]

Hence, Gabriela Mistral's condition: baptized, believing but not practicing her Catholicity, is identifiable with the nominal Catholic of the Latin-American variety and distinguishable from the "fallen-away" Catholic of the United States who does not insist that he is still a Catholic.[34] But her condition of fluctuating from Catholicism to Buddhism, or better still, of merging the two, is not so common: ". . . soy católica, pero también retorna mi viejo fatalismo. La metempsicosis . . . es algo poderoso en mi personalidad"[35] (I am a Catholic, but my old fatalism returns, too. Metempsychosis . . . is something powerful in my personality). Doris Dana confirmed the truth of this powerful factor in Gabriela's personality. Matilde Ladrón de Guevara confessed that she could not follow her in the labyrinth of her theological ideas: "Calló. No quise seguirla por el laberinto de sus ideas teológicas . . . Era cristiana por el amor de los humildes, por el recuerdo del Sermón de la Montaña, por la fraternidad universal. Pero seguramente creía 'muy a mi manera' en Dios y creía poco en los milagros de la revelación. ¿Cómo podía ser católica si creía en la metempsicosis?"[36] (She became silent. I did not wish to follow her in the labyrinth of her theological ideas . . . She was a Christian through her love for the lowly, through her remembrance of the Sermon on the Mount, through universal brotherhood. But she certainly believed in God "very much in her own way," and she believed little in the miracles of revelation. How could she be a Catholic if she believed in metempsychosis?). The answer to Matilde's question is: She could not be—"No podía ser."[37]

When sorrow again came to Gabriela, with the tragic death of her beloved Juan Miguel, she could find no solace in her Catholic religion. She found it necessary to have recourse anew in her "vieja herejía," and "echar atrás mi cristianismo" (old heresy . . . and cast aside my Christianity). Christianity was not embedded in her, but metempsychosis and karma were, as they were also deeply rooted in the Brazilians who kept repeating to her, as if in a litany: "No viene de ahora ni de aquí sino de una orilla oscura que usted no sabe, este golpe, este azotazo y esta ceniza"[38] (It does not come from the here and now but from an obscure shore that you know nothing about, this blow, this severe lashing, and these ashes).

Gabriela's very personal concept of religion, her non-dogmatic manner of praying, her preference for witchcraft rather than for liturgy would define a kind of spirituality which Jacques and Raïssa Maritain term subjective and egocentric:

> One also hears formulated sometimes another series of grievances: ascetical preparations, solitary meditation, the desire for and the experience of infused prayer, all this—some say—arises from a spirituality in which the soul is turned towards itself and seeks itself. Under pretext of seeking mystical union, it abandons itself to in-

> trospection and to a psychological fixation on its own interior states, in which a disguised egoism holds the first place and which many a time would call for the attention of the psychologist or psychoanalyst rather than the spiritual director.[39]

Thus, in her "dark night," "Nocturno de la consumación" ("Nocturn of Consummation"), she complains that it is God who has forgotten her:

> Yo te digo que me has olvidado
> pan de tierra de la insipidez,
> . . . . . .
>
> Como Tú me pusiste en la boca
> la canción por la sola merced;
> como Tú me enseñaste este modo
> de estirarte mi esponja con hiel,
> yo me pongo a cantar tus olvidos,
> por hincarte mi grito otra vez.[40]
>
> (I tell You that You have forgotten me,
> bread of earth of insipidity,
> . . . . . .
>
> Since You placed in my mouth
> song for pleasure alone;
> since You taught me this manner
> of soaking from You my sponge with gall,
> I set about singing your abandonments,
> to hurl at You my cry again.)

In the "Nocturno de la derrota" ("Nocturn of the Defeated

One"), the strong strain of Judaism emerges together with her litany of Christian saints: "Pablo, Santo Francisco, Vicente, el segundo Francisco" (St. Francis de Sales). With the same familiarity she speaks of "Abel, Melquisedec, Lázaro," and confesses:

Yo nací de una carne tajada
en el seco riñón de Israel,
Macabea que da Macabeos,[41]

(I was born of a flesh cleaved
out of the dry center of Israel,
Macabees who produce Macabees,)

These lines appeared in *Tala (Felling),* in the section "Muerte de mi madre" ("Death of My Mother"), but the same strain of compassion for and leaning toward the Hebrew race appears in earlier poems of *Desolación.* "Al oído del Cristo" ("In the Ear of Christ") is a plea to Christ for the condition of "estas pobres gentes del siglo están muertas / de una laxitud, de un miedo, de un frío"[42] (these poor people of the century are dead / with a lassitude, with a fear, with a cold). In "Al pueblo hebreo" ("To the Hebrew People"), she sees Christ and His Mother Mary in the "Raza judía, carne de dolores, río de amargura" (Jewish race, flesh of sorrows, river of bitterness):

En tu mujer camina aún María.
Sobre tu rostro va el perfil de Cristo;

(In your woman, Mary still walks.
On your face, the profile of Christ is outlined;)

Then, her glance turns toward the two in whom Christ forgave so much because they loved much:

> Que tu dolor en Dimas le miraba
> y El dijo a Dimas la palabra inmensa
> y para ungir sus pies busca la trenza
> de Magdalena ¡y la halla ensangrentada![43]
>
> (For your sorrow in Dismas looked at Him
> and He spoke to Dismas the immense word,
> and to anoint His feet, it seeks the braid
> of Magadalen—and finds it blood-stained!)

Her "Credo" bears the impress of the strong and terrible God of the Old Testament, while among "Mis libros" ("My Books"), she pays special tribute to the Bible:

> ¡Biblia, mi noble Biblia, panorama estupendo,
> en donde se quedaron mis ojos largamente,
> tienes sobre los Salmos las lavas más ardientes
> y en su río de fuego mi corazón enciendo![44]
>
> (Oh Bible, my noble Bible, stupendous panorama
> on which my eyes remained for a long time,
> you hold over the psalms the most ardent lava
> and in its river of fire, my heart burns!)

It seems here that not only the artist herself, but also the poetry she produces, becomes a reflection, a description, an expression; at times it is almost an appeal for understanding, and perhaps also sympathy, in behalf of the Jew to whom Judaism remains a haunting echo, a source of possible insights, a luggage of folklore. It is, therefore, a source of inner conflict which she cannot escape and which she must articulate, for it must be permitted to rise to the surface, where she hopes it will be understood.

In her readings, Gabriela found a kindred spirit in Rabindranath Tagore. Perhaps she was attracted by the similarity in their ways of thinking, for he too declined the orthodox paths all his life. This he did with great satisfaction to himself and with almost unalloyed gain to his poetry. For him, too, it took much apprenticeship to life to make him forget his shrinking nervousness. Like hers, his real education came from the whole circumstance and environment of his life. Here he experienced the deepest and the most joyous communion with Nature, and his poetry became the faithful transcript of his soul. The process of his poetic creation brought changes in his religious attitudes, for at times, he seems to understand no dogma save the love and joy which are in the Universe. This, too, occurs in Gabriela, for she ". . . was never moved to literary creation by abstract thought, mere reflection, or pure ideas or feelings. All of her poems were born of an immediate and physical contact with reality, of her concrete and direct relationship to something, whether it was a person, a landscape, or an object. The beings of nature, children, men, and their actions were the sources of her song."[45]

To Tagore, she directed three lyrical commentaries on his poems. In the first, "Sé que también amaré la muerte" ("I know that I shall also love death"), she states that she does not believe that she will be lost after her death. She questions the reason for the fullness of her life and the richness of her heart if after her death she is to be emptied, squeezed out like a pressed-out cane. In "Yo me jacté entre los hombres de que te conocía" ("I boasted among men that I knew You"), she tells God that men have come to question her about Him because they continually find Him in her verses, "derramado como un aroma líquido" (poured-out like a liquid aroma). She boasts: "Yo te pinté al hablar de Ti con la precisión del que pinta los pétalos de la azucena" (While speaking of You, I painted You with the precision of one who paints the petals of a lily). She admits that she did all this to find satisfactory answers for her interrogators, but that, in reality, she has neither seen nor tasted Him. Therefore, she hopes to be pardoned for her "quietism," for that attempt to "see" Him, because, ". . . la espera enloquece y el silencio crea ruidos en torno de los oídos febriles" (. . . waiting drives one mad and silence creates noises around feverish ears):

> Tú, mi Señor, me lo perdonarás. Fué el anhelo de ellos, fué el mío también de mirarte límpido y neto como las hojas de la azucena. A través del desierto, es el ansia de los beduinos la que traza vívidamente el espejismo en la lejanía . . . Estando en silencio para oírte, el latir de mis arterias me pareció la palpitación de tus alas sobre mi cabeza febril, y la di a los hombres como tuya. Pero Tú que comprendes te sonríes con una sonrisa llena de dulzura y tristeza a la par.[46]
>
> (You, my Lord, will pardon me it. It was their eagerness, it was mine also to look at You, limpid and pure, like the petals of the lily. Across the desert, it is the anxiety of the Bedouins which traces vividly the mirage in the distance . . . Remaining in silence in order to hear You, it seemed to me that the pulsing of my arteries was the palpitation of your wings on my feverish head, and I gave it to men as yours. But You who understand smile at me with a smile full of sweetness and sadness at the same time.)

The third commentary, "¡Recógeme, pues, recógeme pronto!" ("Take me back again, then, take me quickly!"), is a plea directed to "mi Dueño," "mi segador extasiado" (My Master; My Enraptured Reaper), that she be not lost among the beings of Nature and forgotten by the Creator. In her plea, she identifies God with sights and sounds and begs Him to sweep her up with a simple movement of His lips, with an imperceptible inclination toward her:

> Mas, de vivir atenta a tus movimientos más sutiles, te conozco tantas ternuras que me hacen confiar. Yo te he visto, yendo de mañana por el campo, recoger evaporada la gotita de rocío que tirita en la cabezuela florida de una hierba y sorberla con menos ruido que el de un beso. Te he visto asimismo dejar disimuladas en el enredo de las zarzamoras las hebras para el nido del tordo. Y he sonreído, muerta de dicha, diciéndome:—Así me recogerá, como a la gotita trémula, antes de que me vuelva fango; así como al pájaro se cuidará de albergarme después de la última hora.[47]
>
> (But, from living attentive to your most subtle movements, I know so many of your tendernesses that make me confide. I have seen You, going along the fields in the morning, gathering the evaporated little dew drop that shivers in the small flowery head of grass and absorbing it with less noise than that of a kiss. I have seen you, in like manner, pass by the hair of the brambleberries, leaving them in the entanglement for the nest of the thrush. And I have smiled, dead with joy, saying to myself: "Thus will He gather me, like the little tremulous drop, before I turn to mud; thus, as He does the bird, will He take care to shelter me after the last hour.)

This kind of Pantheism may also be found in other poems: "El Dios triste" ("The Sad God") finds her wondering if "Aquel tremendo y fuerte Señor . . . no existe" (That tremendous and strong Lord does not exist) as she searches for "el rostro de Dios" (the face of God) among the dying creatures of Nature.[48] In "Paisaje de la Patagonia" ("Countryside of Patagonia"), she contemplates the falling snow and sees "la gran mirada de Dios sobre mí" (the great gaze of God upon me):

> Siempre ella, silenciosa, como la gran mirada de Dios sobre mí; siempre su azahar sobre mi casa; siempre, como el Destino que ni mengua ni pasa, descenderá a cubrirme, terrible y extasiada.[49]
>
> (It, always silent, like the great gaze of God upon me; always, with its blossoms upon my house; always, like Destiny which neither wanes nor passes, it will descend to cover me, terrible and enraptured.)

The same idea is amplified in "Mientras baja la nieve" (While the snow comes down), where she personifies "la divina criatura" (the divine creature) which "ha bajado . . . el valle a conocer" (has come down to know the valley). She compares its falling, "calla-callando" (silent-keeping silence), to the coming of the Virgin, to the coming of dreams: ". . . cae y cae a las puertas / y llama sin llamar. / Así llega la Virgen, y así llegan los sueños" (. . . it falls and falls at the doors / and calls without calling. / Thus the Virgin arrives, and thus do dreams arrive). Then, she is not quite sure whether the falling snow is the message of God, His mantle, His image, or His love:

Tal vez rompió, cayendo y cayendo, el mensaje

de Dios Nuestro Señor.
Tal vez era su manto, tal vez era su imagen,
tal vez no más su amor.[50]

(Perhaps, there broke through, falling and falling,
the message of God Our Lord.
Perhaps, it was His mantle, perhaps, it was His image,
perhaps, no more than His love.)

In "Jesús," there is a confusion of dawn and His face:

Ya es silencio el corro,
ya ninguno canta:
se oye el corazón
en vez de garganta.

¡Y mirando Su rostro arder,
nos va a hallar el amanecer![51]

(Now the group is silent,
now nobody sings:
the heart is heard
instead of the throat.

And watching His face burn,
dawn is going to find us!)

Her avid readings also brought her in close contact with the Russian writers, especially Tolstoy and Dostoievsky, whom she greatly admired. In *The Death of Ivan Ilyich,*[52] Tolstoy presents a thesis that modern life has alienated man from himself. Materialism and rationalism have so externalized the individual that he has lost the feeling and the passion for his own personal existence. Modern man, Tolstoy teaches, has lost the meaning of life, and as with Ivan Ilyich, it will take nothing less than the presence of death to restore this meaning to him. There is an uneasiness in his writings that life has lost its passion, intensity, and meaning; that there is some secret decline in human vitality. Gabriela, all passion and intensity, would subscribe to such thought, and to that of Kierkegaard who complained that times are petty because they lack passion: "This is why my soul always harkens back to Shakespeare and the Old Testament. There one feels that those who speak are men; there they hate; there they love; there they kill the enemy, curse their descendants for generations to come; there they sin." "This passage might almost have been written by Nietzsche, who launches his plea from the diametrically opposite anti-Christian pole. 'Modern man,' says Nietzsche, 'lacks a goal, and his existence is, therefore, purposeless and nihilistic.' "[53]

Gabriela Mistral once made the error of adhering to this last, in the days of her youth in the Valley of Elqui: "En cada uno de nuestros países había en los años de su formación intelectual un Nietzsche criollo. El de Colombia llamábase José María Vargas Vila y ejerció su influencia magistérica en todos los rincones del continente. La maestra chilena fue víctima de aquel sucedáneo nietzscheano antes de abandonar el valle de Elqui"[54] (In each one of our countries there was, in the years of her intellectual formation, a creole Nietzsche. The one of Colombia was called José María Vargas Vila, and he exercised a magisterial influence in every corner of the continent. The Chilean schoolmistress fell victim to that Nietzschean drug before she left the valley of Elqui).

For this, she paid dearly; it cost her admission into Normal School, but this purposeless and nihilistic, existential concept of existence did not long remain with her, for Gabriela's life had meaning and purpose. She did not lack a goal, but too often changed the means to arrive at her goal.

The Dostoievskian characters of *Crime and Punishment, The Idiot, The Brothers Karamazov,* and *The Possessed* inspired her: "Pero mucho más hicieron para ponerla sobre la verdadera pista evangélica los grandes escritores rusos, desde Tolstoi hasta Gorki"[55] (But the great Russian writers, from Tolstoy to Gorki, did much more to place her on the true evangelical course). Dostoievsky's creatures suffer through the powers of the vital energies, being aware that there is a spiritual reality to which they should ascend and which they can reach:

> Not the sociologist, but the poet, is able to describe the labyrinth of the world and the paradise of the heart. Poetry transcends the horizon of society only when integrating the hell and paradise of human life into the symbols of the whole, a task which the sociologist is incapable of realizing.[56]

Gabriela Mistral, a woman of such complex religious beliefs: Christian and Jewess, Buddhist and Hindu, admirer of Tagore, Rilke, Tolstoy, and Dostoievsky, held in her heart and demonstrated in her life a profound love for the seraphic Saint Francis of Assisi. It was his simplicity, his poverty, his closeness to all creatures of God and Nature that attracted her to him. In 1924, she became a member of the Third Order of St. Francis and declared publicly: "En presencia de Dios Omnipotente y para la gloria de la Inmaculada Virgen María y del Bienaventurado Padre Francisco y de Todos los Santos, prometo guardar todo el tiempo de mi vida los mandamientos de Dios y la regla instituída por el mismo Bienaventurado San Francisco según ha sido sancionada por los sumos Pontífices

Nicolás IV y León XIII" (In the presence of Almighty God and for the glory of the Immaculate Virgin Mary and of our Blessed Father Francis and of all the Saints, I promise to keep, for all my life, the commandments of God and the rule instituted by the same blessed Saint Francis, according as it has been sanctioned by the Supreme Pontiffs Nicholas IV and Leo XIII). In an address, given in July of 1956, she applied to the tertiary the words of Pope Pius XII: "Concerning the mission of the tertiaries, the world has need of that Franciscan vision of life. It is your duty, beloved children, to know it thoroughly, to love it with enthusiasm, and above all, to live it with the perfection that your state in life allows."[57]

In 1950, the Franciscan Academy of History conferred on her the Serra Award, because in her life and works she demonstrated the Franciscan ideals to an outstanding degree.[58] *Vea,* Santiago, Chile, bears the message that, before her final interment, the rough brown Habit of St. Francis, symbol of simplicity, and the white cord, symbol of chastity, were placed on her bier. Thus, she returned to her Creator with the apology: "Yo no he sido tu Santo Francisco / con su cuerpo en un arco de 'Amén' "[59] (I have not been your Saint Francis / with his body in an arc of "Amen").

She explains: "Esta tierra de muchas criaturas / me ha llamado y me quiso tener" (This land of many creatures / has called me and wanted to hold me), but on January 10, 1957, another call reached her. She obeyed, returned, and at last, found the God whom she had been seeking all her life. She realized then that

> Desnudos volvemos a nuestro Dueño,
> manchados como el cordero
> de matorrales, gredas, caminos,
> y desnudos volvemos al abra

cuya luz nos muestra desnudos:
y la Patria del arribo
nos mira fija y asombrada.[60]

(Naked we return to our Master,
stained like the lamb
from thickets, marls, and roads,
and naked we return to the haven
whose light shows us naked:
and our Native Land, at our arrival,
looks at us, fixed and astonished.)

After years of searching for God along the many and devious ways of error, she found Him again in the Fold in which she was born. The Reverend William R. Scrill, Church of Our Lady of Loretto, Hempstead, New York, attended her in the last few hours before she died and signed the papers for her Christian burial.[61]

On January 12, in St. Patrick's Cathedral, New York, the Reverend Renato Poblete, S.J., Chilean resident at Fordham University, offered a Solemn Requiem Mass for the repose of her soul. His Eminence Francis Cardinal Spellman presided at the ceremony. Her body was then flown to Chile where President Carlos Ibáñez proclaimed a period of three days mourning for the passage of that noble soul. This is the highest honor that the State and the University of Chile can bestow on anyone. For these three days her body lay in state in the Salón de Honor of the University. Her remains were then carried to the same church where she was first stamped as a Child of God, the Church of the Immaculate Conception, Vicuña.

For Lucila and Gabriela the search for truth and God is over; the mystery of love and suffering is solved. Now, with

God, she knows the joy of having all things in Him, for like a returning, tired child, she hears the invitation: "Rise, clasp My hand, and come,"[62] from the lips of Truth Itself. With the final reassurance: "I am He Whom thou seekest,"[63] the soul is filled with a peace that "surpasses all understanding,"[64] for it is a peace that follows a restless chase after the Grace of God:

> Cincuenta años caminando
> detrás de la Gracia
> . . . . . .
>
> Cosa mejor que las albas,
> y el golpe de ráfaga,
> . . . . . .
>
> Me la gano de camino,
> la pierdo, arribada,
> o me suelto de ella cuando
> ya iba a ser salva,
> y sigo por soledades
> de Ismael sin patria.[65]
>
> (For fifty years, walking
> after Grace
> . . . . . .
>
> A thing better than dawns
> and a blow from the gust of wind,
> . . . . . .
>
> I gain it on the way,
> I lose it, having arrived,

or I free myself from it when
I was about to be saved,
and I follow through the solitudes
of Ismael without a country.)

Thus did this "magnificent rebel" toss about on a sea of doubt, caught, for fifty years, in the storms of spiritual crisis, seeking, finding, losing; now embracing her "cristo, el de las venas vaciadas en ríos"[66] (Christ, He with veins emptied in rivers), now stretching toward Yaweh and begging to lean upon a "Dios terrible y fuerte"[67] (God, terrible and strong), now practicing yoga in her "anhelo de mirarte límpido y neto"[68] (anxiety to look at You, limpid and pure), now losing herself in a pantheistic search for her God by identifying Him with Nature:

> Amarás la belleza, que es la sombra de Dios sobre el Universo.
>
> De toda creación saldrás con vergüenza, porque fue inferior a tu sueño, e inferior a ese sueño de Dios que es la Naturaleza.[69]
>
> (Thou shalt love beauty, for it is the shadow of God upon the Universe.
>
> Of all creation, thou shalt be ashamed, because it was inferior to your dream, and inferior to that dream of God which is Nature.)

For, all her life, she had a "zeal of God, but not according to knowledge,"[70] and this lack of knowledge, deeply rooted and grounded in the Church of Jesus Christ, was the result of a lack of proper religious instruction:

How then shall they call on Him in Whom they have not believed? Or how shall they believe Him, of Whom they have not heard? And how shall they hear, without a preacher?[71]

And now, in the evening of life, she obtains mercy[72] from the God of Mercy:

O the depth of the riches of the wisdom and of the knowledge of God! How incomprehensible are His judgments, and how unsearchable His ways!

For of Him, and by Him, and in Him, are all things: to Him be glory forever. Amen.[73]

CHAPTER IV—FOOTNOTES

1. "Nocturno de la derrota" ("Nocturn of the Defeated One"), *Poesías,* p. 385.

2. ". . . publicamos en seguida el documento aclaratorio, que contiene un error en el nombre de la madre, llamada Petronila.

Parroquia de la Inmaculada Concepción de Vicuña

El infrascrito, Cura y Vicario de esta Parroquia, certifica que a fojas cuatrocientos cincuenta del libro N.° veintiuno de Bautismos se encuentra la partida siguiente:

'En esta iglesia parroquial de Vicuña, a siete días del mes de abril del año de mil ochocientos ochenta y nueve, bauticé solemnemente a Lucila de María, de un día de edad, hija legítima de Jerónimo Godoy y de Peta Alcayaga. Fueron padrinos Mateo Torres y Rosario Alvarez, de que doy fe.—A. Olivares, C. y V.' " See Virgilio Figueroa, *La divina Gabriela,* pp. 46-47. See also p. 52, n. 7 of the present study, concerning the date of Gabriela's birth.

(" . . . we publish here the clarifying document which contains an error in the name of the mother, called Petronila.

Parish of the Immaculate Conception of Vicuña

The undersigned, Priest and Vicar of this Parish, certifies that on page four hundred fifty of the book No. twenty-one of Baptisms, the following account is found:

'In this parish church of Vicuña, on the seventh day of the month of April of the year one thousand eight hundred eighty-nine, I solemnly baptized Lucila of Mary, of one day of age, legitimate daughter of Jerónimo Godoy and of Peta Alcayaga. Mateo Torres and Rosario Alvarez were the Godparents, of which I give faith.—A. Olivares, Curate and Vicar.' ")

3. Annie Besant Wood (1847-1933), an English writer on social and religious topics, was born in London. All her lightning changes of belief were conditioned by her emotional nature. Through the writings of and personal encounter with Helena Blavatsky, she became an avowed Theosophist. She succeeded Blavatsky as head of the Esoteric School of Theosophy (the school which holds that doctrine is imparted only to the fit and the disciplined initiates in secret organizations). She became President of the Theosophical Society in 1907 and remained in this office until her death. She toured the world with the young Hindu Krishnamurti, the "new Messiah." She is the founder of the Central Hindu College at Benares and the author of some hundred books and pamphlets on the "aggregate of precious knowledge, the ancient Wisdom, Theosophy."

4. Arce de Vázquez, p. 3.

5. Personal interview, Pound Ridge, New York, October 30, 1965.

6. *Rebelde . . .* ("Rebel"), p. 3.

7. Ladrón de Guevara, p. 34.

8. Gabriela Mistral, "El sentido religioso de la vida" ("The Religious Meaning of Life"), *Boletín del Instituto de Literatura Chilena,* III (1963), 20.

9. Augustine, p. 21.

10. Francis de Sales, p. 121.

11. Stanley R. Hopper, *Spiritual Problems in Contemporary Literature* (New York, 1957), p. 277.

12. See p. 132, n. 18.

13. See John F. Bannon and Peter M. Dunne, S.J., *Latin America: An Historical Survey,* rev. ed. (Milwaukee, 1958). Clarence H. Haring, *The Spanish Empire in America* (New York, 1947). J. Lloyd Mecham, *Church and State in Latin America, A History of Politico-Ecclesiastical Relations* (Chapel Hill, N. C., 1934).

14. *Real Patronato:* A series of papal grants and concessions governing the relationship of Church and State. *Regia pase:* The Crown's right to approve papal decrees, bulls, ordinations, and the like, before these might be promulgated in the Indies.

The Crown added other rights, by way of usurpation: that of reviewing the decrees of ecclesiastical councils and synods held in the Indies and that of intervening in the affairs of the colonial Church in all matters short of dogma and doctrine. The exercise of most of these rights, the king reserved to himself or to his Council of the Indies. Some of the lesser matters were put under the jurisdiction of viceroys. The monarch thus became little short of vice-pope.

15. In Chile, in 1881, President Domingo Santa María was elected on the liberal platform which included the classical Church-State disputes concerning civil marriage and freedom of religion. The President, in his message to congress, June 1, 1883, declared that the time had come for the liberals to realize their oldest and most precious aspirations—lay cemeteries, civil marriage, civil register of births, and liberty of conscience. The man who led the fight in these matters against the conservatives was the brilliant Jose Manuel Balmaceda. This typical Latin intellectual had once studied for the priesthood in the Seminario de Santiago, but his reading of philosophical and scientific works had shaken his religious faith, as happened to so many during those decades, and he became a skeptic and a manner of atheist. He regarded the Church as a sort of despot and once declared: "The Church marches, in a sense, against the liberal current of the century." He claimed that the Church through her "privileges" encroached upon the prerogatives of the sovereign State. In January, 1884, another law made obligatory the civil ceremony of marriage before a civic official. Divorce became legalized. See Bannon and Dunne, pp. 420-421.

16. William J. Coleman of the Maryknoll Fathers states that Latin American Catholicism has a fourfold distinction: "First there is 'formal' Catholicism, or simply the Catholic Faith as professed and fully practiced by one we popularly call a 'real' Catholic. Such a Catholic seriously accepts the doctrine and discipline of the Church as given through her official representatives, the bishops and priests. The 'real' Catholic is easily identified as a Catholic in every aspect of his life, be it the religious, the social, the economic, or the political.

Opposed to the formal or practicing Catholic is the 'nominal' Catholic. The 'nominal' Catholic of the Latin-American variety should not be considered the counterpart of the 'fallen-away' Catholic in the United States. Unlike the latter, he insists that he is 'muy católico,' and wishes to be known and considered a Catholic in every way except the practical.

The third and fourth types—'cultural' and 'folk'—are described as follows: 'Cultural Catholicism, sometimes often referred to as social Catholicism, implies the social organization of the Church as a way of life in terms of her impinging on other wishes and forms, such as a preference for a particular type of music or a specific form of ecclesiastical art, or for a way of life within the Catholic framework as it defines itself in ethnic and regional expression. Finally, folk Catholicism, sometimes spoken of as popular Catholicism, is Catholic practice that emanates from the people and finds its expression in indigenous practices and customs only distantly related to the Church's formal aspect but not, as a rule, in conflict with them.' In these two kinds of Catholicism, one sees the national colorings that the Faith has received from its sojourn in respective countries and in the different epochs of the history of the Church.

The carnival and the 'fiesta' are, for instance, classical expressions of these Catholicisms. They illustrate the Catholic missionary principle that whatever is good or indifferent in the indigenous culture of a people must be retained; and that their Catholicism must be grafted on the Catholicism of the missionary."

See Coleman, *Latin American Catholicism, A Self-Evaluation* (Maryknoll, 1958, p. 2). Father Coleman recommends the excellent article of Allen Spitzer, "Aspects of Religious Life in Tepotzlán," *Anthropological Quarterly,* XXX (1957), 1-17, for the use of this fourfold division of Catholicism, and also that of Joseph N. Moody, "The Dechristianization of the French Working Class," *Review of Politics,* XX (1958), 46-69. Here, Mr. Moody has a classification of French Catholics into (1) detached, (2) seasonable conformists, (3) observants, and (4) devout, applicable also in Latin America.

17. Some hold that this dual Catholicism is a product of modern irreligion and materialism. Others hold that it is an inevitable result of the crisis suffered by the Church when revolution overtook it as it did in France in 1789. Still others affirm that it is traceable to the origins of the Church in the age of Castilian imperialism. With the passing of the years and the coming of independence for Spain's former colonies, in 1810-1824, the centuries-old politico-ecclesiastical system of royal patronage and royal vicariate was broken, but the political advantage of the absorption of the Church by the State was not lost on the caudillos of the new republics. Consequently, a generation of ecclesiastical chaos ensued. With the exile or flight of most of the bishops and archbishops and the major religious superiors of the Orders, the leadership of the Church came to an abrupt end. The secular clergy was equally affected, and there was no chance of replacing the priests, since seminaries were nationalized as part of the universities and entrance requirements of an impossible nature were imposed by the civil government.

The solution of the crisis of the Church was to establish direct contact between the Holy See and the new republics through the medium of apostolic delegations and nunciatures. Chile was the first republic to establish this contact, through its plenipotentiary, Ignacio Cienfuegos, who appeared in Rome in 1822, through the interest of Cardinal Gonsalvi, and through an apostolic delegate in the person of Archbishop Giovanni Muzi. This delegate was empowered to consecrate three titular bishops: two for the vacant Sees of Santiago and Concepción, and a third who would succeed him as resident apostolic delegate for all countries to which he would travel. The plan failed, however, foundering on the cornerstone of patronage. Eventually the republics established individual relations with the Holy see. (See Coleman, pp. 4-5.)

18. Personal letter, Montevideo, Uruguay, December 15, 1965.

19. Personal letter, Toulouse, France, November 18, 1965.

20. The answer to the first question was given by stating that the vast majority of Catholics are "sólo de nombre" ("in name only"). Though baptized and believing in the Catholic Faith, they do not practice their religion, nor do they allow it to influence their lives to any appreciable degree. The answer to the second question was that the average person in

Latin America receives an appalling minimum of religious instruction and is a nominal Catholic for that reason. Though born and baptized and even reared in the Catholic Faith, he inherits a traditional and devitalized form of Catholicism, often with a curious mixture of religious sentiments and practices that bear no relation to the real substance of his Faith. His religion is thus an external ritualism of routinized practices which becomes all the more evident in the case of the large minorities of Indians, and which is unfairly called "pagan Catholicism." The definite intermixture of pagan and other superstitious practices with old Catholic customs is typical of "folk Catholicism," yet it can be identified with a not fully developed form of Catholic Christianity.

The answer to the third question showed an obvious discrepancy between that which a Catholic is expected to do and what he actually does. His Catholicism consists of a traditional set of pious customs, a superficial substitute for those demands of a vital nature that the Catholic Church makes upon life. The same individualistic and ritualistic concept of religion projects itself in both family and professional life. In the latter there is the influence of liberalism and its philosophy of exaggerated individualism, resulting in a very attenuated awareness of the Mystical Body on the part of the liberal Catholic who lives a religious life disassociated from the vital forms that the Church could give such a Catholic as a member of the Mystical Body. (See Coleman, pp. 20-22.)

21. Religious ignorance is the major cause of an alarming spiritual crisis in Latin America today, quickened by progress with its materialistic overtones. But the languid spiritual life responsible for such a crisis comes actually from one hundred fifty years of rabid secularism. An added hampering factor is that many modern Latin American states have tried to use the ancient Spanish system of royal patronage, or regalism, under which the State presents the names of candidates for a vacant bishopric and sometimes interferes with the administration of the Sacraments and the teaching of Catholic doctrine.

These conditions, along with social and economic evils, are responsible for the scarcity of priests, which in turn results in the widespread religious ignorance of the people. It is not surprising then that an estimated seventy per cent of Latin America's Catholics do not know the fundamentals of their religion. It is true that they have a traditional sort of religiosity, consisting of a general idea of God and some popular saints. Many regard some Sacraments, such as marriage, as merely a prelude to social festivities. This religious ignorance prevails not only among the illiterate, but also among the educated. It is due largely to the lack of proper religious education.

Of the twenty and one half million children and youths receiving some sort of schooling, only two and one half million receive regular religious instruction in Catholic institutions. Perhaps about five million are given occasional instruction at public schools or in catechism centers. But this is considered by many as having no lasting results. In fact, most of the government systems of education are highly secularized; and militant agnostics teach the masses and write for them.

In some regions of Latin America, only six per cent or less of the men go to church and receive the Sacraments, and only ten or twelve of every one hundred women. In other areas, about fourteen per cent of the people fulfill their Easter duties, more than half die without having received the last rites, and concubinage and abortions are common. Although nearly ninety-five per cent of the Latin Americans are baptized Catholics, only about one third have made their first Communion. See *Latin America, A Challenge to Catholics* (Washington, D.C.), pp. 13-14.

22. Father Edwin Ryan affirms this truth: "But the greatest need is that of priests. There are parts of South America where the people never see a priest because there is none to send them. For instance, in Paraguay there are about ninety priests for the whole population of the Republic, which is about 900,000. And of these priests about half are in the capital (Asunción). That leaves less than fifty to minister to 800,000 people in a vast region where travel is difficult and often impossible." See Edwin Ryan, *The Church in the South American Republics* (New York, 1932), p. 50.

A publication of the Latin American Bishops' Council carried the following lament: "This is the desolate situation we see in all the Latin-American countries: countless parishes without a priest; untold villages without the slightest spiritual assistance; seminaries almost empty; the basic institution of the family in danger of disintegration; such vital works as teaching the catechism, administering the Sacraments, observances of feasts, organization of the lay apostolate—all sadly forfeited. And with so many burdens falling on the parish priest, the parish is never well-organized." See Fonseca, pp. 18-19.

Fonseca continues: "The causes of the Catholic losses that followed are many. The iniquities of history, the influence of anticlericals, and a new paganism begotten by secularism in society brought war and decimation in the ranks of the priesthood." See Fonseca, p. 20.

23. Bannon and Dunne, p. 321.

24. "These spiritual impulses vary greatly from age to age and are often profoundly different from anything that the adult experiences in his religious life. At first, indeed, they are wholly natural and largely unconscious. Yet they are the foundations from which true spirituality gradually arises. The more we understand these early impulses, the better we are able to give neither too much nor too little as we help the children to grow in body, mind and spirit." See Eve Lewis, *Children and their Religion* (New York, 1962), p. 5.

25. Saavedra Molina, pp. xxix-xxx.

26. Jerónimo Godoy, "Angel de la Guarda" ("Guardian Angel"), in Figueroa, p. 42. Lucila's love for and faith in her Guardian Angel continued throughout her days. In *Ternura* ("Tenderness"), she describes the Angel to her pupils:

Es verdad, no es un cuento:

hay un Angel Guardián
que te toma y te lleva como el viento
y con los niños va por donde van.

(It is true; it's not a tale:
there is a Guardian Angel
who takes you and carries you like the wind,
and with the children, he goes where they go.)

She knows that "Tiene cabellos suaves / ojos dulces y graves / cuerpo, manos y pies de alas (He has gentle hairs / sweet and grave eyes / body, hands, and feet of wings). She warns: "cuando su seña te pone el pecado / recoge tu alma y el cuerpo te deja" (when his mark records sin on you / he takes back your soul and leaves you your body). See *Poesías,* pp. 341-342.

27. Sidonia Carmen Rosenbaum, *Modern Women Poets of Spanish America* (New York, 1945), p. 172.

28. Doris Dana confirmed the fact that Gabriela Mistral remembered Emelina as a kind of "Doña Perfecta," and her mother as one who shared her playfulness, tenderness, and sense of humor.

29. Paul, *Romans* viii. 35-39.

30. Ladrón de Guevara, pp. 44-45.

31. Ladrón de Guevara, pp. 44-45.

32. "It is through the liturgy that the Church says what she is and becomes what she should be, the fellowship of Christians with one another and with their head. According to the philosophical statement that activity follows upon being, that Christian community, being that redeemed community, must express what it is. It does this chiefly by repeating to itself —not merely by rote or by memory, but by a representation—that act by which it came into existence as the worshipping fellowship, the holy people of God.

This is brought out in Article 2 of the Constitution on the Liturgy: 'For the liturgy, through which the work of our redemption is accomplished, most of all in the divine sacrifice of the Eucharist, is the outstanding means whereby the faithful may express in their lives and manifest to others the mystery of Christ and the real nature of the true Church.' And in Article 6, it is described how that which the apostles proclaimed, and which is proclaimed throughout the world by the living witness of the Church, is effected 'by means of sacrifice and sacraments, around which the entire liturgical life revolves. . . .'" See John R. Sheets, S.J., "The Mystery of the Church and the Liturgy," *Worship,* XXXVIII (1964), 617-618.

33. Personal interview, Pound Ridge, New York, October 30, 1965.

34. "Out of the Church-State struggle there has developed a division in Latin-American politics which is strange to the Anglo, namely clericalism and anticlericalism. Not to be overlooked in connection with this matter is the following fact, psychologically impossible as it may seem to the

Anglo observer. In his own mind, the anticlerical can make a fine distinction between what he believes, namely, his faith or creed, and what he does in his politics. He can thus consider himself a Catholic and yet be an ardent anticlerical at one and the same time.

Among the many factors which bred anticlericalism in Latin America is the materialistic or antireligious philosophy of the Enlightenment and the later positivist philosophy of Auguste Comte, adopted enthusiastically by many of the political leaders; the sometimes fanatical opposition to the Church of Freemasonry; the unrealistic democratic idealism of many liberal leaders; selfishness, greed, and ambition or mere careerism on the part of many politicians; and finally, the natural extremism of the Latin character which . . . knows not the art of compromise." See Bannon and Dunne, p. 321.

35. Ladrón de Guevara, p. 46.

36. *Ibid.*

37. "In Article 10 we read: 'The liturgy is the summit toward which the activity of the Church is directed; at the same time, it is the fount from which all her power flows.' . . . God is a jealous God. He will not give his glory to another. He cannot be indifferent to his glorification. Isaiah declared this as Yahweh's spokesman: 'I the Lord, this is my name; I will not give my glory to another . . .' (Is. 42:8). Thus God has not been indifferent to man's efforts to encounter and adore him. In consequence, at a point in history God took the initiative, stepped into man's life of worship, and dictated the form of that worship. . . . This worship would suffice until the day of fulfillment when the type and figure would pass away and God would receive a worship adequate to his infinite perfection. In that day, his Son would step into our valley and become man's perfect spokesman, man's perfect worshipper of the Father, the high priest of all creation. . . . This worship of fulfillment, . . . reached its crowning expression in the sacrificial surrender upon the cross. It received its ritual transposition, its re-enactment, in sacred signs, in the celebration of the paschal supper, wherein Christ offered the action of Calvary and the resurrection of Easter morning in anticipation, and then gave to his first priests the mandate: 'Do this in remembrance of me' (Luke 22:20). . . . And liturgy today is but the representation of that awesome action, a representing 'in mysterio' and in ritual sign of the saving events of Calvary and Easter. . . . The Christian must realize that the law of salvation is this: salvation in community . . . that the Christian life is not a combat fought by an isolated individual on a lonely battleground . . . we achieve salvation only in and with the Christian community." See John H. Koenig, "College Theology and Community Worship," *Worship,* XXXVIII (1964), 635-637. The above-mentioned Article 10 and Articles 2, 6, p. 175, n. 32, refer to *The Constitution on the Sacred Liturgy of the Second Vatican Council,* Paulist Press (Glen Rock, N. J., 1964).

38. Ladrón de Guevara, p. 42.

39. Maritain, *Liturgy and Contemplation* (New York, 1960), p. 64.

40. "Nocturno de la consumación," *Poesías,* pp. 382-383.

41. "Nocturno de la derrota" ("Nocturn of the Defeated One"), *Poesías,* p. 387.

42. "Al oído del Cristo" ("In the Ear of Christ"), *Poesías,* p. 5.

43. "Al pueblo hebreo" ("To the Hebrew People"), *Poesías,* pp. 8-9.

44. "Mis libros" ("My Books"), *Poesías,* p. 33.

45. Arce de Vázquez, p. 145.

46. "Comentarios a poemas de Rabindranath Tagore" ("Commentaries on Poems of Rabindranath Tagore"), *Desolación,* p. 151.

47. "Comentarios a poemas de Rabindranath Tagore" ("Commentaries on Poems of Rabindranath Tagore"), *Desolación,* pp. 151-152.

48. "El Dios triste" ("The Sad God"), *Poesías,* pp. 37-38.

49. "Paisajes de la Patagonia" ("Countrysides of Patagonia"), *Poesías,* pp. 123-124.

50. "Mientras baja la nieve" ("While the snow comes down"), *Poesías,* p. 324.

51. "Jesús," *Poesías,* p. 232.

52. "Martin Heidegger owes much of his influence to what he has done with Tolstoy. The central section of his main work, *Being and Time,* deals at length with death. It contains a footnote (original ed., 1927, p. 254): 'L. N. Tolstoy, in his story, *The Death of Ivan Ilyich,* has presented the phenomenon of the shattering and the collapse of this *one dies.*' 'One dies' refers to the attitude of those who admit that one dies, but who do not seriously confront the fact that they themselves will die. . . . Heidegger on death is for the most part an unacknowledged commentary on *The Death of Ivan Ilyich;* . . .

Tolstoy drew his inspiration in large measure from the Gospels. His intelligence and senstivity were of the highest order. And whether we classify him as a Christian or a heretic, his late writings remain to challenge every reader who is honestly concerned with the New Testament or, generally, with religion.

. . . Tolstoy and Dostoievsky were contemporaries, Russian to the core, . . . and deeply concerned with Christianity. But their interpretations of Christianity were as different as their temperaments and their artistic techniques." See Walter Kaufmann, *Religion from Tolstoy to Camus* (New York, 1961), pp. 7-8.

53. Hopper, p. 144.

54. Espinoza, p. 100.

55. Espinoza, p. 100.

56. Hopper, p. 24.

57. "Truly Apostolic," *Franciscan Herald and Form,* XXXVII (1956), 419. See also Chacón y Calvo, "Gabriela Mistral en una asamblea franciscana (Gabriela Mistral in a Franciscan Assembly), *Boletín de la Academia Cubana de la lengua* (Bulletin of the Cuban Academy of Language), VI (1957), 111-118.

58. "Inter-American Notes: The Serra Award," *The Americas,* VII (1951), 281-282. "The Serra Award of the Americas for 1950," *Books Abroad,* XXV (1951), 219.

59. "Nocturno de la derrota" ("Nocturn of the Defeated One"), *Poesías,* p. 386. See also Salvador Bueno, "La actualidad literaria: la muerte de Gabriela Mistral" ("The Present Literary Time: The Death of Gabriela Mistral"), *Boletín Comisión Cubana de la UNESCO* (Cuban Commission Bulletin of UNESCO), VI (1957), 20. Arturo Capdevila, "¡Paz, Gabriela Mistral!" ("Peace, Gabriela Mistral!"), *La Nueva Democracia* (The New Democracy), XXXVII (1957), 18-22.

60. "El regreso" ("The Return"), *Poesías,* p. 745.

61. "All I can say, which is public knowledge anyway, is that I attended her in the last few hours of her life; when she died, I signed the necessary papers for her Christian burial." Personal letter, Hempstead, New York, August 15, 1964.

According to Doris Dana's report of the deathbed scene, it can be reasonably assumed that Gabriela Mistral received conditional absolution from Father Scrill. Although not a Catholic herself, Miss Dana sent for the hospital Chaplain, Father Scrill. When Gabriela regained consciousness, she resented the fact that Doris had so acted. Miss Dana feels that she was desperately clinging to her fading life, and that, to her, the presence of the priest, ready to administer the last rites of the Church, meant certain and imminent death. Whether or not this explains her resentment is not certain. What is certain is that she did not go to confession. When she lapsed into unconsciousness again, the priest administered the last rites. Therefore, to the end, she remained "católica muy a su manera" (Catholic very much in her own way).

62. Francis Thompson, "The Hound of Heaven," *Works,* II, 112.

63. *Ibid.,* p. 113.

64. Paul, Philipians, iv.7.

65. "Memoria de la Gracia" ("Memory of Grace"), *Poesías,* pp. 757-758.

66. "Al oído del Cristo" ("In the Ear of Christ"), *Poesías,* p. 5.

67. "Credo" ("Creed"), *Poesías,* p. 32.

68. "Comentarios a poemas de Rabindranath Tagore" ("Commentaries on Poems of Rabindranath Tagore"), *Desolación,* p. 151.

69. "El arte, decálogo del artista" ("Art, Decalogue of the Artist"), *Desolación,* pp. 149-150.

70. Paul, Romans, x.2.

71. *Ibid.,* x.14.

72. Since Martin C. Taylor, in his doctoral dissertation, *Religious Sensibility in the Life and Poetry of Gabriela Mistral* (University Microfilms, Ann Arbor, Michigan, 1964), did not have the information offered on p. 178, n. 61, of the present study, he explains on p. 54: "The irony is that Gabriela did not request the last sacraments, but instead chose spiritual release from sin in the tradition of the Jew. It is highly probable that she was rejecting the Catholic Church to affirm once more, and for the last time, her estrangement from, and independence of, institutionalized religion.[33] Yet it is fitting that her last gesture should betoken a fidelity to the Jewish tradition, because in spirit, she had allied herself with the persecuted Jews, including the martyred Jesus, 'King of the Jews.' And

her life cycle closed as it had begun with the sound of an ancient Hebrew chant, recalling the Edenic Elqui Valley and the voice of a wizened grandmother who recited wondrous tales of the Old Testament."

His fn. 33 reads as follows: "In *Gabriela Mistral: la errante solitaria* (Gabriela Mistral: The Wandering Recluse) (Santiago, 1958), pp. 101-103, Josué Monsalve's clinical account of Gabriela's last days is in sharp conflict with the view I'm taking. He neither supports nor denies this version, but instead asserts that she took a Cross to the hospital and that she received extreme unction, January 2, two days before lapsing into a coma: 'El ocho Gabriela recibió la bendición apostólica impartida por un padre jesuíta chileno. El miércoles anterior, le habían puesto la santa extremaunción. Con estos actos, la mujer que había sido criticada por sacerdotes por sus ideas religiosas y por haber practicado otras, moría como una conversa en el seno de la religión católica.' (On the eighth, Gabriela received the Apostolic blessing imparted by a Chilean Jesuit Father. On the Wednesday before, they had given her holy Extreme-Unction. With these acts, the woman who had been criticized by priests for her religious ideas and for having practiced others died like a convert in the bosom of the Catholic religion.) There are still many doubtful points which only Doris Dana and the Archbishop of the diocese can solve. An appeal to both for information proved futile."

The clarified "doubtful points" regarding Gabriela's last days reveal that there is partial truth in both Taylor's and Monsalve's accounts. Gabriela brought both the Cross and the record "Kol Nidre" into the hospital with her, for to the end, she continued to profess her love for Jesus Christ of the New Testament and Jehovah of the Old. She was not "rejecting the Catholic Church," for Miss Dana affirmed that she never considered herself out of it. She did receive Extreme Unction. She did receive the privilege of Catholic funeral ceremonies in St. Patrick's Cathedral, New York City. It is true, therefore, that "her life cycle closed as it had begun," but in the Roman Catholic ritual of the Sacraments of Baptism and Extreme Unction.

73. Romans xi.33-36.

chapter V

POETRY AND GABRIELA MISTRAL

1. The spirit of the poet

> . . . Gabriela était essentiellement poète (c'était le fond de son être), . . . et cela explique déjà bien des choses, . . .[1]
>
> (. . . Gabriela wes essentially a poet [this was the very essence of her being], . . . and that already explains many things.)

The words of Jacques Maritain define the essence of Gabriela Mistral, the poet.[2] Her spirit is passion, passion saturated with the obsession of death. The marriage of passion and death produced her first offspring, *Desolación*. For, "emotion produces poetry when it is remembered in tranquillity,"[3] and the greatest poets are seldom content to affirm values without seeking for a way to bring them into unity. This is what Norberto Pinilla calls "el proceso de elaboración subconsciente hasta que aflora a la conciencia y se estiliza en formas logradas, cuando se trata de un verdadero artista"[4] (the process of subconscious elaboration, until it blossoms in the consciousness and is stylized in successful forms, when it is a question of a true artist).

The unity of Gabriela's poetry is her tragic sense of love, love that gives itself unto emptiness and demands to receive in fullness: the emptiness of desolation and the fullness of

ctivity, bearing the impress of her
uctifies during her lifetime in four
ición (*Desolation*), 1922; *Ternura*
la (*Felling*), 1938; *Lagar I* (*Wine*
et evolves from "desolation" to "ten-
to "wine press." The two volumes,
blished in Chile, *Recado de Chile*
Lagar II (*Wine Press II*), form the
life and reveal the poet grown to her

etic development of Gabriela Mistral
isolated mind, isolated in its nobility,
sionary reflections which acquire in-
ications. Her "song of thought" finds
echo in every human heart, for remembering her own tragedy, she converts it into balm for sick-at-heart mankind. She returns from her particular sorrow with hands scarred, but ladened with solace enough to reach the universal. It is that which marks the difference between the character ennobled by suffering and the one embittered by it, the distinction enriched by the thought of William Blake:

Tell me what is the night or day to one o'erflowed with woe?
Tell me what is a thought? And of what substance is it made?
Tell me what is a joy? And in what gardens do joys grow?

If thou returnest to the present moment of affliction,
Wilt thou bring comforts on thy wings, and dews and honey
and balm,
Or poison from the desert wilds, from the eyes of the envier?[6]

And when Gabriela returns, she remembers from whence she came; she remembers the factors that led to her formation.[7]

Desolación, a volume of seventy-three poems arranged under the titles of "Vida" ("Life"), "Escuela" ("School"), "Infantiles" ("Childish things"), "Dolor" ("Sorrow"), "Naturaleza" ("Nature"), a collection of poetic prose writings, and four "Canciones de cuna" ("Cradle Songs"), bears the imprint of her broken heart. She knows it and apologizes for it:

> Dios me perdone este libro amargo y los hombres que sienten la vida como dulzura me lo perdonen también. En estos poemas queda sangrando un pasado doloroso, en el cual la canción se ensangrentó para aliviarme. Lo dejo tras de mí como a la hondonada sombría y por laderas más clementes subo hacia las mesetas espirituales donde una ancha luz caerá, por fin, sobre mis días. Yo cantaré desde ellas las palabras de la esperanza, sin volver a mirar mi corazón como lo quiso un misericordioso, para "consolar a los hombres."[8]
>
> (May God pardon me this bitter book, and may men who feel life as sweetness also pardon me it.
> In these poems, a dolorous past remains bleeding, in which the song bled in order to relieve me. I leave it behind me like a gloomy ravine, and along more clement slopes, I rise toward spiritual plateaus where a great light will fall, at last, upon my days. From them, I shall sing the words of hope, without turning to look at my heart, as a merciful one wished it, "in order to console men.")

This "Voto" ("Vow"), found on the last page of the book, recalls her bitterness, the painful past, and the finding of hope and artistic creation as a catharsis. She proposes to renounce subjectivity and to embrace more objective lyricism "para consolar a los hombres" (in order to console men).

2. Immortal themes: love and death

Y tembló de amor, toda su primavera ardiente,
y ahora, al otoño, anégase de verdad y tristeza.
El "de morir tenemos" pasa sobre su frente,
en todo agudo bronce, cuando la noche empieza.[9]

(And he trembled with love, all his ardent springtime,
and now, in autumn, he is submerged in truth and sadness.
The thought, "we have to die," passes over his forehead,
all in sharp bronze, when the night begins.)

The prevailing and pervading themes expounded in *Desolación* are tragic death and passionate love. The book opens with "El pensador de Rodin" ("The Thinker of Rodin"), ". . . este hombre que medita en la muerte" (. . . this man who meditates on death), and continues with lamentations: ". . . del primer llanto a la última agonía;" "Cristo, el de las carnes en gajos abiertas;" "Raza judía, carne de dolores, . . ." "Tú no beses mi boca. Vendrá el instante lleno de luz menguada, en que estaré sin labios sobre un mojado suelo" (. . . from the first cry to the last agony; Christ, He with His flesh opened in sections; Jewish race, flesh of sorrows, . . ; You may not kiss my mouth. There will come an instant full of failing light, in which I shall be without lips on a dampened ground). This constant mingles with love as her heart throbs through "Los sonetos de la muerte" ("Sonnets on Death"):

Del nicho helado en que los hombres te pusieron,
te bajaré a la tierra humilde y soleada.
Que he de dormirme en ella los hombres no supieron,
y que hemos de soñar sobre la misma almohada.

Me alejaré cantando mis venganzas hermosas,
¡porque a ese hondor recóndito la mano de ninguna
bajará a disputarme tu puñado de huesos![10]

(From the frozen niche in which men placed you,
I shall lower you to the lowly and sun-dried earth.
That I have to sleep in it, men did not know,
and that we have to dream upon the same pillow.

I shall withdraw singing my sweet vengeances,
for to that recondite depth, the hand of no one
will come down to dispute with me your handful of bones!)

In tragic despair, she raises her heart to God and questions: "¿Cómo quedan, Señor, durmiendo los suicidos?" (How, O Lord, do suicides remain sleeping?). Then she tries the lover's coquetry to move the justice of God to have mercy on the suicide: "mientras los otros siguen llamándote Justicia, / ¡no te llamaré nunca otra cosa que Amor!" (while others continue to call You Justice, / I shall never call You anything but Love!). She dares to tell Him that He should understand: "¡Tú, que vas a juzgarme, lo comprendes, Señor!" (You, who are going to judge me, You understand it, O Lord!). And again: "¡No importa! Tú comprendes: ¡yo le amaba, le amaba!" (It doesn't matter! You understand: I loved him, I loved him!). She defines love as a bitter experience: "Y amor (bien sabes de eso) es amargo ejercicio; / un mantener los párpados de lágrimas mojados" (And love—You know about it very well—is a bitter exercise; / a maintaining of eyelids wet with tears). Womanlike, she proclaims that she will continue to plague Him until He grants her request:

Aquí me estoy, Señor, con la cara caída

sobre el polvo, parlándote un crepúsculo entero,
o todos los crepúsculos a que alcance la vida,
si tardas en decirme la palabra que espero.

(Here I am, O Lord, with my face fallen
on the dust, speaking to you for an entire twilight,
or all the twilights to which life may aspire,
if You delay in telling me the word for which I hope.)

Finally, she tries another artifice: "¡toda la tierra tuya sabrá que perdonaste!"[11] (this whole earth of yours will know that you have pardoned!).

The grief that envelops her is so oppressive and so aggressive that it brings on dynamic, restless interrogations and foolish demands, but love must needs speak foolishly to ease its pain and to satisfy its impatience. Again and again, she takes up her quarrel. In such a state, her soul knows no respite from complaints; it never tires of stating its anxieties in every manner possible until a remedy be found.

In "Coplas" ("Couplets"), she regrets that she can no longer remember his face and fears lest it be her soul and not his image for which she is searching:

> Tal vez lo que yo he pedido
> no es tu imagen, es mi alma,
> mi alma en la que yo cavé
> tu rostro como una llaga.
>
> Cuando la vida me hiera,
> ¿adónde buscar tu cara,
> si ahora ya tienes polvo
> hasta dentro de mi alma?[12]

(Perhaps that for which I have begged
is not your image; it is my soul,
my soul in which I carved
your face like a wound.

When life wounds me,
where shall I look for your face,
if you are now already dust
even deep within my soul?)

The poems of the section "Dolor" appear to follow a logical sequence in the story of her first love from "El encuentro" ("The Encounter") to the tragic denouement in "Los huesos de los muertos." "¡Y éstas no pueden nunca más besar!"[13] ("The Bones of the Dead." And these can never kiss again!). However, "Dios lo quiere" ("God Wants It") and "Nocturno" ("Nocturn") reveal the presence of another love story. When Matilde Ladrón de Guevara asked Gabriela to whom she was referring when she declared: "La tierra se hace madrastra / si tu alma vende a mi alma" (The earth will become a stepmother / if your soul sells my soul), she answered quite simply: "Fue un segundo amor"[14] (It was a second love). Margot Arce de Vázquez affirms that "Nocturno" ("Nocturn"), too, alludes to this second love: ". . . el 'Nocturno' expresa la crisis de la segunda, de la más decisiva"[15] (. . . "Nocturn" expresses the crisis of the second, of the most decisive one). Dulce María Loynaz offers more relevant information: ". . . le oí decir, con el consiguiente asombro, que el novio aquel que le fuera doblemente arrobatado, no había sido en verdad su único amor" (. . . I heard her say, with the consequent astonishment, that that sweetheart over whom she was doubly enraptured had not been, in truth, her only love). She clarifies: "Estaba ella en la treintena, que es cuando las pasiones alcanzan plenitud en nuestro pecho; pero estaba además en su camino, en el que era ya su verdadero rumbo. Y el hombre no la dejaba andar, no la quería allí, tenía celos del glorioso destino de su amada"[16] (She was in her thirties, which is when the passions reach plenitude in our hearts; but, besides, she was on her road, on that which was already her true destination. And the man would not let her go; he did not want her there; he was jealous of the glorious destiny of his beloved). Hence, although according to this testimony it was Gabriela herself who terminated the second affair, she resumes her lamentations and again directs them to God. In a veritable "Eloi, Eloi, lamma sabacthani" (My God, my God, why have You forsaken me?), she cries out:

> Padre Nuestro que estás en los cielos,
> ¿por qué te has olvidado de mí?
> . . . . . .
> ¡Llevo abierto también mi costado,
> y no quieres mirar hacia mí!
>
> Y perdida en la noche, levanto
> el clamor aprendido de Ti:
> ¡Padre Nuestro que estás en los cielos,
> por qué te has olvidado de mí![17]
>
> (Our Father who art in heaven,
> why have You forsaken me?
> . . . . . .
> I, too, bear my side opened,
> and You don't care to look upon me!
>
> And lost in the night, I raise
> the cry learned from You:

Our Father who art in heaven,
why have You forsaken me!)

The name of her first love, Romelio Ureta, has been handed down to posterity; the name of the second, according to Dulce María Loynaz, has been interred with Gabriela: "Ese hombre, cuyo nombre se llevó a la tumba, ¿la vería al fin muerta? ¿Se atrevería a allegarse, como un desconocido, como un número más entre la fila, hasta la gran mujer yacente que lo amara un día?"[18] (That man, whose name she carried to the tomb, did he see her, at last, dead? Did he dare to draw near, like a stranger, like just another number on the line, to the great woman lying there, who loved him one day?).

Margot Arce de Vázquez throws more light on his identity, but gives a somewhat contradictory description of the love affair:

> Shortly after this first literary triumph, she met under romantic and somewhat strange circumstances a young poet from Santiago; for him she felt a passion, more intense and more decisive than her first love. A short while later, however, he married a wealthy young lady of the capital's high social circles. The cruel blow moved her to ask for her transfer to Punta Arenas in the extreme south of Chile, an inhospitable, desolate region. There she remained for two years, exiled and overwhelmed with sorrow. It was then, having decided to leave Chile, that she accepted the invitation from the Mexican government. The most moving and impassioned poems of *Desolación,* the very title of that anguished book, express with ardent eloquence her heartbreaking disillusion.[19]

Doris Dana, however, knows the name of Gabriela's second

love, declared that it was Gabriela herself who ended the love affair, and explained that neither love had the shattering impact upon Gabriela that her poems would indicate. "She was writing as a poet," Miss Dana clarified, "and, as a poet, she knew no half measures, no restraints."[20]

However the story runs, the fact remains that Gabriela the poet tasted the desolation of death and drank deep of the pangs of love. As Vicente Aleixandre put it: "Todo está en el nítido / temblor de la lágrima / que brilla en tus ojos, Gabriela"[21] (All is in the resplendent trembling of the tear that shines in your eyes, Gabriela). Twice she knew the torture of violent separation and the gnawing pain of jealousy. Twice she wondered at the gentleness of the wind, the earth in flower, the peacefulness of the road, the melody of a song, when

> El pasó con otra;
> yo le vi pasar.
> Siempre dulce el viento
> y el camino en paz.
> ¡Y estos ojos míseros
> le vieron pasar!
>
> El besó a la otra
> . . . . . .
> ¡Y no untó mi sangre
> la extensión del mar!
>
> Y él irá con otra
> por la eternidad![22]
>
> (He passed by with another;
> I saw him pass by.

Always sweet the wind
and the road in peace.
And these miserable eyes
saw him pass by!

He kissed another
. . . . . .
And my blood did not smear
the expanse of the sea!

And he will go with another
for all eternity!)

She understood the transforming quality of love: "Como soy reina y fui mendiga, . . ." "Si tú me miras, yo me vuelvo hermosa . . . / y desconocerán mi faz gloriosa . . ." (Since I am a queen and I was a beggar, . . . If you look at me, I shall become beautiful . . . / and they will not recognize my glorious face). Love produced a sense of unworthiness in her in the presence of the beloved: "Tengo vergüenza de mi boca triste, / de mi voz rota y mis rodillas rudas" (I am ashamed of my sad mouth, / of my broken voice, and of my rude knees). She experienced the numb disbelief of his death: "Yo me olvidé que se hizo / ceniza tu pie ligero, / y, como en los buenos tiempos, / salí a encontrarte al sendero" (I forgot that your light step had become ashes, / and, as in those good times, / I went out to the path to meet you). And finally, the futility of the future without him rendered her helpless and hopeless: "Yo no tengo otro oficio / después del callado de amarte, / que este oficio de lágrimas, duro, / que tú me dejaste"[23] (I have no other duty / after ceasing to love you, / than this unbearable duty of tears, / which you have left me).

In her unique and individual contribution to poetry, love

plays a very important part in *Desolación*. In *Tala* (*Felling*), it is transformed into universal love. *Lagar* (*Wine Press*), as Eugenio Florit so poetically expressed it, "continues her ecumenical love and intensifies another characteristic: the image of death, not as the tragedy of her first book, but as a mystery, as the ineffable, God.[24] These themes are interwoven with others like a shuttle that weaves in and out of a tapestry."[25] The mystery of death loses the torment of tragedy as she calls it "La vieja Empadronada," "La Contra-Madre del mundo," "La Convida-gentes"[26] (The Old Census-Taker, The Counter-Mother of the World, The Inviter of People). She predicts for herself a silent death in a strange land:

> Y va a morirse en medio de nosotros,
> en una noche en la que más padezca,
> con solo su destino por almohada,
> de una muerte callada y "extranjera."[27]

> (And she is going to die in our midst,
> in a night in which she will suffer most,
> with only her destiny for a pillow,
> of a death, silent and strange.)

Three of her unpublished poems in *Recado de Chile* intensify this mingling of death and exile, this never arriving and never stopping "at home": "La ruta," "Despedida," "Emigración de pájaros" ("The Route," "Farewell," "Emigration of Birds"):

> ¿A dónde es que tú me llevas
> que nunca arribas ni paras?
> O es, dí, que nunca tendremos

eso que llaman "la casa"
donde yo duerma sin miedo?

Ya me voy porque me llama
un silbo que es de mi Dueño,
llama con una inefable
punzada de rayo recto;
dulce-agudo es el llamado
que al partir le conocemos.

Nosotros sí nos perdemos
mientras que ellos nunca fallan.
Bajarán cuando divisen
playa suya acostumbrada.

(Where is it that you carry me,
where you never arrive and never stop?
Or is it, tell me, that we shall never have
that which they call "home"
where I may sleep without fear?

Now I am going because there calls me
a whisper which belongs to my Master,
He calls with an ineffable
piercing of a straight lightning flash;
sweet-sharp is the call
which, on leaving, we shall recognize.

We, yes, we lose ourselves
while they never fail.
They swoop down when they descry
their accustomed shore.)

Thus does the theme of death become in Gabriela, as in Emily Dickinson, a mysterious and phantasmal entity. The poetry of both women is an outlet for suffering "which exists within them by some inexplicable mystery: their privileged capacity to suffer, a condition which comes from the very entrails of their being."[28] It is not surprising, then, that their songs take the form of prayer in moments of fulfillment as well as in those of affliction, for the poet knows that in his moments of agony, he is bringing forth the child of his ecstasies.

Love, sorrow, and death, interwoven and intermingled, are the constants of Gabriela's poetry:

> El dolor y la muerte acompañan este amor desde su aurora hasta su ocaso y arrancan al verso, aún en los breves momentos de felicidad, resonancias sombrías, matices sutiles que enlazan el temor con el deleite, la angustia con la ternura.
>
> A semejanza de Unamuno, quiere trascender lo pasajero del placer y de los lazos temporales y vencer a la muerte.[29]
>
> (Sorrow and death accompany this love from its first appearance to its decline, and they root out the verse, even in her brief moments of happiness, somber resonances, subtle blendings which entwine fear with delight, anguish with tenderness.
>
> Like Unamuno, she wishes to transcend the transitoriness of pleasure and of temporal ties and conquer death.)

3. Concept of Divinity

Gabriela Mistral was a woman of deep religious fervor. It was natural for her to think about God, as natural as breathing. She found Him everywhere and conversed with Him freely. Hers might have been the same "hymn of the universe" sung by Chardin: "Lord God, my dignity as a man forbids me to shut my eyes to this . . .; therefore, lest I succumb to the temptation to curse the universe and the Maker of the universe, teach me to adore it by seeing you hidden within it. Say once again to me, Lord, those great and liberating words, the words which are at once revealing light and effective power: 'Hoc est Corpus meum.' "[30] She would have thrilled with this bold encounter with reality and would have found in its milieu, at once divine and cosmic, an echo of her own "sentido religioso de la vida" (religious sense of life). Chardin speaks to God: "Lord, it is you who, through the imperceptible goadings of sense-beauty, penetrated my heart in order to make its life flow out into yourself. You came down into me by means of a tiny scrap of created reality; and then, suddenly, you unfurled your immensity before my eyes and displayed yourself to me as Universal Being."[31] Gabriela Mistral explains: "Entre los artistas son religiosos los que, fuera de la capacidad para crear, tienen al mirar el mundo exterior la intuición del misterio, y saben que la rosa es algo más que una rosa y la montaña algo más que una montaña; ven el sentido místico de la belleza y hallan en las suavidades de las hierbas y de las nubes de verano la insinuación de una mayor suavidad, que está en la mano de Dios"[32] (Among the artists, they are religious who, apart from their capacity to create, have, on looking at the exterior world, the intuition of mystery, and they know that the rose is something more than a rose and that the mountain is something more than a mountain; they see the mystical meaning of beauty and find in the smoothnesses of herbs and of the clouds the insinuation of a greater suavity, which is in the hand of God).

This "intuición del misterio" (intuition of mystery) is also described by Jacques Maritain when, referring to the Oriental artist, he states: "Il regarde les Choses, il médite sur le mystère de leur apparence visible et sur le mystère de leur secrète force vitale; . . . Mais parce que l'art oriental est essentiellement religieux ou d'inspiration religieuse, il est en communion avec les Choses non pour l'amour des Choses, mais pour l'amour d'une autre réalité—invisible et adorable—dont les Choses sont les signes, et qu'à travers les Choses l'art révèle en même temps que les Choses"[33] (He looks at Things, he meditates on the mystery of their visible appearance and on the mystery of their secret vital force; . . . But because Oriental art is essentially religious or of religious inspiration, he is in communion with Things, not for the love of Things, but for the love of another reality—invisible and adorable—of which Things are symbols, and which, through Things, art reveals at the same time as Things).

Gabriela Mistral further clarifies the idea and concludes by defining it: "Les roe el corazón como una herida el ansia de lo perfecto y el solo imaginar la perfección y ansiarla con tanta angustia, les dice que lo que ansían *debe existir*. Después de su lucha entre lo concebido y lo realizado, en la cual fueron vencidos, se hace en ellos una infinita humildad, porque se sienten vasos limitados de una ilimitada hermosura. La ilimitada hermosura es Dios . . ."[34] (The anxiety for the perfect gnaws at their hearts like a wound and, only imagining perfection and desiring it with so much anguish, tells them that what they so much desire *must exist*. After their struggle between the conceived and the realized, in which they were conquered, there rises within them an infinite humility, because they feel themselves limited vessels of an unlimited beauty. The unlimited beauty is God . . .).

This was, indeed, the keystone of her spiritual philosophy or intuition: she saw God within herself and permeating everything in the universe, big or small. The poet in her was subdued by the woman of God. He claimed the whole of her person, all her activities, all her relationships.

Her mature religion was spiritual in its conception of God and of the good He bestows and demands. It was ethical, for she believed that it must manifest itself in moral and social responsibility. It sprang from an experience of the presence of God which had no patience with illusion, but which grasped the relationship between the spiritual and the natural, the eternal and the temporal, and knows that man belongs to both levels or orders.

Yet, her religion was not mysticism, for it lacked the unifying principle indispensable in its conception of God. Gabriela's conception of God passed through varying stages. At times, she seemed to understand no dogma save the joy, the love, and the sorrow which are in the universe. Sometimes she has compassion for God, and sometimes she argues with Him. Now she loves Him; now she fears Him. At times He is her Christ Crucified; at times He is the strong and terrible God of the Old Testament.[35] Sometimes He is vague; sometimes, certain. Thus, throughout her books of poems, there are expressions of "al Señor fuerte," "Cristo, el de las venas vaciadas en ríos," "que aun Jesús padece," "¡Yo cantaré cuando / te hayan desclavado!" "el estupor de Dios," "creo en mi corazón, el reclinado / en el pecho de Dios terrible y fuerte" (To the strong Lord; Christ, He with his veins emptied in rivers; for Jesus still suffers; I shall sing when they have taken the nails out of you; the stupor of God; I believe in my heart, the one reclined on the heart of God terrible and strong).

Then He takes on a pantheistic guise. He becomes "un Dios de otoño, un Dios sin ardor y sin canto" (a God of autumn, a God without ardor and without song). He is a vengeful, cunning divinity: "Dios no quiere que tú tengas /

sol si conmigo no marchas" (God does not wish that you have / any sun if you don't walk with me). He is love: "¡es un viento de Dios, que pasa hendiéndome" (it is a wind of God, which passes going through me). He abandons His creatures: "y no quieres volverte hacia mí!" (and You don't wish to turn toward me!). He is "lo Eterno," "nuestro Dueño," "el Unico" (The Eternal One; our Master; The Only One). It is He who "en los vientos te bate la frente" (in the winds, He beats against your forehead). It is He who rocks the child to sleep: "que es Dios en la sombra / el que va meciendo" (for it is God in the shadow / who is rocking). He is "la gran mirada de Dios"[36] (the great gaze of God).

In her "Dos canciones del Zodiaco" ("Two Songs of the Zodiac"): "Canción de Virgo" and "Canción de Taurus" ("Song of Virgo" and "Song of Taurus"), she identifies the mythical Christ with the Christ Child:

> Dormido irás creciendo;
> creciendo harás la Ley
> y escogerás ser Cristo
> o escogerás ser Rey.
>
> Hijito de Dios Padre
> en brazos de mujer.[37]

> (Asleep, you will keep on growing;
> growing you will make the Law
> and you will choose to be Christ
> or you will choose to be King.
>
> Little Son of God the Father
> in the arms of a woman.)

In the falling snow, she sees the message, the cloak, the image, the love of God:

Tal vez rompió, cayendo y cayendo, el mensaje
de Dios Nuestro Señor.
Tal vez era su manto, tal vez era su imagen,
tal vez no más su amor.[38]

(Perhaps there broke through, falling and falling, the message
of God Our Lord.
Perhaps it was His cloak, perhaps it was His image,
perhaps nothing more than His love.)

Her litany of names and allusions continues throughout her poetry, showing the pronounced aspect of religion in them, for true poets must have a pronounced religion; they hold themselves as a link between earth and heaven.[39] William Blake expresses a similar thought:

Trembling I sit day and night, my friends are astonished at me,
Yet they forgive my wanderings, I rest not from my great task!
To open the Eternal Worlds, to open the immortal Eyes
Of man inwards into the Worlds of Thought: into Eternity
Ever expanding in the Bosom of God, the Human Imagination.[40]

4. Nature

¡En el cerco del valle de Elqui,
bajo la luna de fantasma,
no sabemos si somos hombres
o somos peñas arrobadas![41]

(In the encirclement of the valley of Elqui,
beneath the phantom moon,
we know not whether we are men
or enchanted rocks!)

The childhood of Lucila Godoy was spent in the Andean valley of Elqui. Here she was in constant touch with the land and with nature's beings that inhabit it. Here she "drew the bolt of nature's secrecies and made them shapers of her own moods or wailful or divine."[42] Here, the external landscape became internal, as she "lived, breathed, suffered, and loved it intensely."[43] Here, as Chardin put it, she absorbed "the unique essence of the universe":

> The man who is wholly taken up with the demands of everyday living or whose "sole" interest is in the outward appearances of things seldom gains more than a glimpse, at best, of this second phase in our sense-perceptions, that in which the world, having entered into us, then withdraws from us and bears us away with it: he can have only a very dim awareness of that aureole, thrilling and inundating our being, through which is disclosed to us at "every" point of contact the unique essence of the universe.[44]

Thus, is she grouped with typical Latin-American writers whose "arte americano ha descubierto nuestro paisaje más verdadero . . . el rol profundamente humanizador de la obra artística, y su inescapable misión en el desarollo de nuestra cultura de hoy, tan desligada de las vestustísimas sublimidades de las culturas precolombinas como asimismo de lo que la cultura occidental hoy en crisis espera ciertamente de nosotros"[45] (American art has discovered our most true landscape

. . . the profoundly humanizing role of artistic work and its inescapable mission in the development of our culture today, so far removed from the very ancient sublimities of the Pre-Colombian cultures and also from that which Western culture today in crisis certainly expects from us).

In this respect, perhaps, *Tala* (*Felling*) is her most representative book. In the section "América," she has two hymns: "Sol del trópico" ("Sun of the Tropics") and "Cordillera" ("Mountain Range"), which Eugenio Florit considers the "deep and the most fundamental essence of our land and the very air which we breathe."[46] Gabriela herself considers it the best of her work: "Créame, Sybila, que *Tala* es mi verdadera obra . . . mucho más interesante que *Desolación,* aunque a usted le parezca extraño. Más tarde la leerá y se acordará de mí. Es la raíz de lo indoamericano"[47] (Believe me, Sibyl, that *Tala* is my real work . . . much more interesting than *Desolación,* although it may seem strange to you. Later you will read it and you will remember me. It is the root of the Indo-American).

She is indeed "la mujer americana" (The American Woman) as she sings to the "Sol de los Incas, sol de los Mayas, sol de montañas y de valles, Sol del Cuzco, Sol de México" (Sun of the Incas, sun of the Mayas, sun of mountains and of valleys, Sun of Cuzco, Sun of Mexico). Years of absence from her beloved *América* had produced in her a physical longing. She complains that she tread on foreign soils, ate mercenary fruit on hard tables, drank weakened mead from dull glasses, and murmured dying prayers, as she sang barbaric hymns to herself. She compares herself to native plants and native birds that blossom and bathe in the healing warmth of this sun and begs to be possessed by and absorbed in it:

> ¡Como el maguey, como la yuca,

como el cántaro del peruano,
como la jícara de Uruapan,
como la quena de mil años,
a ti me vuelvo, a ti me entrego,
en ti me abro, en ti me baño!
Tómame como los tomaste,
el poro al poro, el gajo al gajo,
y ponme entre ellos a vivir,
pasmada dentro de tu pasmo.[48]

(Like the maguey, like the yuca,
like the pitcher of the Peruvian,
like the chocolate cup of Uruapan,
like the Indian flute of a thousand years,
I turn to you, I give myself to you,
In you, I open up; in you, I bathe!
Take me as you took them,
pore to pore, branch to branch,
and place me among them to live,
astonished in your astonishment.)

It takes but two lines of "Cordillera" to learn how she loved the mountain range when she was a child and how she missed it in her absence:

que de niños nos enloquece
y hace morir cuando nos falta;[49]

(which, when children, drives us mad
and makes us die when we miss it.)

She admired the culture of the Inca, the Maya, the Aztec, and held that the essence of America is to be found in its indigenous element. Her Americanism is always tinged with this Indianism. Juan Ramón Jiménez says of her: "Gabriela Mistral siente el indigenismo porque lo tiene dentro"[50] (Gabriela Mistral feels the indigenousness because she carries it within herself). In her lengthy poem, "El maíz" ("Indian Corn"), she recalls Anáhuac, Quetzalcóatl, "el indio que los cruza como que no parece" (the Indian who crosses them as one who does not appear) and symbolically proclaims the end of Mexico with the death of the Indian corn:

y México se acaba
donde el maíz se muere.[51]

(and Mexico ends
where the corn dies.)

To the Mexican peak Ixtlazihuatl she gives her praise, her love, and her reason for both:

Te doy mi amor, montaña mexicana;
como una virgen tú eres deleitosa;
. . . . . .

Y yo te llevo cual tu criatura,
te llevo aquí en mi corazón tajeado,
que me crié en tus pechos de amargura,
¡y derramé mi vida en tus costados![52]

(I give you my love, O Mexican mountain;
like a virgin are you delightful;
. . . . . .

And I bear you as your creature,

I carry you here in my cleaved heart,
for I was nurtured in your breasts of bitterness,
and I poured out my life in your sides!)

In *Lagar* (*Wine Press*), Gabriela continues the theme of the natural beauty of the Americas as a source of inspiration, as she sings of the "Amapola de California" ("Poppy of California"); "Hallazgo de Palmar" ("The Finding of Palms"), with reference to the palm tree of Chile which produces an exquisite honey; "La piedra de Parahibuna" ("The Stone of Parahibuna"), with children who whiten her skirts; "Muerte del mar" ("Death of the Sea"), a fantasy of a surrealistic nightmare in which the sea basin is drained and reveals an oppressive landscape; "Ocotillo" ("Little Okote Pine"), the American cactus; "Palmas de Cuba" ("Cuban Palms"), which she must find or remain orphaned, which she must taste or be embittered. In "Ceiba seca" ("Dry Silkcotton Tree"), "Espiga Uruguaya" ("Uruguayan Corn Tassel"), "Poda de rosal" ("Pruning of the Rose Bush"), "Poda de almendro" ("Pruning of the Almond Tree"), and "Hijo árbol" ("Son Tree"), "Gabriela captures both the earthly and cosmic sense of these beings; they appear to her as steps that link her to God and to the earth as understandable words and sings of the earthly and the Eternal. At times this objective vision, so realistic and penetrating it impels the poet to communion with the universe, gives way, through some image or analogy, to a subjective, personal reference."[53]

This capturing of the earthly and cosmic sense of beings is perceptible in "Cosas" ("Things"), where she declares:

Amo las cosas que nunca tuve
con las otras que ya no tengo:[54]

(I love the things I never had
with others that I have not now:)

Here she touches silent water which gives her a strange thought; she plays with this water as with a fish or with a mystery. She searches for a verse which she has lost. An aroma comes to her; she remembers children; a river sounds, the Elqui of her childhood; the Pacific, the stone of Oaxaca or Guatemala, the memory of her father. Then, she falls asleep:

Al dormirme queda desnuda;
no sé por qué yo la volteo.
Y tal vez nunca la he tenido
y es mi sepulcro lo que veo . . .[55]

(When I fall asleep, it is naked;
I don't know why I turn it over.
And perhaps I've never had it
and it is my tomb I see . . .)

The same phenomenon occurs in "Materias" ("Substances"). Here, bread personified, takes on a feeling of loneliness:

y no hay nadie tampoco en la casa
sino este pan abierto en un plato,
que con su cuerpo me reconoce
y con el mío yo reconozco.

. . . . . .
los dos en este silencio humano
hasta que seamos otra vez uno
y nuestro día se haya acabado . . .[56]

(and neither is there anyone in the house
except this opened bread on a plate,
which with his body recognizes me,
and with mine, I recognize it.

. . . .

the two of us in this human silence,
until we are one again
and our day has ended . . .)

"Sal" ("Salt") is but a mysterious union and a strangely common origin of both the material and the poet. She states that the salt searches for her because both have come from the waves and their brine-sterns to a quiet and recondite house:

Ambas éramos de las olas
y sus espejos de salmuera,
y del mar libre nos trajeron
a una casa profunda y quieta:
y el puñado de Sal y yo,
en beguinas o en prisioneras,
las dos llorando, las dos cautivas,
atravesamos por la puerta . . .[57]

(We were both from the waves
and their brine-sterns,
and from the free sea they carried us
to a house profound and quiet;
and the handful of Salt and I,
as "blesseds"[58] or as prisoners,
the two of us crying, the two of us captives,
cross the threshold.)

"Agua" ("Water") repeats the nostalgic theme of absent loved places:

> Hay países que yo recuerdo
> como recuerdo mis infancias.
> Son países de mar o río,
> . . . . . .
>
> Me han traído a país sin río,
> tierras-Agar, tierras sin agua;[59]
>
> (There are countries which I remember
> as I remember my childhood.
> They are countries of sea or of river,
> . . . . . .
>
> They have taken me to a country without rivers,
> Agar-countries, countries without water;)

Here, as in "Cascada en sequedal" ("Cascade in Dry Soil") and "El aire" ("Air"), there is a certain dematerialization of water, a personification of things which makes them capable of union and communion with the author whose love for them converts them into immortal beings who make up an eternal landscape: "¡agua, madre mía, / e hija mía, el agua!"[60] (water, my mother, / and my daughter, the water!). Now she sleeps "como la madre del hijo, / rota del Aire . . ."[61] (like the mother of the child, / broken from the Air).

"País de la ausencia" ("Land Of Absence"), one of the poems with "Cosas" ("Things") in the section called by the Portuguese name "Saudade" ("Soledades"),[62] reveals again the longing for the persons and things she loved. She speaks of the things she lost: "Perdí cordilleras . . . / perdí huertos de oro / dulces de vivir" (I lost mountain ranges . . . / I lost orchards of gold / sweet things of life), and prophesies her death in a strange land: "y en país sin nombre / me voy a morir" (and in a country without a name / I am going to die). She lives in pure time and negates the reality of space: "más ligero que ángel / . . . con edad de siempre, / sin edad feliz" (lighter than angel / . . . with age of eternity, / without age of joy). She seemed distracted and removed from reality, yet she felt its presence with intensity. The value of the past, the distant, and the lost are felt in the "Land of Absence":

> Me nació de cosas
> que no son país;
> de patrias y patrias
> que tuve y perdí;
> de la criaturas
> que yo vi morir;
> de lo que era mío
> y se fue de mí.[63]
>
> (It was born to me of things
> that are not country;
> of lands and lands
> which I had and lost;
> of the creatures
> I saw die;
> of that which was mine
> and went from me.)

She seems to be moving in a void where actual countries like Chile, Mexico, and the United States are not important. Only the formless and nameless one is real to her as she keeps repeating: "Y en país sin nombre / me voy a morir" (And in a country without name / I am going to die).

Her "valle de Elqui" is so close to her heart that she pictures it possessing a regal charm which it passes on to all who love it:

> Pero en el valle de Elqui, donde
> son cien montañas o son más,
> cantan las otras que vinieron
> y las que vienen cantarán:
>
> "En la tierra seremos reinas,
> y de verídico reinar,
> y siendo grandes nuestros reinos,
> llegaremos todas al mar."[64]
>
> (But in the valley of Elqui, where
> there are one hundred mountains, or there are more,
> the others who came sing,
> and those who are coming, will sing:
>
> "In the land we shall be queens,
> and we shall really reign,
> and since our kingdoms are great,
> we shall all reach the sea.")

"La tierra es dulce cual humano labio" (Land is sweet as a human lip) as she still waits for her old love: "Miro correr las aguas de los años, / . . . / Antiguo Amor, te espero todavía"[65] (I watch the waters of the years flow by, / . . . / O my old Love, I still wait for you). She sinks her eyes into the horizon, and suddenly a star falls down to her breast and awakens her. She calls to her incredulous neighbors to come and see: "¿No veis que en las sábanas / echa luz y tiembla?" (Don't you see that in the sheets / she gives out light and trembles?). She knows that because the star has come down to her, the land will give produce and the sheep will not die. All bless her, but her love bids them be silent while her child-star sleeps:

¡Ay, dejad dormir
mi niñita estrella!

Luz, echa su cuerpo
y luz sus pupilas,
y la miro y lloro,
¡que es mía y es mía![66]

(Ah, let her sleep,
my little child-star!

Light, her body gives out,
and light, her eyes,
and I look at her and weep,
for she is mine, and she is mine!)

Who is this woman, or rather, what is she, that she can thus identify herself with all the creatures of nature? She is at home with the elements; she makes a child of the stars. She knows why sugar cane is hollow and why roses have thorns. She touches a putrid, stagnant pool and converts it into a pure, cottony, aerial foam, while a tree and a bird stare, incredulous at its transmutation.[67] "Suspended in the dripping well of her imagination the commonest object becomes encrusted with imagery, the least idea blazes and scintillates in the subtle oxygen of her mind."[68]

Why is it that the language of Nature which is but a stir, a silence, unintelligible to the sound of man, becomes intelligible to this woman as she "dabbles her fingers in the day-fall and becomes gold-dusty with tumbling amidst the stars."[69] A San Juan de la Cruz complains that the babbling of Nature leaves him dying with its "no sé qué que quedan balbuciendo"[70] (I know not what they keep stammering), a Francis Thompson admits its vanity: "For, ah! we know not what each other says,"[71] and Gabriela Mistral can boast: "En la luz del mundo / yo me he confundido"[72] (In the light of the world / I have confounded myself).

In Gabriela Mistral, there is something deeper, something more mysterious than the poet's inspired faculty to commune with Nature. Is it perhaps her firm belief in metempsychosis, her conviction that in a previous existence she had a different mode of being? Was not this, as she herself kept repeating, that powerful factor in her personality? ". . . pero también retorna mi viejo fatalismo. La metempsicosis . . . Es algo poderoso en mi personalidad. A veces sé que he vivido otras vidas; a veces ignoro todo, pero creo en las reencarnaciones"[73] (. . . but my old fatalism also returns. Metempsychosis . . . It is something powerful in my personality. Sometimes I know that I have lived other lives; sometimes I don't know anything, but I do believe in reincarnation).

5. Motherhood

> Me ha besado y ya soy otra: otra, por el latido que duplica el de mis venas; otra, por el aliento que se percibe entre mi aliento.[74]
>
> (He kissed me and now I am another; another, in the pulse that duplicates that of my veins; another, in the breath that is perceived in my breath.)

In spirit, mind, and heart, Gabriela Mistral was a mother.[75] In body, she was one by baptism of desire. So much did she desire to bear children of her own that, when this was denied her, she embraced the children of others and shared with them her maternal love. With deep tenderness she cared for these children, for she considered them the product of a painful but divine condition. To this condition, she dedicated an entire section of *Desolación,* and called it "Poemas de las Madres" ("Mothers' Poems"). Here, in a note, she gives her reason for the dedication. She had observed a crude man fling an ugly phrase at a woman heavy with child. As the woman blushed, Gabriela felt toward her all the solidity of her sex, the infinite pity of one woman for another, and firmly resolved to proclaim the sacredness of maternity:

> —Es una de nosotros quien debe decir (ya que los hombres no lo han dicho) la santidad de este estado doloroso y divino. Si la misión del arte es embellecerlo todo en una inmensa misericordia, ¿por qué no hemos purificado, a los ojos de los impuros, "esto"?
>
> Y escribí los poemas que preceden, con intención casi religiosa.[76]
>
> (It is one of us who should declare [since men have not declared it] the sanctity of this dolorous and divine state. If the mission of art is to beautify all in an immense act of mercy, why have we not purified "this" in the eyes of the impure?
>
> And I wrote the poems which precede, with an intention almost religious.)

She regrets that some women who, in order to remain chaste and find it necessary to close their eyes to realities, made a ruinous commentary on the poems and even suggested that she eliminate them from her book. She pities their sad plight and resolves the more that the poems shall remain, for they sing of "la Vida total" (the total Life):

> En esta obra egotista, empequeñecida a mis propios ojos por ese egotismo, tales prosas humanas tal vez sean lo único en que se canta la Vida total. ¡Había de eliminarlas?
>
> ¡No! Aquí quedan, dedicadas a las mujeres capaces de ver que la santidad de la vida comienza en la maternidad, la cual es, por lo tanto, sagrada. Sientan ellas la honda ternura con que una mujer que apacienta por la Tierra los hijos ajenos, mira a las madres de todos los niños del mundo![77]
>
> (In this egotistical work, belittled before my very eyes by that egotism, such human prose perhaps is the only one in which the total Life is sung. Had I to eliminate them?
>
> No! Here they remain, dedicated to women who are capable of seeing that the sanctity of life begins in motherhood, which is, for that reason, sacred. Let them feel the deep tenderness with which a woman who shepherds all over the Earth the children of others looks at the mothers of all the children of the world!)

With a boldness, forgivable only because of her avowed touch of sacredness, she wrests from the innermost recesses of the heart of woman thoughts heretofore hardly admitted even to herself. For, if one would try to describe Gabriela Mistral with one single word, that word would be intensity. She wastes no time in scratching surfaces; she must explode them and lay bear to their depths the chasms hidden beneath. Prudery should avoid these pages, for it will neither desire nor understand them. In its scandal, it will again incur the ironic pity of their author, who would add another sacrament to the seven already instituted by Christ to give grace.

Thus, for one transfigured moment, she becomes the expectant mother with an exhalation of flowers on her breath, all because of the one who "descansa en mis entrañas blandamente"[78] (rests in my entrails mildly). She wonders what the child will be like, and in her musings, she touches rose petals, for she wants their softness for his cheeks; she plays in a tangle of brambles, for she wants his hair dark and tangled that way, but if his hair be brownish with the rich color of the red clays that potters love, or stringy and as plain as her life has been, it doesn't matter. She watches the hollows in the mountains when they are filling with mist, and in the mist she traces the shape of a little girl, but more than anything else, she wants the child's look to have the sweetness of "his" look and the child's voice to have the timbre of "his" voice when he speaks to her, for "en el que viene quiero amar a aquél que me besara"[79] (in him who is coming, I wish to love him who would kiss me).

In "Sabiduría" ("Wisdom"), she learns why for twenty summers she has basked in the warm sun and gathered beautiful flowers: ". . . me traspasó la luz para la dulzura que entregaría"[80] (. . . the light pierced me through for the sweetness that it would transfer). That which is deep within her comes into being, drop by drop, from the wine of her veins. She prays to receive from the hands of God the clay from which he will be made, and when she reads a poem for him, her beauty burns her like a live coal so that he may catch from her flesh a fire that can never be extinguished.

In "La dulzura" ("Sweetness"), she shares her maternity with creatures of Nature:

> Hurgo con miedo de ternura en las yerbas donde anidan codornices. Y voy por el campo silenciosa, cautelosamente: Creo que árboles y cosas tienen hijos dormidos, sobre los que velan inclinados.[81]
>
> (With tender fear, I poke about the grass where they nest quails. And silently, cautiously, I go about the field: I believe that trees and things have sleeping children over whom they incline, keeping watch.)

She is daring in "La hermana" ("The Sister"), where she takes home another woman, a woman plowing in the fields with "caderas henchidas, como las mías, por el amor" (hips filled up, like mine, for love) and showers upon her all manner of tenderness with the hope that she will supply for her deficiency: "Y si mi seno no es generoso, mi hijo allegará al suyo, rico, sus labios"[82] (And if my breast is not generous, my son will approach hers, rich, his lips). She is even more daring in "El ruego" ("The Plea"), where she gives God a new name, "El Henchidor" (The Filler), in order to beg of Him "el licor de la vida, abundoso. Mi hijo llegará buscándolo con sed" (the beverage of life, abundant. My child will approach seeking it with thirst); in "Sensitiva" ("Sensitive"), she dares to describe all the changing vicissitudes of her state. In "El dolor eterno" ("Eternal Sorrow"), "Por él" ("For Him"), "La quietud" ("Tranquillity"), "Ropitas blancas" ("Little White Clothes"), and "Imagen de la tierra" ("Image of the Earth"), she pours forth all her craving for motherhood, mingled again with her love for Nature:

> Voy conociendo el sentido maternal de las cosas. La montaña que me mira, también es madre, y por las tardes la neblina juega como un niño por sus hombros y sus rodillas.[83]

(I am understanding the maternal meaning of things. The mountain which looks at me is also a mother, and in the afternoons, the mist plays like a child on her shoulders and her knees.)

In "Al esposo" ("To the Husband") and "La madre" ("The Mother"), she leaves nothing unsaid. In the first, she begs her husband to forgive her clumsiness and to treat her with more love and kindness. In the second, she and her mother become sisters as together they discuss all the intimacies of maternity. She cries out with the pangs of childbirth in "El amanecer" ("Dawn") and calls on God, Infinite Sweetness, to release the child gently. In "La sagrada ley" ("The Sacred Law"), childbirth and eternity become one and the same thing:

—¿Quién soy yo, me digo, para tener un hijo en mis rodillas? Y yo misma respondo:

—Una que amó, y cuyo amor pidió, al recibir el beso, la eternidad.[84]

(Whom am I, I say to myself, to have a child within my knees? And I myself answer me:

One who loved, and whose love begged, on receiving the kiss, for eternity.)

The second part of this section of poems for mothers is dedicated to "La madre más triste" ("The Saddest Mother"). Here, there are two prose poems: "Arrojada" ("Thrown Out"), which briefly describes the plight of a young mother who is thrown out by her father and who fears that her child will be born before she reaches the village, and "¿Para qué viniste?" ("Why Did You Come?"), which is the story of a young mother deserted by her husband. She questions her unborn child and answers him:

> ¿Para qué viniste, si él que te trajo te odió al sentirte en mi vientre?
>
> ¡Pero no! Para mí viniste; para mí que estaba sola, sola hasta cuando me oprimía él entre sus brazos, hijo mío.[85]
>
> (Why did you come, if he who brought you hated you on feeling you in my womb?
>
> But no! You came for me; for me who was alone, alone until he pressed me within his arms, my son.)

Gabriela Mistral loved her own mother dearly. She dedicated part of *Tala* to "Muerte de mi madre" ("Death of My Mother"), and explains in a note the reason for this dedication:

> Ella se me volvió una larga y sombría posada; se me hizo un país en que viví cinco o siete años, país amado a causa de la muerte, odioso a causa de la volteadura de mi alma en una larga crisis religiosa.[86]
>
> (She provided me with a long and gloomy lodging; she made for me a land in which I lived five or seven years, a land loved because of death, hateful because of the overturning of my soul in a long religious crisis.)

In her anguish, she wonders whether her mother knows that she is searching for her, whether she is with her or within her: ". . . o vas en mí por terrible convenio, / sin responderme con tu cuerpo sordo, / siempre por el rosario de los cerros, / que cobran sangre para entregar gozo" (or you go within me by a terrible pact, / without answering me with your deaf body, / always along the rosary of hills, / that collect blood in order to give pleasure). She falls into "Nocturno de la consumación" ("Nocturn of Consummation") and "Nocturno de la derrota" ("Nocturn of the Defeated One"), where she confesses: "Yo nací de una carne tajada / en el seco riñon de Israel" (I was born of a flesh cleaved /out of the dry center of Israel). She continues with "Nocturno de los tejedores viejos," "Nocturno de José Asunción," "Nocturno del descendimiento" ("Nocturn of the Old Weavers," "Nocturn of José Asunción," "Nocturn of the Descent"), and concludes with "Locas letanías"[87] ("Crazy Litanies"), with its tone of "la esperanza y cuenta su remate a quienes se cuidan de mi alma y poco saben de mí desde que vivo errante"[88] (hope, and it recounts its end to those who care for my soul and know little about me since I have been living an errant life).

It is strange that this woman who so loved and respected her own mother, who adorned the state of motherhood with an unheard-of brilliance, wrote so little in her poetry about the Mother of God.[89] Besides several poetic allusions to Mary, she has only one poem, "A la Virgen de la colina" ("To the Virgin of the Hill"), dedicated to her. This absence of Mary continues throughout her unpublished volumes,[90] while two of her contemporaries: Juana de Ibarbourou in Uruguay and Marie Noël in France devote entire volumes in praise of the Blessed Virgin Mary. The first sings *Los loores de Nuestra Señora* (Praises of Our Lady); the second, *Le Rosaire des Joies* (The Rosary of Joys).[91] Yet, Gabriela is not unaware of Mary's powerful assistance:

> Ahora estoy dando verso y llanto
> a la lumbre de tu mirar.
> . . . . . .

Miedo extraño en mis carnes mora.
¡Si tú callas, qué voy a hacer![92]

(Now I am giving forth verse and tears
in the splendor of your gaze.
. . . . . .

A strange fear inhabits my flesh.
If you are silent, what am I going to do!)

6. Children

Closely linked to her respect for motherhood are Gabriela's all-embracing love for children and her role as a teacher.[93] To children, she devotes sections of all her books in "Canciones de cuna" ("Cradle Songs"), "Rondas" ("Rounds"), "Jugarretas" ("Tricks"), "Cuenta-mundo" ("World-Account"), "Casi escolares" ("Almost Scholastic"), and "Cuentos" ("Tales"). In her unpublished *Recado de Chile* (*Message of Chile*), she has written reminders labeled "Notas para hacer" ("Notes to make"). Here she declares her intention: "Hacer hablar al niño en chileno y que hable bastante" (To make the child speak in Chilean, and make him speak enough). In *Largar II* (*Wine Press II*), she has written another group of "Jugarretas" ("Tricks") and "Rondas" ("Rounds"). In "Vagabundaje" ("Roaming"), she sings a "Canción de las niñas catalanas" ("Song of Catalan Children"). In "Sin clasificar" ("Without Classifying"), she writes of "Niños" ("Children"), and "Nino siciliano" ("Sicilian Child"), as well as a new "Canción de cuna" ("Cradle Song").

In the first group, "Cradle Songs," she begs the "velloncito de mi carne" (little fleece of my flesh) to keep close to her; she assures her child that she is not lonely; she cradles him, feeling the hand of God in the darkness; to the sway of her cradle swinging, the whole world goes to sleep, while she tells her babe: ". . . duérmete sonriendo, / que es Dios en la sombra / el que va meciendo"[94] (. . . go to sleep smiling, / for it is God in the shadow / who is rocking). She sings to him of his "Encantamiento," "La madre triste," "Suavidades" ("Delightfulness," "The Sad Mother," "Gentilities"). In her "Canción amarga" ("Bitter Song"), she plays with him "a la reina con el rey"[95] (as the queen with the king). In "Miedo" ("Fear"), she does not wish to have her child a swallow, a princess, or a queen, for each state would involve a painful separation from her. Through "Corderito" ("Little Lamb"), "Rocío" ("Dew"), "Hallazgo" ("Finding"), she continues her cradle songs, then begs in "Mi canción" ("My Song"):

> La canción que yo prestaba
> al despierto y al dormido
> ahora que me han herido
>   ¡cántenme![96]
>
> (The song which I rendered
> on waking and sleeping
> now that they have wounded me
>   let them sing to me!)

In "Niño mexicano" ("Mexican Child"), as she combs the hair of a Mexican child, an eternity of ages peers at her through his eyes, reminding her of her everlasting desire to care for little ones:

> Me miran con vida eterna
> sus ojos negri-azulados,
> y como en costumbre eterna,

yo lo peino de mis manos.[97]

(They look at me with eternal life,
his black-blue eyes,
and, as in eternal custom,
I comb him with my hands.)

"Rondas" is a series of twenty rounds in which, while singing and dancing with children, she continues her preoccupation with Nature and with eternity. In her song, she carries them to the waves of the sea, to the foot of the mountains, to the woods where the chant of children and birds meet together in a kiss of the wind. As usual, not satisfied with the infinite, she desires an infinite round:

¡Haremos la ronda infinita!
¡La iremos al bosque a trenzar,
la haremos al pie de los montes
y en todas las playas del mar![98]

(We shall make the infinite round!
We shall go to the woods to frolic,
we shall make it at the foot of the mountains
and on all the shores of the sea!)

In these rounds, especially in "Los que no danzan" ("They Who Do Not Dance"), Margot Arce de Vázquez perceives, through the affirmation of life, love, and peace, the conception of the poems as an attempt to create a true antidance macabre:

> Sin caer nunca en la superficialidad ni en la cursilería sensiblera, estos poemas están al alcance del entendi-

miento y la imaginación de los niños y despiertan y afinan su sensibilidad con graciosas ficciones poéticas, con la nobleza de los pensamientos elevados. Entre todo el grupo se destacan las "Rondas," consteladas en torno al motivo de la armonía universal. . . . que alcanza su culminación en el momento en que Cristo penetra en el corro transfigurándolo en experiencia mística. Los movimientos de la danza, las pequeñas acciones como momentos significativos, la rica plasticidad de la descripción, la belleza del símbolo y de las imágenes encierran muchas posibilidades de ejecución dramática.[99]

(Without ever falling either into superficiality or perceptible bad taste, these poems are within the reach of the understanding and of the imagination of children, and they awaken and refine their sensibility with gracious poetic fiction, with the nobility of elevated thoughts. From this entire group, the "Rounds" are outstanding, like constellations moving about the universal harmony. . . . which reaches its culmination at the moment in which Christ penetrates the circle, transfiguring it in mystical experience. The movements of the dance, the small actions like significant moments, the rich plasticity of the description, the beauty of the symbol and of the images embrace many possibilities of dramatic execution.)

The mystical experience to which Margot Arce de Vázquez refers seems but a fusion, or rather a confusion, between the vision of the face of God and the sight of dawn:

¡Y mirando Su rostro arder
nos va a hallar el amanecer![100]

(And watching His face burn,
dawn is going to find us!)

She continues her games through "Jugarretas" ("Tricks"), in "La pajita" ("Little Straw"), "La rata" ("The Rat"), "El papagayo" ("The Parrot"), and "El pavo real" ("The Peacock"). She enchants her listeners through "Cuenta-mundo" ("World Account") as air, light, water, rainbow, butterflies, fruit, mountain, fire, and earth take on human qualities and demand human tenderness.

The twenty-one poems of "Casi escolares" ("Almost Scholarly") include her constant themes: she pours her heart over "piececitos de niños" (little feet of children) and "manitas de los niños" (little hands of children); she urges the sower: "echa la simiente" (sow the seed); she dabbles with "nubes blancas, nieve, promesas de las estrellas" (white clouds, snow, promises of the stars). In the falling snow, she hears the silent message of God, sees His mantle, feels His love. She asks the stars to bear witness to her purity and goodness; she remembers her mother and begs: "déjame decirte dulzuras extremas" (let me tell you extreme sweetnesses). She sings of "Doña Primavera" ("Lady Spring"), who goes about "loca de soles" (crazy with suns), and of "verano rey" (King Summer), from whom "el río corre en huída de tu castigo ardoroso" (the river runs in flight from your fiery chastisement). She directs her hymns to "las escuelas Gabriela Mistral" (the Gabriela Mistral schools), to "el árbol" (the tree), and to God. The last, together with "Hablando al Padre" ("Speaking to the Father"), is a prayer of petition with a constant refrain of "Dame" ("Give me"), as opposed to the mystic's surrender and "Suscipe" ("Take").

Her "Cuentos" ("Tales") are delightful nature and animal stories, including the beloved "Caperucita Roja" ("Little Red

Riding Hood"). Among them is the story of the ugly root that brings forth the beautiful rose bush:

> —¡Oh Dios! ¡Cómo lo que abajo era hilacha áspera y parda, se torna arriba seda rosada! ¡Oh Dios! ¡Como hay fealdades que son prolongaciones de belleza! . . .[101]
>
> (Oh God! How what below was ravelled thread, dark and knotty, becomes above rose-colored silk! Oh God! How many ugly things there are that are prolongations of beauty! . . .)

This abundance of poems, fashioned after the style of children's folklore and intended for the spiritual and moral formation of her pupils, achieves the intense simplicity of true songs of the people. Gabriela Mistral expertly approaches the soul of the child from the child's point of view in affectionate, rhythmic language.

More than twenty years of teaching deepened Gabriela's capacity for love and understanding of children. She looked upon her work as a Christian duty, as an exercise of charity whose function was to awaken the heart and mind of the child to moral, spiritual, and physical beauty. For this vocation, the teacher must guard as a precious pearl her own spiritual beauty and moral integrity.[102] For this reason, she lays down in "La maestra rural" ("The Rural Schoolmistress") the qualities of a teacher: "Pura, pobre, alegre, dulce ser" (Pure, poor, happy, sweet being). She utters a subtle warning to both teachers and parents that a child bears more of the impress of a teacher than of a parent upon his character:

Cien veces la miraste, ninguna vez la viste
y en el solar de tu hijo, de ella hay más que de ti.

Pasó por él su fina, su delicada esteva,
abriendo surcos donde alojar perfección.
La albada de virtudes de que lento se nieva
es suya. Campesina, ¿no le pides perdón?[103]

(A hundred times you looked at her, not once did you see her,
and deep down in your child, there is more of her than there is of you.

Through him there passed her fine, her delicate plow handle,
opening furrows in which to lodge perfection.
The dawn of virtues in which, slowly, he becomes snow-white
is hers. Country-woman, do you not ask her pardon?)

When the teacher falls asleep in God, the Father sings for her the cradle songs she composed for His little ones, as peace rains abundantly over her heart. She had borne her soul like an overflowing vase in order to pour forth the ambrosia of all eternity; her life, a dilated breach through which the Father manifested His brilliance, shone as the stars, and now:

Por eso aún el polvo de sus huesos sustenta
púrpura de rosales de violento llamear.
¡Y el cuidador de tumbas, como aroma, me cuenta,
las plantas del que huella sus huesos, al pasar![104]

(For that, even the dust of her bones bear
purple from rose bushes of intense blazing.
And the caretaker of tombs, like aroma, recounts for me
the plants he smells from her bones, on passing!)

In "La encina" ("The Oak"), she compares the teacher to

the majestic oak. She repeats the idea that a true teacher must suffer and begs to venerate her wounds: ". . . ¡Noble encina, / déjame que te bese en el tronco llagado" (Noble oak, / permit me to kiss your wounded trunk), as she sees in the lofty branches the magisterial arms outstretched in benediction: "que con la diestra en alto, tu macizo sagrado / largamente bendiga, como hechura divina!" (that with your right hand on high, your sacred massiveness may bless copiously, like divine workmanship!). Then, as she enumerates the noble tasks of the teacher, she declares that they have sanctified her, that they have stamped her with immortal beauty, that autumn cannot touch her youth:

De tanto albergar nido, de tanto albergar canto,
de tanto hacer tu seno aromosa tibieza,
de tanto dar servicio, y tanto dar amor,

todo tu leño heroico se ha vuelto, encina, santo.
Se te ha hecho en la fronda inmortal la belleza,
¡y pasará el otoño sin tocar tu verdor![105]

(From so much sheltering nests, from so much sheltering song,
from so much making of your breast fragrant coolness,
from so much giving service, and so much giving love,

all your heroic wood has become, O Oak, holy.
You have shaped for yourself beauty in your immortal foliage,
and autumn will pass without touching your verdure!)

7. Chile

Danzamos en tierra chilena,
más bella que Lía y Raquel;

la tierra que amasa a los hombres
de labios y pecho sin hiel . . .

La tierra más verde de huertos,
la tierra más rubia de mies,
la tierra más roja de viñas,
¡qué dulce que roza los pies![106]

(We dance on Chilean land,
more beautiful than Leah and Rachel;
the land which molds men
of lips and breast without gall . . .

The land more green than orchards,
the land more yellow than ripe wheat,
the land more red than vines,
how gently it scrapes the feet!)

Although Gabriela Mistral traveled the world over, her heart kept reverting to her native Chile, to the scenes of her childhood and of her girlhood, to her sorrows and to her joys. Her nostalgia for Chile is one of the pronounced motifs of her poetry. To it she wrote and dedicated one of her last volumes of poetry, *Recado de Chile* (*Message of Chile*). One of her aims, written in her "Notas para hacer" ("Notes to make"), was "contar en metáforas la largura de Chile, sus tres climas, etc." (to relate in metaphors the length of Chile, its three climates, etc.). Here, she has five poems entitled "Araucanos" ("Araucanians"), three "Araucarias" ("Tall Pine Trees"), two "Aromas" ("Fragrances"), two "Atacama" ("Chilean desert"), and one each of "Salitre" ("Nitrate") and "Cobre" ("Copper"). Another section sings of "Provincias de Chile—norte al sur" ("Provinces of Chile—North to South"). The province "Bío-Bío" attracts her attention, as does the onomatopoeic river of "Trozas del 'Poema de Chile'" ("Fragments of the 'Poem of Chile'"), which are found in *Poesías:*

> Yo no quiero que me atajen
> sin que vea el río lento
> que cuchichea dos sílabas
> como quien fía secreto.
> Dice Bío-Bío, y dícelo
> en dos estremecimientos.
> Me he de tender a beberlo
> hasta que corra mis tuétanos . . .[107]
>
> (I do not wish them to stop me
> without my seeing the slow river
> that whispers two syllables,
> like one who confides a secret.
> It says "Bío-Bío," and it says it
> in two tremblings.
> I must stretch out to drink it
> until my very marrow runs.)

Chile, until 1967, was the only country of Latin America that produced a Nobel Prize Winner,[108] and "Chile," says Andrés Bello, "es el único de los pueblos modernos cuya fundación ha sido inmortalizada por un poema épico" (is the only modern country whose foundation has been immortalized by an epic poem). Menéndez y Pelayo adds: "Ni hay tampoco literatura del Nuevo Mundo que tenga tan noble principio como la de Chile, la cual empieza nada menos que con 'La Araucana,' obra de ingenio español, ciertamente, pero tan ligada con el suelo que su autor pisó como conquistador, y con las gentes que allí venció, admiró y compadeció a un tiempo, que sería grave omisión dejar de saludar de paso la noble figura de Ercilla, mucho más cuando su poema sirvió de tipo a todos los de materia histórica, compuestos en América, o sobre América, durante la época colonial"[109] (Neither is there any literature of the New World that has such a noble beginning as that of Chile, which begins with nothing less than "The Araucanian," the work of the ingenious Spaniard, certainly, but so bound to the soil that its author tread as a conquistador, and with the peoples whom he conquered, admired, and with whom he sympathized at the same time, that it would be a grave omission to fail to salute on passing the noble figure of Ercilla, much more so when his poem served as model for all those of historical subject composed in America, or on America, during the colonial epoch).

Yet, "Alone" reveals a secret in his "Interpretación de Gabriela Mistral" ("Interpretation of Gabriela Mistral"), a secret which he guarded in silence during her lifetime. He alleges that Gabriela did not love Chile; that she looked upon Chileans as hostile, suspicious people; that the Chile she loved was her remote corner in the valley of Elqui:[110] "La apoteosis de Gabriela Mistral permitiría decir sobre ella ciertas verdades, particularmente una; que antes habrían debido dejarse en silencio: más allá de cualquier crítica, hállase fuera de todo posible daño: los altares son intangibles. Digámoslo, pues, sin reticencias. Gabriela Mistral no amaba a Chile. Amaba su Monte Grande natal y, por extensión, el valle de Elqui, el campo y la montaña, la gente montañesa y campesina, sus días infantiles. Más allá divisaba un pueblo extraño, hostil, bastante sospechoso que no la inspiraba afecto y con el cual sentíase en oposición"[111] (The apotheosis of Gabriela Mistral would permit telling certain truths about her, particularly one which previously had to be left in silence: beyond any criticism whatsoever, it is found out of the reach of any possible damage: the altars are untouchable. Let us say it, then, without any reticence. Gabriela Mistral did not love Chile. She loved her native Monte Grande and, by extension, the Valley of Elqui, the country and the mountain, the mountain and country people, her childhood days. Beyond that, she descried a strange country, hostile, rather suspicious, which did not inspire affection in her and with which she felt in opposition).

This impassioned child of Monte Grande, this heart of vehement impulses and powerful fantasies, traveled many roads and stopped under many trees to give of her tremendous self. So strong is her communing with all creatures that in her burning verses "roots rise from the ground, take wings, and flutter from the soil in which she stands."[112]

SUMMARY

Gabriela Mistral's importance as a poet, as "without a doubt, one of the most extraordinary poets the Spanish language has ever produced,"[113] does not stem from the perfection of form in her verses. There are few pleasing consonants, little of the musicality and sensuous beauty that produce the audio-visual effects in the work of Juan Ramón Jiménez. She brought the archaisms and colloquial diction of the road and fields to her verses and married them with the deep roots of her painful biography. While she did not dwell upon the form at the expense of the spirit, she did not lack the ability of handling metric forms. Sometimes perfect forms and irregular unpolished ones are found side by side. She seems more concerned with the precision and expressiveness of the word than with the meter of the verse lines. Her critics, in general, agree that her poetic lines are dictated rather by emotion than by concern for form.

Allison Peers states: "We need have no hesitation in saying that for form, as such, Gabriela Mistral cares very little. She seems to shun mere grace; to find satisfaction in a certain brusqueness and asperity. Careless rhymes are not uncommon in her work, nor are lines that halt and almost break down entirely. . . . The poet's best lines, however, are dictated rather by emotion than by concern for form. Her artistic devices are few and of almost negligible importance . . ."[114]

Torres Ríoseco affirms: "Pudiera ser también que Gabriela desdeñara las leyes métricas por considerarlas enemigas de la originalidad y de la poesía vital. Y podría ser también que Gabriela, autodidacta orgullosa, desconociera muchas de estas regulaciones convencionales. De todos modos la dicotomía es innegable"[115] (It could also be that Gabriela despised metrical laws because she considered them enemies of originality and vital poetry. And it could also be that Gabriela, proud and self-taught, did not know many of these conventional regulations. At any rate, dichotomy is undeniable).

Katherine Anne Porter alleges: "In the precious sense, Gabriela Mistral has no culture, no system of esthetics. She makes no calculated effects, no verbal refinements; . . . If she is modern, it is in her independence of traditional forms. She has not troubled even to master the sonnet thoroughly: within her limited choice of forms, all very rough-hewn, she creates many moods out of a sheer capacity for pure song and by the intensity of her feeling."[116]

Margaret Bates, at first, appears to be in harmony with these critics, as she declares:

> Sometimes her efforts to exteriorize her disheveled and burning inspiration fall short of formal perfection; her feelings rush forward disorderly and are put down on paper in the rough. The critics enamored of the "good

> rules" look askance at these explosions, but Gabriela, in true Hispanic fashion, turns her back on easy elegance, deliberately eschews the smooth-flowing, and revels in the rough-hewn and rugged. This "bárbara" certainly has not passed through Grecian paths. Even her tender notes have been called, "almost ferocious." Her frankness scandalized the routinists. The dynamic Hispanic genius pays little homage to formal tidiness. The cool-headed poets, content with the resonance of the ivory tower, cannot belong to this school with its rugged rural notes and primitive earthiness.[117]

Later, however, she refutes Luis Alberto Sánchez's declaration of "carelessness" in Gabriela[118] and terms it "rightness of certain irregularities."[119] To defend this statement, she appeals to Gerardo Diego's "anormalidad necesaria"[120] and Amado Alonso's "cuidadoso descuido"[121] (necessary abnormality and careful carelessness). In her evaluation of Gabriela's "Poema de Chile," Doctor Bates insists that: "It was Gabriela's *modus operandi* (manner of operating) in all her poetry, not only in the 'Poema,' to correct her rough draft until the corrections began to menace legibility . . . The correcting would continue in subsequent copies until Gabriela felt she could no longer improve upon the poem. Gabriela always found correcting very onerous. . . . correcting and eliminating was such hard work that she called it a 'tala,' a chopping down of trees in a huge forest."[122]

Ortiz-Vargas admits of this carelessness, but holds that "it has given her a unique place among contemporary writers of Hispanic America, for she remains herself in all her faults and in all her virtues as a poet. If, at times, she is careless in the technique of her verse, she is always profound, and there is always a deep-rooted meaning to all her words. She does not write poetry for the sake of pleasing the ear with musical rhymes, but rather to unburden a heart heavy with pain and to deliver the message of a soul eternally sad."[123]

Juan Marín attributes her receiving the Nobel Prize not to "una simple apreciación de méritos literarios. Pues Gabriela Mistral no podría en ningún caso ser apreciada como una versificadora más o menos afortunada en sus metros y rimas, . . ." (a simple appreciation of literary merits. For, Gabriela Mistral could not in any case be appreciated as a versifier more or less fortunate in her meters and rhymes, . . .). He attributes the award to "un mensaje moral, mensaje que iba dirigido a toda la humanidad; un 'recado,' como solía decir, para todos los hombres y, especialmente, para los más humildes y más sufridos que pueblan la tierra"[124] (a moral message, a message which was directed to all humanity; a "recado," as she used to call it, for all men and, especially, for the most lowly and the most suffering of all who people the earth). Perhaps she best portrays her love of the humble and suffering in her poetic description of the lily's attempt to discover from her beautiful neighbors, the rose, jasmine, poppy, violet, if they knew Christ. The owner of the lily had told that pure white flower that it resembled Christ. Since none of these lovely flowers knew Christ, they decided to ask the lowly thistle who answered: "Sí, ha pasado por este camino y le he tocado los vestidos, yo, un triste cardo!" (Yes, He has passed along this way and I have touched his garments, I, a lowly thistle!). The lily asked: "¿Y es verdad que se me parece?" (And is it true that He looks like me?). The thistle answered: "Sólo un poco y cuando la luna te pone dolor. Tú levantas demasiado la cabeza. Él la lleva un poco inclinada, pero su manto es albo como tu copo y eres harto feliz de parecértele. Nadie lo comparará nunca con el cardo polvoroso"[125] (Only a little and when the moon makes you look sorrowful. You raise your head too much. He carries His inclined a little, but His mantle is white like your white bulb, and you are exceedingly fortunate to look like Him. No one will ever compare Him to the dusty thistle).

It appears, then, by conjunction of opinion, that the poetry of Gabriela Mistral remains, as Margot Arce de Vázquez affirms: ". . . reacción frente al rubendarismo: poesía sin forma atildada, sin virtuosismos verbales, sin evocaciones de épocas galantes o aristocráticas; poesía de una alma campesina, primitiva y fuerte como la tierra,[126] y de un acento muy puro donde faltan los ecos supercultos de Francia, achaque de modernistas.[127] . . . esta poesía posee el médito de la originalidad cabal, de la voz propia, auténtica, lograda con voluntad consciente. La afirmación en ella del yo íntimo, ajeno a lo extraño, la hace profundamente humana, y por humana, de valor universal"[128] (reaction against Rubén Darío's style: poetry without an adorned form, without verbal virtuosities, without evocations of gallant or aristocratic epochs; poetry of a soul of the country, primitive and strong like the earth, and of a very pure accent, where the super-elegant echoes of France are lacking, a pretext of modernism. . . . this poetry possesses the merit of perfect originality, of the proper voice, authentic, arrived at with conscious will. The affirmation in it of the intimate ego, foreign to the extraneous, makes it profoundly human, and because it is human, of universal worth).

Ginés de Albareda holds that Gabriela Mistral owes as much to her poetry as she does to her breathing and that Spain makes her poetic triumph its own: "Cuando decimos 'su poesía' nos referimos a toda su obra: verso, prosa, biografías, ensayos, artículos, porque en todo momento y en cualquiera de sus manifestaciones literarias, Gabriela es poeta y se debe a su poesía como a su respiración. Ella lo ha dicho: 'Hace el trópico sus poetas como hace los poros de la piña:

traspasados de esencia.' España hace suyo el triunfo de Gabriela Mistral. . . . nombrarla con frase de Eugenio d'ors, 'Angel de la Guarda de la República de Chile' "[129] (When we say "her poetry," we refer to all her work: verse, prose, biographies, essays, articles, because at every moment and in any of her literary manifestations, Gabriela is a poet, and she owes herself to her poetry as she does to her respiration. She has said it: "The tropics make their poets as they make the pores of the pine: pierced through with perfume." Spain makes the triumph of Gabriela Mistral its own. . . . to name her with the phrase of Eugenio d'Ors, "Guardian Angel of the Republic of Chile").

Perhaps her greatest adventure with poetry takes place in "La flor del aire" ("The Flower of the Air"). In twenty assonant stanzas, in an old-fashioned ballad form, she pictures poetry as a mistress of all who pass her way. She meets this mistress in her path, halfway across the meadow. Four times, Poetry sends her to gather flowers: white, red, golden, without color. These colorless ones are the idea of pure poetry, the "unmediated vision," the ". . . striving for pure representation, which we have sometimes called the imageless vision; for poetry is at one with the other arts in seeking, though by varying means, visibility without image, audibility without sound, perception without percepts."[130]

In this experience with pure poetry, Gabriela Mistral approaches the idea of "la poesía desnuda" (the naked poetry) of Juan Ramón Jiménez and "lo evanescente" (the evanescent) of Adolfo Bécquer.[131] In this experience, the poetess obeys, surrendering to her destiny like a picker who is blind, while she follows her mistress to the brink where Time dissolves:

con estas flores sin color,
ni blanquecinas ni bermejas,

hasta mi entrega sobre el límito,
cuando mi Tiempo se disuelva . . .[132]

(with these flowers without color,
neither whitish nor reddish,
until my surrender on the brink,
when my Time dissolves).

CHAPTER V—FOOTNOTES

1. Personal letter received from Jacques Maritain, Toulouse, France, November 18, 1965. He and his late wife, Raïssa, were Gabriela's friends and confidants. Raïssa was even closer to Gabriela than Monsieur Maritain, as he states in his letter: "C'est à Raïssa que Gabriela s'était confiée" (It was in Raïssa that Gabriela confided).

2. ". . . No puedo llamarla 'poetisa,' que suena a poeta a medias; y Gabriela es todo un poeta." (I cannot call her "poetess," for it sounds like half a poet; and Gabriela is all of a poet.) See Carlos D. Hamilton, "Gabriela de Hispanoamérica," *Revista Iberoamericana,* XXIII (1958), 84.

3. Charles A. Bennett, *A Philosophical Study of Mysticism,* 2nd ed. (New Haven, 1923), p. 3.

4. Norberto Pinilla, *Biografía de Gabriela Mistral* (Santiago, Chile, 1945), p. 28.

5. *Recado de Chile* and *Lagar II* have been microfilmed from Gabriela's notebooks and placed in the manuscript room of the New York Public Library, 42nd Street. The two volumes of poetry, together with Gabriela's personal notes, make up the nineteen films in the Mistral microfilm collection. These may not be read or reproduced without the express permission of Miss Doris Dana, Literary Executrix, Estate of Gabriela Mistral. The permission was granted to me when Mr. Hill, the Keeper of Manuscripts, received from Miss Dana a letter authorizing him to permit me to see and to study the Mistral collection. Passages from these works are cited in the present study with the permission of Miss Doris Dana.

6. William Blake, "Song of Thought," *Symbolic Poems of William Blake,* ed. Frederick E. Pierce (New Haven, 1915), pp. 1-2.

7. Doris Dana gave me a copy of the following interview which she found among Gabriela's papers. Miss Dana does not know who the questioner was. She presumes that it was a radio interview. It was never printed in Gabriela's lifetime, but when Miss Dana toured the United States, lecturing on Gabriela Mistral, she used the interview, and several newspapers printed it:

Entrevista con Gabriela Mistral
1941

—¿Qué factores de la realidad social de su país, hecho de conciencia, libro o afecto han orientado su vocación actual?
—Tal vez mi soledad. Hay que hablar consigo cuando se está muy sola, porque la soledad es una antesala de la muerte o de la locura . . .
—¿Qué disciplinas de estudio han influído más en su orientación literaria?
—Siempre leí mucho, pero sólo aproveché de las ramas y los libros que tenían amarras en mi temperamento: en la literatura un poco o muy llana del "sentido trágico" de la vida. Leo libros científicos, en especial geografías y botánicas; de filosofía, me quedé con la religión, y de ésta, con la pura mística.
—La experiencia subjetiva del escritor, ¿en qué medida cree Ud. que debe proyectarse en la creación literaria?
—Siempre y todo lo posible.
—¿Ha hecho autobiografía en su propia obra, y en cuáles?
—El poeta hace casi siempre autobiografía, pero no como se lo creen, con ingenuidad, sus lectores.
—Para una mayor inteligencia interamericana en estos momentos, ¿qué estima usted indispensable y urgente?
—Ser puros y fuertes y no aceptar, dentro de nosotros, la derrota de la cultura y la religión.
—(What factors of the social reality of your country, deed of conscience, book, or affection have influenced your present vocation?
—(Perhaps my solitude. One must speak to oneself when one is very much alone, because solitude is an anteroom of death or of insanity . . .
—(What study disciplines have influenced you most in your literary orientation?
—(I have always read a great deal, but I have profited only from the branches and the books which had attractions for my temperament: in literature, a little or very evidently those which treat of the "tragic sense of life." I read scientific books, especially those on geography and botany; of philosophy, I stay with religion, and of this, with pure mysticism.
—As for the subjective experience of the writer, to what measure, do you think, should it project itself in literary creation?
—Always and as much as possible.
—Have you written autobiography in your own works, and in which ones?
—The poet almost always writes autobiography, but not as his readers, with ingenuity, think.
—For a greater interamerican understanding in these times, what do you consider indispensable and urgent?
—To be pure and strong and not to accept within ourselves the destruction of culture and religion.)

8. "Voto" ("Vow"), *Desolación,* p. 174.
9. "El pensador de Rodin" ("The Thinker of Rodin"), *Poesías,* p. 3.

10. "Los sonetos de la muerte" ("Sonnets on Death"), *Poesías,* p. 81.

11. "Interrogaciones," "Los sonetos de la muerte," "El ruego" ("Interrogations," "Sonnets on Death," "The Entreaty"), *Poesías,* pp. 84-85, 83, 100-101.

12. "Coplas" ("Couplets"), *Poesías,* p. 110.

13. "Los huesos de los muertos" ("The Bones of the Dead"), *Poesías,* p. 111.

14. "Dios lo quiere" ("God Wants It"), *Poesías,* p. 68.

15. Arce de Vázquez, p. 30.

16. Loynaz, cxl.

17. "Nocturno" ("Nocturn"), *Poesías,* pp. 79-80.

18. Loynaz, cxli.

19. Arce de Vázquez, *The Poet and Her Work,* pp. 4-5.

20. Personal interview with Doris Dana, October 30, 1965.

21. Vicente Aleixandre, "A Gabriela Mistral" ("To Gabriela Mistral"), *Gabriela Mistral, Premio Nobel* (Gabriela Mistral, Nobel Prize) (Madrid, 1946), p. 87.

22. "Balada" ("Ballad"), *Poesías,* pp. 75-76.

23. "Desvelada" ("Vigilant"), "Vergüenza" ("Shame"), "La espera inútil" ("Useless Waiting"), "Coplas" ("Couplets"), *Poesías,* pp. 72, 73, 86, 91. The last quotation in the above paragraph recalls the lira in "El cántico espiritual" ("The Spiritual Canticle") of San Juan de la Cruz: "ni ya tengo otro oficio; / que ya sólo en amar es mi ejercicio" (Nor do I now have any other duty; / for now only loving is my exercise). However, it was not this lira which she copied by hand into her notebook, but the three that relate the complete surrender of the Bride to her Bridegroom: "En la interior bodega / de mi Amado bebí, . . ." "Allí me dió su pecho, . . ." ". . . que andando enamorada, / me hice perdidiza, y fuí ganada" (In the interior wine cellar / of my Beloved, I drank, . . . There He gave me His heart, ... that going about lovesick, / I became lost, and I was found). With these, there are the last two liras which describe the final state of the unitive way: ". . . en la noche serena / con llama que consume y no da pena" (in the serene night / with a flame that consumes and gives no pain). "Que nadie lo miraba . . ." (For no one looked at it . . .).

24. Doris Dana stated that Gabriela Mistral was constantly preoccupied with the mystery of all things: God, the soul, life, death, the hereafter, nature. She permitted me to examine a book of Hebrew poetry which belonged to Gabriela. On every page where the words "misterio" (mystery) or "destierro" (exile) appeared Gabriela had underlined them. She had singled out a paragraph in the preface and underlined five of its words: "El afán del poeta se vuelca en los ámbitos de su mundo interior, gusta de hacer introspección, *se enfrenta con su alma,* como para pedirle cuentas de su gestión, y descúbrela a modo de pura centella de las luces del Señor" (The anxiety of the poet is capsized in the limits of his interior world; he enjoys introspection; *he comes face to face with his soul,* as if to ask it to render an account of its conduct and discover it as if by a

pure flash of the lights of the Lord). In *Poesía Hebraica,* selección y traducción del Dr. J. Millas Vallicrosa (Hebrew Poetry, selection and translation of Dr. J. Millas Vallicrosa) (Barcelona, 1953), p. xvii.

25. Eugenio Florit, "Landscape in Gabriela Mistral," lecture given at Ladycliff College, New York, April 28, 1964.

26. "Canción de la muerte" ("Song of Death"), *Poesías,* p. 202.

27. "La extranjera" ("The Stranger"), *Poesías,* p. 516.

28. Florit, *op. cit.*

29. Arce de Vázquez, pp. 48-49.

30. Pierre Teilhard de Chardin, *Hymn of the Universe,* trans. Simon Bartholomew (New York, 1961), p. 90.

31. *Ibid.,* p. 91.

32. Gabriela Mistral, "El sentido religioso de la vida" ("The Religious Sense of Life"), *Boletín del Instituto de Literatura Chilena* (Bulletin of the Institute of Chilean Literature), III (1963), 21.

33. Jacques Maritain, "La poésie, l'homme et les choses" ("Poetry, Man, and Things"), *La Table Ronde* (The Round Table), CCXV (1965), 12.

34. "El sentido religioso de la vida" ("The Religious Sense of Life"), p. 21.

35. Doris Dana stated that Gabriela loved Jehovah of the Old Testament and Jesus Christ of the New Testament. She believed that Jesus Christ was the promised Messiah and revered Him as God made man. She spent hours reflecting on this mystery, but just as many hours meditating upon the mystery of life and death and the eternal, the mysteries in nature and nature's creatures.

36. The quotations cited on pp. 196-197 are taken from *Poesías,* pp. 3, 5, 10, 19, 23, 32, 37, 55, 69, 67, 79, 746, 745, 321, 166, 124.

37. "Canción de Taurus" ("Song of Taurus"), *Poesías,* p. 177.

38. "Mientras baja la nieve" ("While the snow comes down"), *Poesías,* p. 324.

39. "Every definition of poetry that is felt to be at all true to its deeper meaning tries to express the prophetic element. And the great poets themselves have often felt that they were voices of a higher wisdom, that 'poetry hath some participation of divineness.' The best minds have always held poetry to be in some sort a revelation, and the critics are not so very wrong in sometimes seeing more in great poems than the poets themselves were conscious of writing. Milton, writing of the conditions under which poetry is possible, says: 'This is not to be obtained but by devout prayer to that Eternal Spirit that can enrich with all utterance and knowledge and sends His Seraphim with the hallowed fire of his altar to touch and purify the lips of whom He pleases.' Even a child of nature like Robert Burns felt that he was a dedicated spirit.

'Poet and prophet differ greatly in our loose modern notions of them,' says Carlyle. 'In some old languages the titles are synonymous: *vates* means both Prophet and Poet, and indeed at all times Prophet and Poet, well-understood, have much kindred meaning. Fundamentally indeed they are still the same; in this most important respect especially, that they have penetrated both of them into the sacred mystery of the universe. Whoever may forget this divine mystery, as the realized thought of God, the *vates*, whether Prophet or Poet, has penetrated into it, is a man sent hither to make it more impressively known to us.'

Tennyson has clearly expressed his thought of the Poet's calling:

> He saw through life and death, through good and ill,
> He saw through his own soul;
> The marvel of the everlasting will,
> An open scroll,
> Before him lay.

Rare gifts of nature, the eye that reads the everlasting will, the apostleship of light, truth, liberty, the power to see the life and meaning beneath all forms—such a man is verily sent of God.

As the Bible has been the food for the loftiest imagination . . . so poetry sustains the faculty of faith, casts over the common things of life an ideal light, pierces the veil of sense and reads the spiritual truths of man and the universe, is a witness for God and the spirit of immortality. So an interpretation of the poets has its place in the studies of religion . . . the great poets are voices to the soul. Dante and Goethe, Shakespeare and Milton, Wordsworth and Tennyson and Browning are prophets of the spiritual life as truly as Augustine and Luther and Calvin and Wesley and Newman. 'The poets even as prophets, / Have . . . Heaven's gift, a sense that fits them to perceive / Objects unseen before.'" See Arthur S. Hoyt, *The Spiritual Message of Modern English Poetry* (New York, 1924), pp. 5-8.

40. William Blake, "Jerusalem," in Helen C. White, *The Mysticism of William Blake* (Madison, Wisconsin, 1924), p. 179.
41. "Cordillera" ("Mountain Range"), *Poesías,* p. 466.
42. Francis Thompson, "The Hound of Heaven," *Works,* I, 189.
43. Florit, "Landscape . . ."
44. Chardin, *Hymn,* p. 80.
45. Julio Molina Müller, "Naturaleza americana y estilo en Gabriela Mistral" ("American Nature and Style in Gabriela Mistral"), *Homenaje,* p. 110.
46. Florit, "Landscape . . ."
47. Ladrón de Guevara, p. 26.
48. "Sol del trópico" ("Sun of the Tropics"), *Poesías,* pp. 460-461.
49. "Cordillera" ("Mountain Range"), *Poesías,* p. 463.
50. Juan Ramón Jiménez, *El Modernismo* (Modernism), ed. Ricardo Gullón y Eugenio Fernández Méndez (Madrid, 1962), p. 148.
51. "El maíz" ("Indian Corn"), *Poesías,* p. 471.
52. "El Ixtlazihuatl," *Poesías,* p. 145.
53. Arce de Vázquez, *The Poet . . .,* p. 75.
54. "Cosas" ("Things"), *Poesías,* p. 524.
55. "Cosas" ("Things"), *Poesías,* p. 526.
56. "Pan" ("Bread"), *Poesías,* pp. 442-443.

57. "Sal" ("Salt"), *Poesías,* pp. 445-446.

58. The word "beguinas" refers to "beatas" or blesseds who form part of certain religious communities existing in Belgium. They do not take vows, but they do observe the evangelical counsels. They live in common in "beguinajes" and dress in black robes, white hoods, and wear a crucifix on their hearts. They are either widows or virgins. They flourished in Belgium and Germany during the thirteenth century. They were suppressed, in 1311, by the Council of Vienne (France). Pope John XXIII again authorized them on the condition that they submit to ecclesiastical authority. The word "beguinería" or "beatería" refers to religious hypocrisy.

59. "Agua" ("Water"), *Poesías,* p. 447.

60. "Cascada en sequedal" ("Cascade in Dry Soil"), *Poesías,* p. 450. It is interesting to note how Gabriela's love of nature and especially of the sea is transferred even to her reading and translating of American and English poetry. Among those found in her notebook are Joyce Kilmer's "Trees" and John Masefield's "Sea Fever," which she calls "Fiebre de mar" and translates: "Debo volver otra vez a los mares, / al mar y al cielo solitarios / y únicamente pido un alto barco / y una estrella que sirve de llante."

61. "El aire" ("The Air"), *Poesías,* p. 453. Neither *Recado de Chile* (Message of Chile) nor *Lagar II* (Wine Press II) contains a poem on "el aire" (the air), but the theme of "el mar" (the sea) continues in *Lagar II* with "Montaña y mar," "Al mar," "Ronda del mar." ("Mountain and Sea," "To the Sea" "Round of the Sea.")

62. "Suelo creer con Stefan George en un futuro préstamo de lengua a lengua latina. Por lo menos, en el de ciertas palabras, logro definitivo del genio de cada una de ellas, expresiones inconmovibles en su rango de palabras 'verdaderas.' Sin empacho encabezo una sección de este libro, rematado en el dulce suelo y el dulce aire portugueses, con esta palabra 'Saudade.' Ya sé que dan por equivalente de ella la castellana 'soledades.' La sustitución vale por España; en América el sustantivo 'soledad' no se aplica sino en su sentido inmediate, único que allá le conocemos."

(I am in the habit of believing with Stefan George in a future borrowing of one Latin language from another. At least, in that of certain words, I find definitive of the genius of each one of them expressions inflexible in their range of "true" words. Without embarrassment, I head one section of this book, completed in the sweet Portuguese soil and air, with this word "Saudade." I already know that they give as its equivalent the Castilian "solitudes." The substitution is good for Spain; in America, the substantive "solitude" is only applied in its strict sense, the only one that we know there.) See Gabriela Mistral, "Excusa de unas notas" ("Excuse for Some Notes"), *Poesías,* p. 806.

63. "País de la ausencia" ("Land of Absence"), *Poesías,* pp. 513-515.

64. "Todas íbamos a ser reinas" ("We Were All Going To Be Queens"), *Poesías,* p. 523.

65. "Canciones del solveig" ("Solveig Songs"), *Poesías,* p. 147.

66. "Estrellita" ("Little Star"), *Poesías,* pp. 211-212.

67. "Prosa-escolar-Cuentos" ("Student-Prose-Tales"), *Desolación,* pp. 163-174.
68. Francis Thompson, "Shelley," *Works,* III, p. 18.
69. Francis Thompson, "Shelley," *Works,* III, p. 18.
70. San Juan de la Cruz, "El cántico espiritual" ("The Spiritual Canticle"), *Poesías,* p. 33.
71. Francis Thompson, "The Hound Of Heaven," *Works,* I, p. 110.
72. "Poeta" ("Poet"), *Poesías,* p. 562.
73. Ladrón de Guevara, p. 46.
74. "Me ha besado" ("He kissed me"), *Desolación,* p. 123.
75. "A mother is by definition a giver of life. She is by definition a woman who prolongs herself into another. She is by definition a person preoccupied with the other. If the virgin is a mother, she is by that fact altruistic. Yet it is ironical that the popular supposition is that the virgin is isolated and self-centered, that she has a heart that is pure but cold, almost as ice is pure but cold. In reality, however, and ideally, the virgin should be the warmest of all women, the most poured out into others, because she belongs to all, not only to a few. If anything, the virgin needs a heart that is bigger than the wife's, a love that is loftier, an other-concern that is more ardent. She is par excellence an other-lover." See Thomas Dubay, S.M., "Virginial Motherhood," *Review for Religious,* XXIV (1965), 756.
76. "Nota" ("Note"), *Desolación,* pp. 130-131.
77. "Nota" ("Note"), *Desolación,* pp. 130-131.
78. "Me ha besado" ("He Kissed Me"), *Desolación,* p. 123.
79. "¿Cómo será?" ("How will he be?"), *Desolación,* pp. 123-124.
80. "Sabiduría" ("Wisdom"), *Desolación,* p. 124.
81. "La dulzura" ("Sweetness"), *Desolación,* p. 125.
82. "La hermana" ("The Sister"), *Desolación,* p. 125.
83. "Poemas de las madres" ("Poems for Mothers"), *Desolación,* pp. 125-128.
84. "La sagrada ley" ("The Sacred Law"), *Desolación,* pp. 129-130.
85. "¿Para qué viniste?" ("Why Did You Come"), *Desolación,* p. 130.
86. "Muerte de mi madre" ("Death of My Mother"), ("Nota"), *Poesías,* p. 803.
87. "Muerte de mi madre" ("Death of My Mother"), *Poesías,* pp. 377-398.
88. "Muerte de mi madre" ("Death of My Mother"), ("Nota"), *Poesías,* p. 803.
89. In the bibliography compiled by Alfonso M. Escudero, O.S.A., "La prosa de Gabriela Mistral" ("Gabriela Mistral's Prose"), *Homenaje,* pp. 250-265, there are listed four articles which refer to Mary, the Mother of God: no. 109, "Divulgación religiosa, Sentido de la letanías: Virgen de las Vírgenes," no. 121. ("Religious Publication, Meaning of the Litanies: Virgin of Virgins"). "Alabanza a la Virgen," no. 133 ("Praise to the Virgin"), "El fervor de Lourdes (I)," no. 135, "El fervor de Lourdes (II), ("Fervor of Lourdes"). These prose works appeared in *El Mercurio,*

Santiago and *El Mercurio,* Antofagasta, in 1925-1926.

90. Martin C. Taylor, p. 143, offers the following explanation: "To the Jew, maternity, not virginity, was praiseworthy, and to him the thought of Jehovah becoming incarnate would be incredible; in fact, the Virgin-birth, so far from being an invention of Jewish Christians, must have been a severe stumbling block to them in accepting their new faith. The Council of Ephesus, in 431, declared the concept of the Virgin-birth in order to show Mary free of sin, including intercourse, menstrual flow, and afterbirth. Perhaps for these reasons Gabriela Mistral's poetry underplays Mary's importance. She appears among offensive barn animals, clumsy and unaccustomed to her task, rather than as the medieval painters conceive of her, adorned with a nimbus and regal vestments." The declaration of the Council of Ephesus, however, was not "to show Mary free of sin," for these acts are not sinful but, on the contrary, ordained by God for the procreation of the human species. The declaration of the Council was to proclaim Mary's perpetual virginity before, during, and after the birth of her Divine Son.

In his second chapter, "The Hebraic Tradition," Doctor Tayor explores la Mistral's "identification with the Hebrew spirit," pp. 51-53: "She learned to identify herself in life and poetry with its (the Bible's) characters; the Bible's multiple allusions to nature become synchronous with her own time and place, and she 'talked' with its unswerving, righteous God. Rather than being a Jew in the modern sense, Gabriela seems to have assimilated the spirit of the Hebrews of Biblical times. Mention has been made of her ability to quote whole passages from the Bible, of the parallels which critics found to Job and Jeremiah, and of the association of nature in the Bible to the paradisiacal Elqui Valley. But no comment is more apt than that by Díaz Arrieta, who says: 'Hebrea de corazón, tal vez de raza . . . dejamos el problema a los etnólogos e investigadores . . . el genio bíblico traza su círculo en torno a Gabriela Mistral y la define' " (Hebrew of heart, perhaps of race . . . we leave the problem to Ethnologists and investigators . . . the Biblical genius traces its circle about Gabriela Mistral and defines her).

". . . one must see three different, parallel relationships, . . . which contribute to a total vision of the poet's stand vis-à-vis Judaism. The first is that the study of the Bible led to an affinity with Biblical characters, kindled a Hebrew spirit . . . and provided the groundwork for the Biblical allusions in the poetry. Second, preoccupation with present-day Jewish social problems is part of her encompassing humanitarian feeling for the persecuted. . . . The third point is that Gabriela's personal suffering and her own feeling of persecution, . . . became associated in her feelings with the Jewish people, who symbolize the outcast."

91. *Le Rosaire des Joies* ("The Rosary of Joys") (Paris, 1930) is a volume of meditations on the Joyful Mysteries of the Rosary which speak of Mary's wonder and love.

92. "A la Virgen de la Colina" ("To the Virgin of the Hill"), *Poesías,* p. 28.

93. The magnificent prayer, "Oración de la maestra" ("Teacher's Prayer"), has been discussed in Chapter I of the present study. Apart from this prayer, Gabriela has written articles on the role of the teacher. In her poetry, only two poems deal with the subject: "La maestra rural" ("The Rural Schoolmistress") and "La encina" ("The Oak"). Since Chapter V is a discussion of her poetry, only the two teacher poems will be treated and will be included in the same section with children.

94. "Me tuviste" ("You Had Me"), *Poesías,* p. 166.

95. "Canción amarga" ("Bitter Song"), *Poesías,* p. 182.

96. "Mi canción" ("My Song"), *Poesías,* p. 204.

97. "Niño mexicano" ("Mexican Child"), *Poesías,* pp. 206-207.

98. "¿En dónde tejemos la ronda?" ("Where Shall We Weave the Round?"), *Poesías,* p. 216.

99. Arce de Vázquez, *Persona* . . ., pp. 41-42.

100. "Jesús" ("Jesus"), *Poesías,* p. 232.

101. "La raíz del rosal" ("The Root of the Rose Bush"), *Desolación,* p. 170.

102. "Even in the natural order one of the most lofty occupations open to man or woman is the exercise of the mysterious causality involved in the act of teaching.

"Unmistakable, too, is the fact that by his mysterious influence the teacher is a parent. A woman who is by profession a teacher is therefore by profession a mother. A woman who is a spiritual-supernatural teacher is a spiritual-supernatural mother. She is an image of the Father's fruitfulness in the inner trinitarian life in His conceiving His Word through a most calm, integral, pure generation. She, too, conceives this Word in the souls of men by her example and by her instruction. Even though she gives birth to the Word in an infinitely inferior manner, yet her fruitfulness is awesome. And still further, she imitates Father and Son breathing forth in love their common nature into their mutual Gift when she somehow brings a child to the loftiest of human acts, the act of supernatural love for God." See Dubay, S.M., pp. 750-751.

103. "La maestra rural" ("The Rural Schoolmistress"), *Poesías,* p. 52.

104. "La maestra rural" ("The Rural Schoolmistress"), *Poesías,* p. 53.

105. "La encina" ("The Oak"), *Poesías,* pp. 54-55.

106. "Tierra chilena" ("Chilean Land"), *Poesías,* p. 220.

107. "Bío-Bío," *Poesías,* p. 507.

108. Miguel Angel Asturias, Guatemala's novelist of the poor and the oppressed, was awarded the Nobel Prize for Literature in 1967.

109. Marcelino Menéndez y Pelayo, "Chile," *Historia de la poesía hispanoamericana* (History of Spanish American Poetry), ed. Enrique Sánchez Reyes (Santander, 1948), II, 220.

110. Doris Dana denied this statement of "Alone's." She affirmed that Gabriela loved Chile passionately. She recalled with nostalgic loneliness all its beauty, and all its creatures: creatures of nature and creatures of men. "One would have to listen to her reminiscences or watch her attempt to put Chile into poetry to realize just how much she loved her native

country. But," she admitted, "it is true that some Chileans, through their envy and jealousy, made her suffer."

111. "Alone," "Interpretación de Gabriela Mistral" ("Interpretation of Gabriela Mistral"), *Homenaje,* p. 15. Gabriela Mistral was, no doubt, referring to these hostile people in her "Notas para hacer" ("Notes to make") when she wrote: "Contar finalmente el que no me dejan volver" (Relate finally the fact that they won't let me return).

112. Florit, "Landscape . . ."

113. *Ibid.*

114. E. Allison Peers, "Gabriela Mistral, The Chilean Schoolmistress who won the Nobel Prize for Literature, 1945," *Institute of Hispanic Studies* (Liverpool, 1946), pp. 12-13.

115. A. Torres Ríoseco, *Gabriela Mistral* (Valencia, 1962), p. 13.

116. Katherine Anne Porter, "Latin America's Mystic Poet," *The Literary Digest International Book Review,* IV (1926), 308.

117. Margaret Bates, "Gabriela Mistral," *The Americas,* III (1946), 175.

118. Luis Alberto Sánchez, "Un ser y una voz inconfundibles" ("An Unmistakable Being and Voice"), *Cuadernos,* XXIII (1957), 22-23.

119. Margaret Bates, "Apropos an article on Gabriela Mistral," *The Americas,* XIV (1957), 146.

120. Gerardo Diego, "Imperfección y albricia" ("Imperfection and Reward"), *Gabriela Mistral, Premio Nobel: Homenaje a Gabriela Mistral* (Madrid, 1946), p. 39: "Como la erupción volcánica en su tierra chilena, así, cuando menos se piensa, salta en el verso de Gabriela la anormalidad necesaria, la abrupta llama interior que la compromete y agrieta. Llamar imperfección a tal estallido, libre y forzoso a un tiempo, es incomprender." (Like the volcanic eruption in her Chilean land, thus, when one least expects it, there erupts in the verse of Gabriela the necessary abnormality, the abrupt interior flame that binds and cracks her. To call such an explosion, free and compulsory at the same time, an imperfection, is not to understand.)

121. Amado Alonso, *Poesía y estilo de Pablo Neruda* (Poetry and Style of Pablo Neruda) (Buenos Aires, 1951), p. 153.

122. Margaret Bates, "Gabriela Mistral's 'Poema de Chile,'" *The Americas,* XVII (1961), 262-263.

123. A. Ortiz-Vargas, "Gabriela Mistral," *Hispanic American Historical Review,* XI (1931), 101.

124. Juan Marín, "Recuerdo de Gabriela Mistral" ("Remembrance of Gabriela Mistral"), *Gabriela Mistral* (Washington, D.C., 1958), pp. 10-11.

125. Gabriela Mistral, "Yo conozco a Cristo" ("I know Christ"), *La Nueva Democracia* (The New Democracy), XXIX (1949), 25.

126. See Jorge Mañach, "Gabriela: Alma y Tierra" ("Gabriela: Soul and Land") *Revista Hispánica Moderna* (Modern Hispanic Review), III (1937), 106-110.

127. See Augusto Iglesias, *Gabriela Mistral y el modernismo en Chile* ("Gabriela Mistral and Modernism in Chile"), (Santiago, Chile, 1950). Eugenio Florit, "Poetisa de una era" ("Poetess of an Era"), *The Americas,* III (1951), 37.

128. Arce de Vázquez, *Persona . . .*, p. 27.

129. Ginés de Albareda, "Figuras literarias del mundo hispánico: Gabriela Mistral" ("Literary Figures of the Hispanic World: Gabriela Mistral"), *Revista Javeriana,* XXXII (1949), 149, 152.

130. Geoffrey H. Hartman, *The Unmediated Vision:* An Interpretation of Wordsworth, Hopkins, Rilke and Valéry (New Haven, 1954), p. 129. See also Jacques Maritain, *Art and Poetry,* trans. E. de P. Matthews (New York, 1943), and Paul Claudel, *Poetic Art,* trans. Renée Spodheim (New York, 1948).

131. J. M. Aguirre, "Bécquer y lo evanescente" ("Béquer and the Evanescent"), *Bulletin of Hispanic Studies,* XLI (1964), 28-39.

132. "La flor del aire" ("The Flower of the Air"), *Poesías,* p. 431.

chapter VI

SUMMARY AND CONCLUSION

1. Summary

Por cuanto soy
gracias te doy:

Por el tener
más que otro ser
capacidad de amor y de emoción,
y el anhelar
y el alcanzar,
ir poniendo en la vida perfección.[1]

(For all that I am
I give Thee thanks:

For having,
more than any other being,
capacity for love and emotion,
and the longing for
and the attaining to
perseverance in placing perfection in my life.)

It would seem that Gabriela Mistral is a mystic.[2] Deep-rooted in her soul there was a powerful tendency toward mysticism.[3] She was aware of this tendency, and for all that she was, she thanked God. She knew that He had given her a tremendous capacity for love and emotion. She sensed that this capacity was greater than that given to any other being. She longed to set order and perfection in her life.

From her earliest childhood, she was a solitary but majestic figure: "From the first there has been about Gabriela Mistral a touch of the loneliness of one of the great heroes of lyric poetry immortalized—nay, created—by Alfred de Vigny. She has always been 'puissante et solitaire' (powerful and solitary)."[4] Lost in her artistic and visionary world, she stands among the religious poets who ". . . tienen la intuición del misterio, y . . . ven el sentido místico de la belleza . . ."[5] (have the intuition of mystery, and . . . see the mystical meaning of beauty). To her are applicable the words which Kenneth Walker spoke of Plotinus: "He retained the feeling that he was living amongst mysteries and miracles until the end of his days."[6] Hers was an interior life,[7] and "solitude in her interior life impels her that more profoundly toward communion with all her kind, with humanity, with all created beings, with God. And in God are joined and perfected all desires."[8] "All her spiritual life with its inward conflicts, shattered hopes, and mystic longings"[9] is revealed in her who seems transplanted from another soil: "Fue en el fondo una perpetua desterrada, una desterrada de sí misma"[10] (She was at heart a perpetual exile, an exile from her very self). She was eulogized as "la peregrina iluminada"[11] (The Illuminated Pilgrim) who, despite her constant public activity, "en soledad vivía, / y en soledad ha puesto ya su nido"[12] (lived in solitude, / and in solitude has now placed her nest).

In this activity and self-sacrifice for her neighbor, especially for children[13] she has been called a lonely soul. She might more properly be described as a lonely body, for her soul, keenly responsive, sent out and received communications on every side. "If her interior life has been spent in a hermitage, her body has roamed over two continents, and she has mingled with the world even more freely than that earlier wanderer-poet, Rubén Darío."[14] This mingling of contemplation and activity is typical of Spanish mysticism which, as Menéndez y Pelayo describes, is not sickly or selfish or inert, but virile, energetic, and robust, even in the pens of women. This, Pedro de Alba noted when he compared the activity of Gabriela with that of Santa Teresa de Avila:

> La reforma de los conventos emprendida por Santa Teresa encontraba correspondencia en las campañas de Gabriela para establecer escuelas y mejorar la educación del pueblo. Las peregrinaciones de la Santa por los campos de Castilla parecen un antecedente de las andanzas de Gabriela por toda la América. En cada lugar visitado por ella quedó un germen de bondad y un estímulo para perseverar en el bien.[15]
>
> (The reform of convents undertaken by Saint Teresa found a counterpart in the campaigns of Gabriela to establish schools and to better the education of the people. The pilgrimages of the Saint along the fields of Castile seem an antecedent to the journeyings of Gabriela through all America. In each place visited by her, there remained a seed of goodness and an incentive to persevere in the good.)

He affirms that in work and in thought, Gabriela bore a close affinity to Santa Teresa; that she loved the language of the mystics;[16] that when she discovered their expressions, she was filled with profound joy. "Místicos batalladores" (warrior mystics), he calls them, as he envisions a Raimundo Lulio in all "the volatility of his nature,"[17] a San Juan de la Cruz, a Fray Luis de León, a Santa Teresa de Avila pass before the enraptured eyes of Gabriela Mistral: "Los místicos batalladores de España disfilaron ante los ojos de Gabriela y ella los siguió como discípula absorta al través de los tiempos. . . . y así completó su visión de la mística española; su espíritu y su idioma se matizaron con las dulces cadencias catalanas"[18] (The warrior mystics of Spain filed before the eyes of Gabriela, and she followed them across the centuries as an absorbed disciple. . . . and thus did she complete her vision of Spanish mysticism; her spirit and her language blended with the sweet Catalan cadences).

Her notebooks, too, testify to the fact that she loved the language of the mystics. In them, she copied those passages of intense love that poured from the pen of San Juan de la Cruz: "En la interior bodega / de mi Amado bebí, . . . / . . . que andando enamorada, / me hice perdidiza, y fui ganada"[19] (In the interior wine cellar of my Beloved I drank, . . . / . . . that going about lovesick, / I lost myself, and was found). Her musing, therefore, and her meditation upon this complete self-surrender, this losing of oneself in order to be possessed by God, would indicate that she understood and desired mystical union; that she sought the presence of God and abandonment to His will.[20] This understanding, seeking, and desiring have won for her the labels: "Mística del futuro"[21] (Mystic of the Future) and "Ejemplo de dignidad espiritual"[22] (Example of Spiritual Dignity).

Her contemplation and activity are in harmony with the spirit of Spanish mysticism, for as David Rubio clarifies, it is not esoteric and mysterious, but rather aspires to influence the moral education of the people and to satisfy their religious fervor.[23]

Gabriela's aspiration to influence the moral education of the people stemmed from a "courage capable of miracles when it surges up from a supernatural spring."[24] This courage she found in Franciscanism: "The social ideals and hidden life of St. Francis[25] impress themselves on our minds in these times, and they follow our every footstep. The hour has come to arouse ourselves and appeal to the religious consciences of the world. We must call on them to follow the way of life of our Patron whom we have willingly taken as our model."[26] And her social ideal rests in the complete absence of xenophobia:

> Cuando digo cristianidad apunto a la ausencia total de xenofobia; lo menos que puede ser un cristiano es un afirmador del género humano y el recto servidor de ello. Me tengo por una especie de necedad trágica el que un ser odie o mofe a su prójimo a causa de su piel, del color de sus ojos, de su talla o de su lengua. Pero me duele mucho apuntar a este tema que es en mí, materia de fuego, un toque de brasa ardiendo. . . . Cualquier sabe que mi pluma ha defendido en cada lugar por donde paso a nuestro indio, estúpidamente denigrado y sobre todo desconocido; a nadie le extrañe que hoy defienda al emigrado blanco por la misma razón.[27]

> (When I say Christianity, I refer to the complete absence of xenophobia; the least a Christian can be is an affirmer of mankind and a just servant of it. I hold as a specimen of tragic stupidity the fact that a person would despise or ridicule his neighbor because of his skin, the color of his eyes, his stature, or his language. But it causes me great sorrow to point out this theme which is in me matter for fire, a touch of burning, a red-hot coal. . . . Everyone knows that in every place through which I have passed,

my pen has defended our Indian, stupidly reviled and, above all, not understood; no one should be surprised that today I defend the white emigrant for the same reason.)

Gabriela's contemplation and activity led Manuel de Montoliu, whom Allison Peers calls "a Catalan of considerable sensibility and insight," to describe her as a mystic. Peers refers to "the common misuse of that word by Spanish writers," and Margaret Bates, after declaring that many critics use the word synonymously with "religious," labels it "a common and lamentable use."[28] Peers admits, however: "But she has that yearning for a closer walk with God which is a prerequisite of the mystic's quest; and at times that sense of God's nearness which can illumine the mystic's way."[29] Katherine Anne Porter observes: "In her religious mysticism she is dogmatic; her imagination is ruled by the doctrines of the Church, having their roots in an intellectual conception of God and of man's relation to God."[30]

Espinosa places her "Credo" side by side with that of the Spanish mystics: "She believes, as the Spanish mystics do, that the heart is the source of love and that the knowledge of God and belief in God proceeds from the love of God. She believes, as does Miguel de Unamuno, that the heart rules the spirit and not the intellect; the will and not reason."[31] Manuel Pedro González perceives the potential mysticism of a great woman: "Under that serene, apparently impassible and imperturbable exterior palpitated a tremendously passionate soul and an ardent temperament capable of achieving the mystic ecstasy in human or divine love . . ."[32] Isabel de Ambía sees her halo of mysticism and sanctity: "He sentido para los niños su ternura de madre universal, y he conocido su noble apostolado de fe y su halo de misticismo, de santidad casi"[33]

(I have felt her tenderness of a universal mother for children, and I have known her noble apostolate of faith and her halo of mysticism, of sanctity almost). Uribe Echevarría selects her "Nocturno del descendimiento," "en el cual vuelve a surgir su vena mística"[34] ("Nocturn of Descent," in which her mystic vein emerges again). Tapia de Renedo, speaking of the Bible, states: ". . . y día tras día, sus ojos no se cansan de beber en estas fuentes sagradas, en estos pasajes inmutables, en estas escenas vividas en que siempre se encuentra el Dios que Gabriela adora, . . ."[35] (. . . and day after day, her eyes never tire of drinking in these sacred fountains, in these immutable passages, in these living scenes in which the God whom Gabriela adores is always found). Oliver Belmas presents four reasons for loving her: "Yo la quiero por americana[36] y por español; por maternal y por mística"[37] (I love her for being American and Spanish; for being maternal and mystic). Antonio Espina feels a wave of emotion passing over his soul when he reads Gabriela and attempts to define it by questioning: "¿Ternura? ¿Desolación? ¿Misticismo?"[38] (Tenderness, Desolation, Mysticism?).

In Gabriela Mistral, there was a deep-seated thirst for immortality, and this "forms the core of every genuinely Spanish soul. This pressing upon eternity determines all the philosophy, all the literary and artistic creation of Spain. This philosophy forces the Spaniard to bring his every act and thought into direct relation with God."[39] The theme immortality permeates her idea of love, of death, of motherhood, of God: "Y es esta certidumbre divina de que la muerte es mentira. Sí, ahora comprendo a Dios"[40] (And it is this divine certitude that death is a lie. Yes, now I understand God). And when this idea becomes confused in metempsychosis, potent in her complex personality, she is sure that she has lived other lives: "Sé que he vivido otras vidas."[41] Her tormented spirit then takes on a close resemblance to Unamuno in his "anhelo de sobrevivirse" (anxiety to outlive himself). "Se asemeja a Unamuno en su afán de eternidad, en la congoja mística y hasta en la sencillez, a veces rebuscada, de la expresión"[42] (She resembles Unamuno in her eagerness for eternity, in the mystical anguish and even in the simplicity of expression, at times affected).

Apart from this powerful tendency toward mysticism which led many critics to label Gabriela Mistral a mystic, a careful observer may attempt to trace the three mystical states in her life and poetry. The first thirty years of her life may be compared to the Purgative Way, for it would seem that God, enamored of her soul, tracks her down from infancy in order to strip and purify her:

> Quien conozca los versos de Gabriela Mistral y su vida, pura y ennoblecida por el sufrimiento, comprenderá sin gran esfuerzo que llegó desde muy temprano, tal vez desde antes de escribir los "Sonetos de la muerte," a esa condición sobrehumana que las gentes de Oriente y los místicos cristianos han llamado la "Absoluta Compasión." Y entenderán que ese amor que Gabriela profesaba . . . derivaba de que para ella la poesía era religión y la religión se había hecho poesía. El amor que tenía por la naturaleza no era un retorno a lo elemental y abstruso; no era el caso dionisíaco. Era la suprema armonía.[43]
>
> (He who knows the verses of Gabriela Mistral and her life, pure and ennobled through suffering, will understand without great effort that she arrived from an early time, perhaps even before she wrote the "Sonnets on Death" at that superhuman condition which the people of the Orient and the Christian mystics have called "Ab-

solute Compassion." And they will understand that that love which Gabriela professed . . . was derived from the fact that for her poetry was religion and religion had become poetry. The love which she had for nature was not a return to the elemental and abstruse; it was not the Dionysiac case. It was supreme harmony.)

This supreme harmony she would convert into the new mysticism: ¿Por qué el arte no ha de ser el nuevo misticismo? ¿Por qué no ha de encender cierto imperativo de santidad? Creo en la belleza como en una técnica que sólo cae en pliegues perfectos sobre el cuerpo de Cristos, de nuevos Cristos"[44] (Why should not art be the new mysticism? Why should it not ignite a certain imperative of sanctity? I believe in beauty as I do in a technique that falls only in perfect folds on the body of Christs, of new Christs).

Ortiz-Vargas describes her embarking on the spiritual way: "With the tragic end of a human life so bitterly and so dearly loved by the poetess as revealed in these sonnets, an end which destroyed for her all possible hopes of happiness on earth, she now turns her tearful eyes, her trembling aspirations, her emptiness of heart, to that mystic kingdom for which she always had a secret longing. She became a sort of lay nun cloistered within the high walls of her own sorrow."[45]

This "emptiness of heart" is the necessary relationship which San Juan de la Cruz establishes between detachment from creatures and possession of God. It is a process of annihilation in which the soul must aim at charity, the memory direct itself toward hope, and the understanding toward faith. Thus, the greater detachment prepares for the greater possession, and only when the emptiness of all creatures is perfect will the possession of the Absolute be perfect. This possession of the Absolute is the unique mark of the mystic: "En dando lugar el alma,—que es quitar de sí todo velo y mancha de criatura . . . —, luego queda esclarecida y transformada en Dios"[46] (The soul, in making room—which is removing from self all veil and stain of creatures . . . —then remains illuminated and transformed in God). St. Paul reiterates the same idea when he exhorts the Corinthians: ". . . let us cleanse ourselves from all defilement of the flesh and of the spirit, perfecting holiness in the fear of God."[47] Francis Thompson questions: "Must Thy harvest fields be dunged with rotten death?"[48] It is Christ's doctrine of the Cross: "If anyone wishes to come after Me, let him deny himself, and take up his cross, and follow Me. . . . but he who loses his life for my sake and for the Gospel's sake will save it."[49]

For the love of God is tremendous, overwhelming, insistent, exclusive. Because His love is so great and so exclusive, it makes the poor, unschooled soul fear the isolating greatness of this same Love. Many there are who go after this Love in the twilight of the "noche oscura del alma" (dark night of the soul) then, through fear, either grope about in darkness trying to light their own candles, because the memory has not been filled with hope, or else turn back and walk no more with Him, because the understanding has not been filled with faith.

Gabriela Mistral lacked the hope and the faith of the mystic. Hence, the experiences which could have led her straight along the road which leads to God caused this same road to fork out into many paths. These experiences, her "noche oscura del alma" (dark night of the soul), briefly reviewed here, might have ended in the Illuminative Way.[50]

At the age of three, she suffered her father's desertion and the ensuing life of hardship and loneliness with her mother and half sister. Later, she endured the accusation and denunciation by her teacher, Doña Adelaida Olivares, and the consequent stoning by her schoolmates. Her "Yo nunca olvido" (I never forget) reveals in some small measure the effects of this traumatic experience on her sensitive personality. Then came her burning zeal for Vargas Vila, her flattery and imitation, and the resultant denial of her admission into Normal School.

Her dedication to reading, studying, and teaching may be evaluated from the sentiments of "La maestra rural" ("The Rural Schoolmistress") and "La oración de la maestra" ("The Teacher's Prayer"). In the first, she lays down the qualities of a devoted teacher: "La maestra era pura. La maestra era pobre. La maestra era alegre. ¡Dulce ser!" (The teacher was pure. The teacher was poor. The teacher was happy. Sweet creature!). She knows that she belongs to Christ and that her kingdom, therefore, is not of this world: "de este predio que es predio de Jesús. Su reino no es humano" (of this property which is the property of Jesus. Her kingdom is not human). Gently she refers to her underlying sorrow: "Su sonrisa[51] fue un modo de llorar con bondad. En su río de mieles, caudaloso, largamente abrevaba sus tigres el dolor" (Her smile was a manner of crying with kindliness. In her abundant river of sweetnesses, her sorrow would soak its cruelties with liberality). And she is aware that her sorrow is but the hand of God purging and emptying her soul to beautify it in order that His beauty may shine upon His little ones:

Como un henchido vaso, traía el alma hecha
para dar ambrosía de toda eternidad;
y era su vida humana la dilatada brecha
que suele abrirse el Padre para echar claridad.

Por eso aún el polvo de sus huesos sustenta
púrpura de rosales de violento llamear.

¡Y el cuidador de tumbas, como aroma, me cuenta,
las plantas del que huella sus huesos, al pasar![52]

(Like an overflowing vessel, she carried her soul, made
to give ambrosia of all eternity;
and her human life was the dilated breach
which the Father is accustomed to open to give forth splendor.

For that, even the dust of her bones bears
purple from rose bushes of intense blazing.
And the caretaker of tombs, like aroma, recounts for me
the plants he smells from her bones, on passing!)

The second, "La oración de la maestra" ("The Teacher's Prayer"), is a complete act of love, humility, and obedience to the Greatest of Teachers and a full realization of the duties and responsibilities of a teacher, so dedicated that she seeks no other reward than that of knowing that she is doing the Divine Will: "Yo no buscaré sino en tu mirada la dulzura de las aprobaciones" (I shall not seek, except in Your glance, the sweetness of approbations). For she knows the penalty for intense teaching and intense loving: "Y, por fin, recuérdame desde la palidez del lienzo de Velázquez, que enseñar y amar intensamente sobre la Tierra es llegar al último día con el lanzazo de Longino en el costado ardiente de amor"[53] (And, finally, from the paleness of the canvas of Velázquez, remind me that to teach and to love intensely here on earth is to arrive on the last day with the lance of Longinus in a side burning with love).

From seventeen to twenty years of age she bore the stigma and the heartbreak of knowing that the man she loved was in love with another woman: "¡Y estos ojos míseros / le vieron pasar! ¡Y no untó mi sangre / la extensión del mar!"[54]

(And these miserable eyes saw him pass by! And my blood did not spill the extension of the sea!). Hers is the kind of pain that Emily Dickinson describes in her poems, the kind from which the victim never fully recovers, the "Hour of Lead" which may not be outlived:

> The Feet, mechanical, go round—
> A wooden way
> Of Ground, or Air, or Ought—
> Regardless grown,
> A Quartz contentment, like a stone—
>
> This is the Hour of Lead—
> Remembered, if outlived,
> As freezing persons recollect the Snow—
> First—Chill—then Stupor—then the letting go—[55]

Before this, she had known the ecstasy of love's requital: "Como soy reina y fui mendiga," "Si tú me miras, yo me vuelvo hermosa," "¡que ya mañana al descender al río / lo que besaste llevará hermosura!"[56] (Since I am a queen and I was a beggar; If you look at me, I shall become beautiful; For now, tomorrow, when I go down to the river, that which you kissed will bear beauty!). Her understanding of love's power to transform is reminiscent of that of San Juan de la Cruz: "Cuando tú me mirabas, / tu gracia en mí tus ojos imprimían" (When You looked at me, Your eyes impressed Your grace upon me), and "después que me miraste, / que gracia y hermosura en mí dejaste"[57] (after You looked at me, what grace and beauty You left in me). But, for San Juan, there was an increase of love, for he was in love with the Immutable One. For Gabriela, there was despair, which she paradoxically calls "Éxtasis" ("Ecstasy"), for she was in love with fickle man. Hence she would cry: "¡Tras de ese instante, ya no resta nada!"[58] (After that instant, now, nothing is left).

For each ecstatic instant
We must an anguish pay
In keen and quivering ratio
To the ecstasy . . .[59]

After the suicide of her sweetheart, Gabriela Mistral poured a litany of lamentations "Al oído del Cristo" ("In the Ear of Christ"):

En esta hora, amarga como un sorbo de mares,
Tú sostenme, Señor.[60]

Padre Nuestro que estás en lo cielos,
¿por qué te has olvidado de mí?[61]

Y yo dijo al Señor: "Por la sendas mortales
le llevan. ¡Sombra amada que no saben guiar!"[62]

¿Cómo quedan, Señor, durmiendo los suicidas?[63]

(In this hour, bitter like a draught of seas,
You sustain me, Lord!

Our Father who art in heaven,
why have you forsaken me?

And I said to the Lord: "Along mortal paths
they bear him. Beloved spirit which they do not know how to guide!

How, O Lord, do the suicides sleep?)

The pathos of her anguished "espera inútil" (useless waiting) reveals that the experience of an unusual intensity was the source of it:

Yo me olvidé que se hizo
ceniza tu pie ligero,
y, como en los buenos tiempos,
salí a encontrarte al sendero.

"Tengo miedo y tengo amor,
¡amado, el paso apresura!"
Iba espesando la noche
y creciendo mi locura.[64]

(I forgot that your light step
was turned to dust,
and, as in the good times,
I went out to the path to meet you.

"I am afraid and I am in love,
Beloved, my step hastens!"
The night kept deepening
and my folly growing.)

All these poignant cries, wrung from her broken heart, asked the same questions and resolved them in paradoxes: Love may be the crowning glory of life, but one becomes fully aware of its transcendent value only when confronted with its extinction by death. Yet, she did not turn to the God of love, except to complain or to beg pardon for her beloved.

And soon, there was another beloved, another whom she threatened with a cunning, vengeful God:

> Dios no quiere que tú tengas
> sol si conmigo no marchas;
> Dios no quiere que tú bebas
> si yo no tiemblo en tu agua;
> no consiente que tú duermas
> sino en mi trenza ahuecada.[65]

> (God will not let you have
> sun unless you walk with me;
> God will not let you drink
> unless I tremble in your water;
> He will not consent to your sleeping
> except in my loosened tresses.)

After this long period of purgation, Gabriela's agony became a search, an unconscious search for God. This search might have ended in the Illuminative Way had she not lacked the unicity of purpose, for

> Gabriela Mistral alzó su espíritu hasta la cumbre bajo el paso de un gran dolor. Aunque tal concepto parezca una paradoja, entraña una verdad y un caso que no es único: el del sufrimiento que aviva el espíritu en vez de abatirlo. Por lo menos, tal acontece a ciertas almas de excepción, predispuestas a la vocinglería cuando las demás callan . . . "El Dolor, aun en el campo de la Psicología y de la Sociología, es un factor de extraordinaria potencia. En la mente humana pesa más un gran dolor que una gran alegría. El dolor une más a los hombres que el placer y la felicidad . . ."[66]

(Gabriela Mistral raised her spirit to the heights beneath the weight of a great sorrow. Although such a concept seems a paradox, it engenders a truth and a case that is not singular: that of suffering which vivifies the spirit instead of casting it down. At least, such a thing occurs to certain exceptional souls predisposed to outcries when others keep silence . . . "Sorrow, even in the field of Psychology and that of Sociology, is a factor of extraordinary potency. A great sorrow weighs more on the human mind than a great joy. Sorrow unites men more than pleasure and felicity . . .")

And again, as Federico de Onís put it:

Alma tremendamente apasionada, grande en todo, después de vaciar en unas cuantas poesías el dolor de su desolación íntima, ha llenado ese vacío con sus preocupaciones por la educación de los niños, la rendición de los humildes y el destino de los pueblos hispánicos. Todo esto en ella no son más que otros modos de expresión del sentimiento cardinal de sus poesías; su ansia insatisfecha de maternidad, que es, a la vez, instinto femenino y anhelo religioso de eternidad.[67]

(A tremendously passionate soul, great in everything, after emptying her sorrow of intimate desolation into a handful of poems, she has filled that emptiness with her preoccupations for the education of children, the redemption of the lowly, and the destiny of the Hispanic peoples. All this in her is nothing more than the cardinal sentiment of her poetry; her unsatisfied eagerness for motherhood which is, at the same time, a feminine instinct and a religious yearning for eternity.)

Therefore, after the purgation, the satisfaction of Gabriela Mistral came not in complete surrender to God, which would have led her along the Illuminative Way to absolute union with Him, but in the transference and sublimation of her particular love to a universal love which embraced the whole world, the children of men and the children of Nature. This transference and sublimation were discussed in the chapters dealing with her personality and her poetry. This love sought the Absolute in "el Dueño," "el rostro de Dios," "el Dios triste" (The Master; The Face of God; The Sad God). In her moments of exaltation, while she contemplated the "heavens that show forth the glory of God and the firmament that declares the works of His Hands,"[68] she would seem another Augustine who complained that there is no health in those who find fault with God's creation, for the whole mystic ascent can be conceived as a movement through visible beauty to its invisible source and thence to "inaccessible Beauty." And the driving force which urges the soul along the way to absolute Truth, Beauty, and Goodness must be love. But, in seeking its goal, the soul must withdraw from all lesser interests: "No apaciente el espíritu en otra cosa que en Dios. Deseche las advertencias de las cosas y traiga paz y recogimiento en el corazón"[69] (Do not feed your spirit on anything but God. Cast away care for things and bear peace and recollection in your heart).

This "Illumination," this calm after the storm, deepened the interiorization of Gabriela and transfigured her, but not to the degree where she looked up and saw only God. This would have led to the Unitive Way of the mystics. Hers was the interiorization of the authentic poet raising himself up to that realm of poetic creation where "todo poeta auténtico halla en el universo y en el yo una misma y grande unidad divina"[70] (every authentic poet finds in the universe and in the ego the same great, divine unity).

> . . . nos encontramos ante la presencia de una mujer genial, que portaba en su carga de metáforas y ensueños, su pesada carga de dolor. . . . porque el dolor es en ella una perturbación, una perturbación espiritual que hunde sus raíces en el inconsciente; terreno al que no intentaremos penetrar. Pero si nos atreveríamos a insinuar que este dolor trasmutado en lirismo deviene de un oscuro resentimiento, de un anhelo inconsciente de dominio, y al cual Nietzsche—antes que Freud—bautizó con tal nombre. El resentimiento, sabemos, constituye una de las más poderosas palancas de la creación artística; como asimismo la tendencia erótica—potente en la Mistral—y que aflora en misticismo y amor universal que proyecta con amplia generosidad hacia las cosas y los seres, en símbolos a imágenes afectivas.[71]
>
> (. . . we find ourselves before the presence of a brilliant woman who carried in her a burden of metaphors and dreams, her heavy burden of sorrow. . . . because sorrow in her is a perturbation, a spiritual perturbation which drowns its roots in the subconscious; a field into which we do not plan to penetrate. But we would dare to insinuate that this sorrow transmuted into lyricism derives from an obscure resentment, from a subconscious eagerness to dominate, and which Nietzsche—before Freud—baptized with such a name. The resentment, we know, constitutes one of the most powerful levers of artistic creation; as likewise the erotic tendency—powerful in Mistral—which blossoms into mysticism and universal love and which projects with ample generosity toward things and creatures in affective symbols and images.)

But San Juan counsels the soul that would seek union with the Absolute:

> Cuando reparas en algo,
> dejas de arrojarte al todo.
> Porque para venir de todo al todo,
> has de dejar del todo al todo.
> Y cuando lo vengas a tener,
> has de tenerlo sin nada querer.
> Porque si quieres tener algo en todo,
> no tienes puro en Dios tu tesoro.[72]
>
> (When you take notice of anything,
> you fail to hurl yourself into everything.
> Because in order to come from all to all,
> you must leave all for all.
> And when you come to possessing it,
> you must possess it without desiring anything.
> For if you wish to possess anything in all,
> you do not hold your treasure pure in God.)

It would seem, therefore, that Gabriela Mistral did not hold "puro en Dios su tesoro" (her treasure pure in God) and that the Unitive Way was for her a union and communion with the "Absolute" and all His creatures. This way lacked that oneness, that unicity of purpose which marks the mystic who has reached the ultimate in man's self-realization, "for when it is perfected, man not only discovers his true self, but finds himself to be mystically one with the God by Whom he has been elevated and transformed. It is supreme freedom, the most perfect fulfillment. It has been called by the Fathers of the Church the 'divinization' (theosis) of man."[73] It is what Dámaso Alonso terms "una enorme polarización"[74] (an enormous polarization).

How far Gabriela's way can be called "Unitive" is difficult to ascertain, for ". . . su tremenda soledad interior era su más hondo poema . . . era reservada en entregar su intimidad"[75] (. . . her tremendous interior solitude was her most profound poem . . . she was reserved in conveying her intimacy). This tremendous interior solitude, this reserve in giving of her intimacy, may very well be what Thomas Merton has termed a contemplation of one's self, for if we try to contemplate God without having turned the face of our inner self entirely in His direction, we end up by contemplating ourselves.

2. Conclusion

Una en mí maté:
yo no la amaba.

La dejé que muriese,
robándole mi entraña.
Se acabó como el águila
que no es alimentada.

. . . . . .
¡ay! olvidadla.
Yo la maté. ¡Vosotras
también matadla![76]

(I killed one in me:
I did not love her.

I left her to die,
robbing her of my entrails.
She ended like the eagle
which is not fed.

. . . .
Ah! Forget her.
I killed her. You
also kill her!)

Gabrelia Mistral is not a mystic. That she was transformed, sublimated, and raised to a more mature level of being is revealed in her own declaration of "La otra" ("The Other One"). She did not love her former self; therefore, she killed her. She left her to die and invited others to do the same to her. This "casting off of the old man and putting on the new,"[77] must be interpreted in the psychological sense, in the religious sense, and in the poetic sense. In the mystical sense, the transformation may be interpreted only in the broad connotation of the word. Unfortunately this connotation has made of mysticism "one of the most abused words in the English language, where it has been used in different and often mutually exclusive senses by religion, poetry, and philosophy; where it has been claimed as an excuse for every kind of occultism, for dilute transcendentalism, vapid symbolism, religious or aesthetic sentimentality, and bad metaphysics."[78] And the Spanish language, as Allison Peers reminds the reader, has done its share in commonly misusing the term. La Mistral herself, in one of her many "Recados"[79] ("Messages"), cautions the reader to be wary of using the term indiscriminately:

> Tengamos cuidado con la palabra mística, que sobajeamos demasiado y que nos lleva frecuentemente a juicios primarios. Pudiese ser Neruda un místico de la materia. Aunque se trata del poeta más corporal que puede darse (por algo es chileno), siguiéndole paso a paso, se sabe de él esta novedad que alegraría a San Juan de la Cruz: la materia en la que se sumerge volun-

tariamente, le repugna de pronto y de una repugnancia que llega hasta la náusea. Neruda no es un adulador de la materia, aunque tanto se restrega en ella; de pronto lo puñetea, y la abre en res como para odiarla mejor . . . Y aquí se desnuda un germen eterno de Castilla.[80]

(Let us take care with the word mysticism, which we exhaust too much and which frequently leads us to primary judgments. Neruda could be a mystic of matter. Although one is treating of the most carnal poet that there could be [He's not a Chilean for nothing]; following him step by step, this novelty is learned from him which would rejoice San Juan de la Cruz: the matter in which he is voluntarily submerged repulses him at once and with a repugnance that reaches to nausea. Neruda is not an adulator of matter, although so much of it rubs off on him; suddenly, he battles with it and pulls it apart as if to hate it the more . . . And here, there is uncovered an eternal germ of Castile.)

The word "mysticism" has, indeed, been very much misused, and is suspect in many quarters, for there are many pseudo-mysticisms, but only one genuine mysticism: that experience in which the soul is completely filled with the love of God and is drawn by God to Himself. This is the only true science or art of the spiritual life, and the price of its achievement is total abnegation of self and complete surrender to God: "Naked I wait Thy Love's uplifted stroke."[81] "True spirituality seeks for bitterness rather than sweetness in God, inclines to suffering more than to consolation, and to be in want of everything for God rather than to possess; to dryness and afflictions rather than to sweet communications, knowing well that this is to follow Christ and deny self, while the other course is perhaps nothing but to seek oneself in God, which is the very opposite of love."[82]

This is the reason why the true mystic prays: "Take, O Lord, . . . all that I am and have. Give me Your love and Your grace, with these I am rich enough and desire nothing more."[83] The prayers that Gabriela has left bear all too frequently a series of "Give me . . ." instead of "Take . . .": "Dame mi parte de alegría. Dame Tú el don de la salud."[84] (Give me my share of joy. You give me the gift of health). All too frequently the "quejas de amor" (complaints of love), which the mystics pour out in their burning love for God, become in Gabriela complaints to God because she is suffering and He has abandoned her: "I find 'El Ruego' ('The Plea') excessively artificial, as different as can be from St. Teresa's reports of her Divine colloquies, which bear the unmistakable hallmark of authenticity. Considered as a passionate monologue, however, the poem is much more effective."[85]

The mystic contemplates Christ on the Cross and envisions all the details of the treachery of His betrayal, His passion, His death, and cannot be consoled. Gabriela contemplates Him and envisions only the details of her own treacherous betrayal, her passion, her death, and complains that God has forgotten her:

> ¡Llevo abierto también mi costado,
> y no quieres mirar hacia mí!
>
> Me vendió el que besó mi mejilla;
> me negó por la túnica ruin.
> Yo en mis versos el rostro con sangre,
> como Tú sobre el paño, le di.
> Y en mi noche del Huerto, me han sido
> Juan cobarde y el Angel hostil.[86]

(I also bear my side wide open,
and You will not look toward me!

He who kissed my cheek sold me;
he denied me for the ruinous tunic.
I in my verses my blood-stained face
I gave him, like Yours on the veil.
And in my night of the Garden, there have been to me
John, cowardly, and the Angel, hostile.)

Here Gabriela is in love not with Christ but with herself. To satisfy self, she turned from Him and tried to find her God "muy a mi manera" (very much in my own way). This is why her "viejo fatalismo" (old fatalism) kept returning; why she sought explanation for her sorrows in karma, metempsychosis; why she preferred "todas las hechicerías y no las liturgias" (all the witchcrafts and not the liturgies); why she sometimes lost herself in a world-soul of Pantheism.

Her "Padre Nuestro . . . ¿por qué te has olvidado de mí?" (Our Father . . . why have You forsaken me?) recalls the observation of Thomas Merton:

> And there are religious men who pray best when they imagine they are rejected by an angry and implacable God. Their prayer and their spirituality consist in the acceptance of apparent rejection. God Himself is less necessary to them than their sentiments of despair. He fits into their lives best when they are tortured by the revenging vulture. Underneath it all is the conviction that God cannot pardon them for wanting to live, for wanting to be perfect and to be free. It is His grace, indeed, which fills them with the insatiable need for life. But their own strange natures only enable them to admit

such a need when it is disguised, at the same time, as a need for punishment.[87]

The mystic contemplates nature and sees his Beloved: "Mi Amado, las montañas, / los valles solitarios nemorosos, / . . ."[88] (My Beloved, the mountains, / the wooded, solitary valleys, / . . .). This is because "su constante, comunicación con el Amado, fuente de toda inspiración, de todo arte, hicieron permisible la posesión de tantos dones"[89] (his constant communication with the Beloved, source of all inspiration, of all art, made permissible the possession of so many gifts). Gabriela contemplates nature and sees "Desolación;" "Arbol muerte;" "Castilla árida, afligida Castilla, Niobe al revés, de ojos secos, te quiero el cielo, presencia grande de su noche y purificación de sus días"[90] (Desolation; Dead Tree; Arid Castile, afflicted Castile, Niobe in reverse, with dry eyes, I love your sky, grand presence of your night and purification of your days).

"I shall only say here that a mystic, by any generally accepted standard, she certainly is not."[91] "Earthbound, she cannot escape with Emily Brontë and Emily Dickinson into the vast consolations of mystical rapture. The final resource of the true mystic lies in the edgeless domain of the mind. Gabriela Mistral cannot wrench herself from her heart. A famine of love is her tragedy, her wrath bruises her."[92] The famine, the tragedy, the wrath, the bruises result not from loving the Infinite, but the finite. "Man is in love and loves what vanishes / What more is there to say?"[93]

Torres Ríoseco states that it is her realistic temperament which is incompatible with her total immersion in God: "Se ha hablado equivocadamente del misticismo de la Mistral. El temperamento realista de este poeta rechaza la inmersión en Dios, en cuanto beatitud; le busca como consuelo, justicia, protección, como se busca a un padre. Es, tal vez, un poeta religioso, y de fuerte influencia bíblica"[94] (One has spoken erroneously of mysticism in la Mistral. The realistic temperament of this poet repels immersion in God, as far as beatitude is concerned; she searches for Him for counsel, justice, protection, as one searches for a Father. She is, perhaps, a religious poet, and of strong biblical influence). And Gabriela herself recognizes the absence of this total commitment when speaking of Sor Juana Inés de la Cruz: "Su actitud aparece más estética que mística. Este último, una mística, no es Sor Juana. Todo su pensamiento está traspasado de cristianismo, pero en el sentido rigurosamente moral. El místico es, casi siempre, mitad ardor y mitad confusión; es el hombre que entra como en una nube ardiente que lo lleva arrobatado. Ella no ha viajado nunca por el país que algunos llaman de la locura, . . ."[95] (Her attitude seems more esthetic than mystical. This last, a mystic, Sor Juana is not. All her thought is transfixed with Christianity, but in the rigorously moral sense. The mystic is, almost always, half ardor and half confusion; he is the man who enters as if into a burning cloud that carries him enraptured. She has never traveled through the country which some have called that of insanity).

"Perhaps the surest way to make 'mystical' a useful literary term is to keep it from meaning the same as 'religious' or 'devotional' or 'meditative.' "[96] When the term "mystical," therefore, is applied to Gabriela Mistral, it must be interpreted as the emergent of her rich, intense interior life and the overflow of her powerful feelings into her activities and her writing. It is the expression of the innate tendency in her toward complete harmony with the transcendental order. But, while she "identifies herself with the forces of the manifest universe, the mystic traverses them and tries to unite with the immutable and unlimited power of the absolute behind them."[97] The craving of the mystic is the craving of a soul unable to rest in symbols of the sensual world. Lope de Vega, in a manner consistent with the genius of his century, captures this craving of the mystic in his "Lágrimas de la Madalena" ("Tears of the Magdalen"). Here, "Mary's soul, and the manifestation of love and grief appear in the relationship of hair, feet, and eyes. These three elements exist together as abstractions capable of infinite combinations, each new combination producing new meaning."[98]

"The mystic sees through the image to see reality. . . . But until he first focuses the image, he will not see through it, he will not be quiet in oneness with God . . ."[99] He will not "attain to that fulness of life for which he was made: to lose himself in that which can be neither seen nor touched; giving himself entirely to this sovereign Object, without belonging either to himself or to others, united to the Unknown by the most noble part of himself. It is the healing of that human incompleteness which is the origin of our divine unrest: the inevitable reaction of the fully conscious, fully living soul upon 'Eternal Truth, True Love, and Loved Eternity.' "[100] "One of the marks of a true mystic is the tenacious and heroic energy with which he pursues a definite ideal."[101] It is the psychology of spiritual ascent:

> The passion that constrains the stars also constrains that starry thing, the soul. Attraction, desire, and union as the fulfillment of desire, this is the way life works, in the highest as in the lowest things. The mystic's outlook is the lover's outlook. It has the same element of wildness, the same quality of selfless and quixotic devotion, the same combination of rapture and humility. . . . mystic and lover, upon different planes, are alike responding to the call of the Spirit of Life. The language of human

> passion is tepid and insignificant beside the language in which the mystics try to tell the splendours of their love.[102]

Arthur Symons, in astonishment of San Juan de la Cruz, cried out: "This monk can give lessons to lovers!" Gabriela Mistral needed no lessons when her passion and despair spilled out from her broken heart. She who would descend to the grave in order to sleep on the same pillow with her lover, who would ascend with a triumphant vengeance because "la mano de ninguna bajará a disputarme tu puñado de huesos"[103] (the hand of no one will descend to dispute with me your handful of bones), knew all the ecstasy and all the longing of finite passions, feeble images of those they could have been had she turned them toward the Infinite One. If she knew that human love transforms, oh, what could have been the transformation that Infinite Beauty would have stamped on her!

". . . the inward transmutation to which the vision compels the mystic, in order that he may be to some extent worthy of that which he has beheld: may take his place within the order of Reality. He has seen the Perfect; he wants to be perfect, too. . . . the only means of obtaining the Absolute lies in adapting ourselves to It. The moral virtues are for him the obligatory ornaments of the Spiritual Marriage. Unless this impulse for perfection be born in him, this travail of the inner life begun, he is no mystic, though he may well be a visionary, a prophet, a 'mystical' poet."[104]

Gabriela Mistral is all of these: visionary, prophet, "mystical" poet.[105] She is a humanitarian, a teacher, a deeply religious woman. She is a philosopher, constantly preoccupied with the deeper emotions aroused by the conflict and tragedy of human life, love, and death. All of these qualities, or each one taken separately, might have earned from the pens and tongues of her ardent admirers the crowning name to end all names: mystic! But, despite her preoccupation with "la intuición del misterio" (the intuition of mystery), her knowledge that "la rosa es algo más que una rosa y la montaña algo más que una montaña" (the rose is something more than a rose and the mountain, something more than a mountain), her insight into "el sentido místico de la belleza" (the mystical meaning of beauty), her encountering "en las suavidades de las hierbas y de las nubes de verano la insinuación de una mayor suavidad, que está en la mano de Dios"[106] (in the suavities of the grass and of the summer clouds the insinuation of a greater suavity, which is in the hand of God), she is not a mystic. This is identification of mysticism with poetry. This is the thought of Pierre Teilhard de Chardin when he "pictures a man who has become conscious of his personal relations with a supreme Person with whom he is led to merge by the whole interplay of cosmic activity. Omega, he towards whom all converges, is concurrently He from whom all radiates. Impossible to place him as a focus at the summit of the universe without at the same time diffusing his presence in the intimate heart of the smallest movement of evolution."[107] It is that to which Concha Zardoya refers when, speaking of Juan Ramón Jiménez, she alludes to "the mystic experience which has nothing to do with theology."[108]

But this is not mysticism in the strict sense of the term. This is not mysticism as it is defined in Chapter II of this discussion and, therefore, Gabriela Mistral cannot be termed a mystic, either in the Catholic connotation of the term or in that of other great religions. That which is indisputable, however, about this "valiant woman" reveals that

> Luchó con un coraje invencible con la vida; había pedido

las cosas sencillas que todos obtienen; en respuesta recibió dolores repetidos y profundos que transformó en sublimas expresiones de belleza; lo que la vida no le dió, ella se lo dió a sí misma y lo entregó a su pueblo para consuelo y purificación de todos los que sufren como enseñanza suprema.[109]

(She struggled with life with an invincible courage; she had asked for the simple things that all obtain; in reply, she received repeated and profound sorrows which she transformed into sublime expressions of beauty; that which life did not give her, she gave to herself, and she gave it to her people for counsel and purification of all those who suffer as a lesson of supreme instruction.)

This is the reason why all who have ever come in contact with her, either personally or through her works, will remember and revere her as another "mujer fuerte" (valiant woman):

Me acuerdo de tu rostro que se fijó en mis días,
mujer de saya azul y de tostada frente,
. . . . . .

Y el lodo de tus pies todavía besara,
porque entre cien mundanas no he encontrado tu cara
¡y aun te sigo en los surcos la sombra con mi canto![110]

(I remember your face which I noted in my days,
woman of blue skirt and of tanned forehead,
. . . . . .

And I would still kiss the mud of your feet,
because among one hundred mundane women, I have not found your face
and I still follow, in the furrows, your spirit with my song!)

CHAPTER VI—FOOTNOTES

1. "Hablando al Padre" ("Speaking to the Father"), *Poesías,* p. 354.

2. See "Mysticism applied to Gabriela Mistral," Chapter I, 2, pp. 25-51 of the present study.

3. Whether or not this tendency may be attributed to the excellent racial heritage formed by the confluence of Basque, Hebrew, and Araucanian blood and whether or not these racial influences were operative in the case of Gabriela Mistral cannot be proved, for the facts are impossible to document. See p. 132, n. 18 of the present study. What is certain is that the tendency was there, and that the tendency was mistaken for fulfillment by many of her critics.

4. Peers, "The Chilean Schoolmistress . . . ," p. 3.

5. Gabriela Mistral, "El sentido religioso . . ." ("The religious meaning . . ."), p. 21.

6. Kenneth Walker, *The Mystic Mind* (New York, 1965), p. 87.

7. A. Guerra, "Vida interior en Gabriela Mistral" ("Interior Life in Gabriela Mistral"), *Grafos,* IV (1936), 5.

8. Clarence Finlayson, "Spanish American Poets: The Life and Ideas of Gabriela Mistral," *The Commonweal,* XXXV (1941), 162.

9. A. Ortiz-Vargas, "Gabriela Mistral, Chile's Teacher Poet," *Poet Lore,* XLVI (1940), 342.

10. Salvador de Madariaga, "Homenaje a Gabriela Mistral" ("Tribute to Gabriela Mistral"), *Diamante,* VII (1958), 3.

11. Pedro de Alba, "Elogio de la Peregrina Iluminada" ("Eulogy in honor of the Illumined Pilgrim"), *La Nueva Democracia* (The New Democracy), XXV (1944), 16-18.

12. San Juan de la Cruz, "El cántico espiritual" ("The Spiritual Canticle"), *Poesías,* p. 37.

13. Andrés Sabella, "El hijo desconocido de Gabriela Mistral" ("The Unknown Child of Gabriela Mistral"), *Atenea,* XXII (1945), 233, 235-236: "Es el niño que esencializará a la niñez entera del Universo en los labios del poeta. El niño a quien los fantasmas, noche a noche, roban a la madre, para sentarle en la falda espectral del padre deshecho, del padre en cuyos besos giran las puertas del más hermoso sueño. . . . Las poesías para niños de Gabriela Mistral resultan la sublimación de su angustia materna despedazada. Gabriela Mistral, madre nívea, integra con la canción el hueco gimiente de su entraña."

(It is the child who, on the lips of the poetess, will make essential the entire childhood of the Universe. The child whom, night after night, phantoms rob from the mother, in order to sit him in the spectral lap of the dead father, of the father in whose arms there revolve the doors of the most beautiful dream. . . . Gabriela Mistral's poems for children result from the sublimation of her lacerated maternal anguish. Gabriela, pure mother, integrates with her song the groaning emptiness of her entrails.)

14. Peers, "The Chilean Schoolmistress . . . ," p. 3.

15. Pedro de Alba, "Hispanismo e indigenismo de Gabriela Mistral" ("Hispanicism and Indigenousness of Gabriela Mistral"), *Homenaje,* pp. 79-80.

16. Angel Valbuena Briones also states: ". . . el lenguaje que emplea es el de los místicos" (. . . the language which she uses is that of the mystics), but he clarifies: ". . . se trata de la necesidad urgente de comunicar en un grito desgarrador la angustia de su vividura" (. . . it is a question of the urgent necessity to communicate the anguish of her living in a heart-rending cry). See "El verso quemante de Gabriela Mistral" ("The Burning Verse of Gabriela Mistral"), *Literatura Hispanoamericana* (Hispanic-American Literature) (Barcelona, 1965), pp. 393-394.

17. E. Allison Peers, *Fool of Love, The Life of Ramon Lull* (London, 1946), p. 9.

18. Pedro de Alba, "Hispanismo . . ." ("Hispanicism . . ."), pp. 79-80. See also "Dádivas espirituales de Gabriela Mistral" ("Spiritual Gifts of Gabriela Mistral"), *La Nueva Democracia* (The New Democracy), XXVII (1947), 52-55.

19. San Juan de la Cruz, "El cántico espiritual" ("The Spiritual Canticle"), *Poesías,* p. 35.

20. *Lagar II,* pp. 19-20. Here, in her own handwriting, Gabriela has her spiritual musings recorded: "Dícele Jesús, tercera vez: 'Simón-Pedro, hijo de Jonás, ¿me amas?" "Tu voluntad, Jesús, se haga ahora en mí." "Ejercicio para buscar la Divina Presencia" (Jesus said to him a third time: "Simon-Peter, son of Jonas, do you love Me?" "Your will, O Jesus, be now done in me." Exercise to search for Divine Providence).

21. César David Rincón, "Gabriela Mistral, mística del futuro" ("Gabriela Mistral, Mystic of the Future"), *Ciencia y Cultura* (Science and Culture), II (1957), 135-148.

22. Rómulo Gallegos, "Ejemplo de dignidad espiritual" ("Example of Spiritual Dignity"), *Cuadernos,* XXIII (1957), 24-25.

23. David Rubio, O.S.A., *The Mystic Soul of Spain* (New York, 1946), p. 71.

24. Gabriela Mistral, "Versicle of Peace," *The Americas,* VII (1951), 282.

25. "Motivos de San Francisco" ("Motifs of Saint Francis") appeared in *El Mercurio,* 1923-1924.

26. "Versicle . . . ," p. 281.

27. "Sobre la xenofobia" ("On Xenophobia"), *La Nueva Democracia* (The New Democracy), XXIX (1949), 22.

28. Bates, "Gabriela Mistral," p. 183.

29. Peers, "The Chilean Schoolmistress . . . ," p. 8.

30. Porter, ". . . Mystic Poet," p. 308. The use of the words "dogmatic" and "doctrines" here are highly debatable. Gabriela Mistral was anything but dogmatic and doctrinal. Chapter IV of the present study deals at length with this point. See Gabriela's own confirmation of the fact, p. 152.

In the second section of this chapter, we shall see that Katherine Anne Porter does not hold that Gabriela is a mystic.

31. Aurelio Macedonio Espinosa, "Gabriela Mistral," *The Americas,* VIII (1951), 11.

32. Manuel Pedro González, "Profile of a Great Woman," *Hispania,* XLI (1958), 429.

33. Isabel de Ambía, "Ante Gabriela Mistral" ("Before Gabriela Mistral"), *Gabriela Mistral, Premio Nobel* (Madrid, 1946), p. 17. See also Honorio Aguilera, "El alma cristiana de Gabriela Mistral" ("The Christian Soul of Gabriela Mistral"), *La Revista Católica de Santiago,* LXVII (1959), 2481-2484. Salvador Cañas, "Gabriela Mistral, los niños y la escuela," ("Gabriela Mistral, Children, and School"), *Cultura,* XIV (1958), 96-100. Rafael Estenger, "Gabriela Mistral, Virgen y Madre" ("Gabriela Mistral, Virgin, and Mother"), *Cuba Contemporánea,* XLIV (1927), 219-224. Margarita de Mayo, "Gabriela Mistral, Maestra" ("Gabriela Mistral, Teacher"), *Cuadernos Hispanoamericanos* (Hispanic-American Notebooks), XXXIII (1958), 360-366. Concha Meléndez, "El magisterio de Gabriela Mistral" ("The Magisterium of Gabriela Mistral"), *Indice* (Index), II (1931), 14-15. E. Montenegro, "La maestra Gabriela Mistral" ("The Teacher Gabriela Mistral"), *Cuba Contemporánea,* XXIX (1922), 351-354.

34. Juan Uribe Echevarría, "Gabriela Mistral; aspectos de su vida y de su obra" ("Gabriela Mistral: Aspects of Her Life and Work"), *Gabriela Mistral* (Washington, D.C., 1958), p. 25.

35. Benito Tapia de Renedo, "Gabriela Mistral," *Mundo Hispánico,* XIII (1960), 50. See also Carlos D. Hamilton, "Raíces bíblicas de la poesía de Gabriela Mistral" ("Biblical Roots of the Poetry of Gabriela Mistral"), *Cuadernos Americanos* (American Notebooks), XX (1961), 201-210, and Eduardo Lecourt, "La Biblia era su aljibe que le daba agua pura diariamente" ("The Bible was her reservoir which supplied her daily with pure water"), *El Mercurio,* January 22, 1957, p. 15, cols. 1-2.

36. See Gabriela Mistral, "El grito" ("The Cry"), *Homenaje,* CXV (1957), 300: "¡América! ¡América! Todo por ella; porque todo nos vendrá de ella desdicha o bien. ¡América y sólo América! ¡Qué embriaguez semejante futuro; qué hermosura; qué reinado vasto para la libertad y las excelencias mayores!" (America, America! Everything for her; because everything will come to us from her, misfortune or blessing. America and only America! What intoxication from such a future; what beauty; what a vast kingdom for liberty and for the greater excellences!)

37. Antonio Oliver Belmas, "Proyección de Gabriela Mistral" ("Projection of Gabriela Mistral"), *Gabriela Mistral, Premio Nobel* (Madrid, 1946), p. 65.

38. Antonio Espina, "Luz-Voz de la poesía" ("Light-Voice of Poetry"), *Gabriela Mistral, Premio Nobel* (Madrid, 1946), p. 46.

39. Rubio, pp. 90-91.

40. "Poemas del éxtasis" ("Poems of Ecstasy"), *Desolación,* pp. 142-143.

41. Gabriela Mistral, in Ladrón de Guevara, *Rebelde magnífica,* p. 46. Two of Gabriela's most intimate friends, Doris Dana and Ester de Cáceres,

have testified to this firm belief in reincarnation. Miss Dana discussed the matter with me, October 30, 1965. Ester de Cáceres mentioned it in a letter from Montevideo, December 15, 1965: "Su religión de infancia fue la Católica. Doris puede mostrarle a Ud. una emocionante foto de Primera Comunión. La formación fue muy pobre como era en estos países en ese tiempo: formación que no nos defendía luego contra el embate del liberalismo. En el caso de Gabriela, esa formación pobre dejó la grieta por donde entró el Budismo . . . sobre todo en cuanto se refiere a la reencarnación" (Her religion from infancy was the Catholic religion. Doris can show you a touching photo of her First Communion. Her formation was very poor, as it was in these countries at that time: formation which did not then protect us from the onslaught of liberalism. In Gabriela's case, that formation left the opening through which Buddhism entered . . . especially in that which refers to reincarnation). Miss Dana stated that perhaps the poem which best expresses this idea is "Ultimo árbol" ("Last Tree"): 'Por si en la segunda vida / no me dan lo que ya dieron / . . . quiero árbol de paradero. / . . . y estoy, de muerta, cantando / debajo de él, sin saberlo" (For if in the second life / they do not give me what they have now given / . . . I desire a tree for a stopping place. / . . . and, dead, I am singing / beneath it, without knowing it). *Poesías,* pp. 797-799.

42. Uribe Echevarría, p. 21.

43. Juan Marín, "Recuerdo de Gabriela Mistral" ("Memory of Gabriela Mistral"), *Gabriela Mistral* (Washington, D.C., 1958), p. 10.

44. Rafael Heliodoro Valle, "Alabanza de Gabriela Mistral" ("Praise of Gabriela Mistral"), *Gabriela Mistral* (Washington, D.C., 1958), p. 35: "De ella conservo un autógrafo escrito el 16 de septiembre de 1922: '¿Por qué. . . ?' " (I preserve an autograph from her written September 16, 1922: "Why . . . ?")

45. Ortiz-Vargas, ". . . , Chile's Teacher Poet," pp. 348-349.

46. San Juan de la Cruz, "Subida del monte Carmelo" ("Ascent to Mount Carmel"), *Poesías,* p. 12.

47. Paul, II Corinthians vi. 14-15.

48. Francis Thompson, "The Hound of Heaven," *Works,* II, 112.

49. Mark viii. 34-35.

50. There is no clear cut division that separates the three mystical states. The beginning of the Illuminative Way does not imply the end of the Purgative. Neither does the beginning of the Unitive Way imply the end of the Purgative and Illuminative. This is clarified by D. M. Hoffman, O.P., in *The Life Within: The Prayer of Union* (N. Y., 1965).

51. See E. M. Allison, "Apunte de su sonrisa" ("Sketch of Her Smile"), *Abside,* XXI (1957), 158-159.

52. Gabriela Mistral, "La maestra rural" ("The Rural Schoolmistress"), *Poesías,* p. 53.

53. Gabriela Mistral, "La oración de la maestra" ("The Teacher's Prayer"), *Desolación,* pp. 121-122. See also Pedro de Alba, "Oración por Gabriela Mistral" ("Prayer by Gabriela Mistral"), *Filosofía y Letras,* XXXI (1957), 237-244.

54. Gabriela Mistral, "Balada" ("Ballad"), *Poesías,* pp. 75-76.

55. Emily Dickinson, *Stairway of Surprise, Emily Dickinson's Poetry,* ed. Charles A. Anderson (New York, 1960), p. 211.

56. "Desvelada," "Vergüenza" ("Vigilant," "Ashamed"), *Poesías,* pp. 72-74.

57. San Juan de la Cruz, "El cántico espiritual" ("The Spiritual Canticle"), *Poesías,* pp. 35-36.

58. "Éxtasis" ("Ecstasy"), *Poesías,* p. 64.

59. Emily Dickinson, "Despair," *Stairway . . . ,* p. 192.

60. "Tribulación" ("Tribulation"), *Poesías,* p. 77.

61. "Nocturno" ("Nocturn"), *Poesías,* p. 79.

62. "Sonetos de la muerte" ("Sonnets on Death"), *Poesías,* p. 83.

63. "Interrogaciones" ("Interrogations"), *Poesías,* p. 84.

64. "La espera inútil" ("Useless Waiting"), *Poesías,* pp. 86-87.

65. "Dios lo quiere" ("God Wishes It"), *Poesías,* pp. 69-70.

66. Julio Saavedra Molina, "Gabriela Mistral: su vida y su obra" ("Gabriela Mistral: Her Life and Her Work"), *Poesías,* pp. xxxv-xxxvi.

67. Federico de Onís, "Gabriela Mistral," *Homenaje,* p. 21.

68. Psalm 18.1.

69. San Juan de la Cruz, "Puntos de amor" ("Points of Love"), *Poesías,* p. 117.

70. Santandreu, "Aspectos del estilo . . ." ("Aspects of Style . . ."), *Homenaje,* p. 175.

71. Santandreu, p. 174.

72. San Juan de la Cruz, "Modo para no impedir al todo" ("Manner of not Preventing Arrival at the All"), *Poesías,* p. 39.

73. Thomas Merton, *The New Man* (New York, 1961), p. 48. See also Philip Marlan, *Monopsychism, Mysticism, Metaconsciousness: Problems of the Soul in the Neoaristotelian and Neoplatonic Tradition* (The Hague, 1963).

74. Dámaso Alonso, *Poesía española: Ensayo de métodos y límites estilísticos* (Spanish Poetry: Essay of Stylistic Methods and Boundaries) (Madrid, 1957), p. 265: "Del amor profano al amor divino, toda la poesía de San Juan de la Cruz es una movilización de partículas y de grandes partes en un sentido determinado: una enorme polarización. Todo en ella viene de los modos y contenidos profanos; toda ella está tensa hacia Dios" (From profane love to divine love, all the poetry of San Juan de la Cruz is a mobilization of particles and of large parts in a determined sense: an enormous polarization. Everything in it comes from profane modes and contents; all of it is tense toward God.)

75. Ladrón de Guevara, p. 48.

76. "La otra" ("The Other One"), *Poesías,* pp. 593-595.

77. Paul, Ephesians iv.22-24.

78. Underhill, *Mysticism,* p. x.

79. " 'Contar' era, en el lenguaje de Gabriela Mistral, lo que es en el de otros escritores; pero, además, significó describir, hablar de, etc. De ahí frases como 'contador del mar,' 'contadores de patria' y otras tan suyas.

Aquí en *Recados: Contando a Chile,* la tenemos hablando de Chile y de sus hombres y de sus cosas." ("To relate," in the language of Gabriela Mistral, was what it is in the language of other writers; but, besides, it signified to describe, to speak about, etc. Hence phrases like "relater of the sea," "relaters of country," and others so much hers. Here in *Messages: Relating to Chile,* we have her speaking of Chile and her men and her things.) Alfonso Escudero, "Prólogo" ("Prologue"), *Recados: Contando a Chile* (Messages: Relating to Chile) (Santaigo, Chile, 1957), p. 7.

80. "Recado sobre Pablo Neruda" ("Message about Pablo Neruda"), *Recados: Contando a Chile* (Messages: Relating to Chile) (Santiago, Chile, 1957), p. 167.

81. Francis Thompson, "The Hound of Heaven," *Works,* II, 110.

82. Bruno, *Three Mystics,* p. 141.

83. Ignatius of Loyola, *Spiritual Exercises,* trans. W. H. Longridge, 2nd ed. (London, 1922), p. 155.

84. "Himno cotidiano" ("Daily Hymn"), *Poesías,* p. 350.

85. Peers, "The Chilean Schoolmistress . . . ," p. 8.

86. "Nocturno" ("Nocturn"), *Poesías,* pp. 79-80.

87. Merton, *The New Man,* p. 32.

88. San Juan de la Cruz, "El cántico espiritual" ("The Spiritual Canticle"), *Poesías,* p. 34.

89. Luis Aguirre Prado, *San Juan de la Cruz: estudio y antología* ("St. John of the Cross: Study and Anthology") (Madrid, 1963), p. 123: "¡Artista perfecto San Juan de la Cruz! Máximo contemplador de la naturaleza, recogía del lenguaje de ésta en cualquiera de sus componentes, y ni aguas, ni montes, ni arboledas, ni besanas tuvieron secreto para él; . . . amó la música y el canto, en el que intervenía directamente; fue dibujante y escultor, . . . Aficiones todas que se conjuntan para la sublimidad de sus poesías." (Perfect artist, St. John of the Cross! Greatest contemplator of nature, he gathered from its language in any of its components whatsoever, and neither waters, nor mountains, nor groves, nor furrows had a secret for him; . . . he loved music and song, in which he directly intervened; he was a painter and a sculptor, . . . All tastes which combine for the sublimity of his poetry.)

90. Gabriela Mistral, "El cielo de Castilla" ("Castile's Sky"), *Premio Nobel,* p. 12.

91. Peers, "The Chilean Schoolmistress . . . ," p. 8.

92. Porter, ". . . Mystic Poet," p. 308.

93. W. B. Yeats, *Collected Poems* (London, 1955), p. 234.

94. Torres Ríoseco, *Gabriela Mistral,* p. 10.

95. Gabriela Mistral, "Silueta de Sor Juana Inés de la Cruz" ("Silhouette of Sor Juana Inés de la Cruz"), *Abside,* XV (1951), 504.

96. Lowry Nelson, Jr. "The Rhetoric of Ineffability: Toward a Definition of Mystical Poetry," *Comparative Literature,* VIII (1956), 324.

97. Jacques and Raïssa Maritain, *The Situation of Poetry,* trans. Marshall Suther (New York, 1955), p. 34.

98. Perry J. Powers, "Lope de Vega and las lágrimas de la Madelena"

("Lope de Vega and the Tears of the Magdalen"), *Comparative Literature,* VIII (1956), 283.

99. John Fandel, "Poets and Mystics," *The Commonweal,* LXXIX (1963), 309.

100. Underhill, *Mysticism,* p. 111.

101. *Ibid.,* p. 109.

102. *Ibid.,* pp. 106-107.

103. "Sonetos de la muerte" ("Sonnets on Death"), *Poesías,* p. 81.

104. Underhill, *Mysticism,* p. 108.

105. "She has been called a mystic poet, but such a definition hardly corresponds to her treatment of the subject or to her attitude. Her religiosity was more a metaphysical explanation of life and death than a theology, more a spiritual need than an ecstasy, as in the case of the true mystic." Manuel Pedro González, "Profile of a Great Woman," p. 430.

106. Gabriela Mistral, "El sentido religioso de la vida" ("The Religious Meaning of Life"), p. 21.

107. Pierre Teilhard de Chardin, *Building the Earth* (Wilkes-Barre, 1965), pp. 82-83.

108. Concha Zardoya, "Twentieth Century Spanish Poetry," Lecture given at Barnard College, April 24, 1966.

109. Gómez Millas, "Oración del Rector" ("Rector's Prayer"), p. 9.

110. Gabriela Mistral, "La mujer fuerte" ("The Valiant Woman"), *Poesías,* p. 15.

BIBLIOGRAPHY

The publications of Gabriela Mistral are listed in several good bibliographies which are recorded here. My compilation in Section I of the bibliography consists of the articles and books which I have consulted in the development of this dissertation. Section II lists the critical studies on Gabriela Mistral which I have consulted. Section III includes the general works dealing with Mysticism, the Psychology of Personality, Religion, and Poetry which afforded invaluable assistance in the present study.

BIBLIOGRAPHY OF BIBLIOGRAPHIES

Albanell, Norah and Mango, Nancy. "Los escritos de Gabriela Mistral y estudios sobre su obra," *Gabriela Mistral.* Washington, D.C., 1958, pp. 49-90.

Arce de Vázquez, Margot. "Bibliography," *Gabriela Mistral, the Poet and her Work,* trans. Helene Masslo Anderson. New York, 1964, pp. 149-152.

Escudero, Alfonso. *La prosa de Gabriela Mistral: fichas de contribución a su inventario.* Santiago, Chile, 1950.

———. "La prosa de Gabriela Mistral: fichas de contribución a su inventario," *Homenaje a Gabriela Mistral* (Santiago, Chile), CIV (1957), 250-265.[1]

1. The first of the two Escudero bibliographies consists of 479 entries; the second, augmented, consists of 549.

Pinilla, Norberto. *Bibliografía crítica sobre Gabriela Mistral.* Santiago, Chile, 1940.

Romo Arreguin, Josefina. "Bibliografía de Gabriela Mistral," *Gabriela Mistral, Premio Nobel.* Madrid, 1946, pp. 8-121.

Rosenbaum, Sidonia Carmen. "Gabriela Mistral," *Revista Hispánica Moderna* (New York), III (1937), 135-140.

———. "Gabriela Mistral," *Modern Women Poets of Spanish America.* New York, 1945, pp. 262-264.[2]

I Selected Works of Gabriela Mistral

A. Poetry

Antología, prólogo de Hernán Díaz Arrieta ("Alone"). Santiago, Chile, 1945.

Antología, prólogo de Ismael Edwards Matte. Santiago, Chile, 1946.

Antología, prólogo de Hernán Díaz Arrieta ("Alone"). Santiago, Chile, 1953.

Desolación. New York, 1922.

Desolación, prólogo de Hernán Díaz Arrieta ("Alone"). Santiago, Chile, 1926.

Desolación, 4th ed. Buenos Aires, 1945.

Lagar I. Santiago, Chile, 1955.

Lagar II (published on microfilm). New York, 1957.

Poesías completas, 2nd ed. Madrid, 1962.

Recado de Chile (published on microfilm). New York, 1957.

Tala. Buenos Aires, 1938.

Ternura. Madrid, 1924.

2. The first of the two Rosenbaum bibliographies has 189 entries. The second is one of seven divisions of the bibliography in her book. This division contains 106 entries. Some of these are repeated from the 1937 list; some are new entries.

B. Prose

"Alabanza a la Virgen," *El Mercurio* (Santiago, Chile), August 23, 1926, p. 3.

"A la mujer mexicana," *El Mercurio* (Santiago, Chile), February 18, 1923, p. 3.

"Breve descripción de Chile,"* *Anales de la Universidad de Chile—Homenaje a Gabriela Mistral,* CXV (1957), 293-299.

"Carta a Benjamín Carrión," *Cuadernos Americanos* (México, D.F.), XV (1956), 289-290.

"Carta a mi biógrafo," *Repertorio Americano* (San José, Costa Rica), XXIX (1934), 8.

"Carta que dirigió a unas amigas," In M. Ladrón de Guevara. *Gabriela Mistral, rebelde magnífica.* Santiago, Chile, 1957, p. 42.

"Cartas a Eugenio Labarca," *Homenaje,* CXV (1957), 266-281.

"Cartas a Matilde Ladrón de Guevara," *Gabriela Mistral, rebelde magnífica.* Santiago, Chile, 1957, pp. 60-162.

"Corazones franceses: Juan María Vianney, cura de Ars," *El Mercurio* (Santiago, Chile), July 14, 1929, p. 5.

"Corazones franceses: San Vicente de Paul," *Repertorio Americano* (San José, Costa Rica), XVII (1928), 377-378.

"Cristo en la escuela," *Repertorio Americano* (San José, Costa Rica), XX (1931), 309-311.

"Divulgación religiosa. Sentido de las letanías: Virgen de las Vírgenes," *El Mercurio* (Santiago, Chile), April 12, 1925, p. 3.

* Further references to this edition will read *Homenaje.*

"El cielo de Castilla," *Gabriela Mistral, Premio Nobel.* Madrid, 1946, pp. 9-12.
"El fervor de Lourdes I," *El Mercurio* (Santiago, Chile), April 10, 1926, p. 7.
"El fervor de Lourdes II," *El Mercurio* (Santiago, Chile), April 15, 1926, p. 1.
"El grito," *Homenaje,* CXV (1957), 300.
"El sentido religioso de la vida," *Boletín del Instituto de Literatura Chilena* (Santiago, Chile), III (1963), 20-23. 20-23.
"El testamento pedagógico," *Educación* (Caracas), VI (1960), 5-7.
Epistolario. Santiago, Chile, 1957.
"Infancia de San Francisco de Asís," *El Mercurio* (Santiago, Chile), October 3, 1926, p. 3.
"Invitación a la lectura de Rainer María Rilke," *Repertorio Americano* (San José, Costa Rica), XVI (1928), 72-76.
José Martí, Versos sencillos: estudio de Gabriela Mistral. Havana, 1939.
"La lengua de Martí," *Revista de la Biblioteca Nacional* (Havana), XVIII (1957), 141-164.
Lecturas para mujeres. México, 1923.
"Los compañeros de San Francisco: Bernardo de Quintaval," *El Mercurio* (Santiago, Chile), October 24, 1926, p. 2.
"Llamado de Gabriela Mistral para el hogar de Cristo," *El Mercurio* (Santiago, Chile), December 7, 1954, no pagination.
"Mensaje sobre los derechos humanos," In M. Ladrón de Guevara. *Gabriela Mistral, rebelde magnífica.* Santiago, Chile, 1957, pp. 170-171.
"Motivos de San Francisco, comentarios a su vida: La madre," *El Mercurio* (Santiago, Chile), April 8, 1923, p. 7.

"Motivos de San Francisco: Los labios," *El Mercurio* (Santiago, Chile), March 16, 1924, p. 3.

"Páginas para Pedro Salinas," *Repertorio Americano* (San José, Costa Rica), XVII (1928), 198.

"Palabras pronunciadas cuando recibió el Premio Nobel," *Les Prix Nobel en 1945*. Stockholm, 1947, pp. 61-62.

"Pienso en Péguy," *Repertorio Americano* (San José, Costa Rica), XLI (1945), 329-330.

"Recado sobre la alameda chilena," *El Mercurio* (Santiago, Chile), August 7, 1945, p. 3.

"Recado sobre Pablo Neruda," *Recados: Contando a Chile*. Santiago, Chile, 1957, pp. 165-169.

Recados: Contando a Chile, prólogo de Alfonso Escudero. Santiago, Chile, 1957.

"Silueta de Sor Juana Inés de la Cruz," *Abside* (México, D.F.), XV (1951), 501-506.

"Sobre la paz y la América Latina," *Repertorio Americano* (San José, Costa Rica), XLVI (1950), 7-11.

"Sobre la xenofobia," *La Nueva Democracia* (New York), XXIX (1949), 22-26.

"Truly Apostolic," *Franciscan Herald and Form* (Chicago), XXXVII (1956), 419.

"Un discurso a la juventud de México," *El Mercurio* (Santiago, Chile), December 18, 1948, p. 1.

" 'Una madrina cubana, chilena, argentina, para cada niño español,' pide Gabriela Mistral," *Repertorio Americano* (San José, Costa Rica), XXXVI (1929), 168.

"Versicle of Peace," *The Americas* (Washington, D.C.), VII (1951), 281-282.

"Yo conozco a Cristo," *La Nueva Democracia* (New York), XXIX (1949), 25.

II Critical Studies on Gabriela Mistral

Adams, Mildred. "Gabriela Mistral," *Mexican Life* (Mexico, D.F.), XXII (1946), 27, 61-63.

Aguilera, Honorio. "El alma cristiana de Gabriela Mistral," *La Revista Católica* (Santiago, Chile), LXVII (1959), 2481-2484.

Alarcón, Abel. "*Desolación,* poemas por Gabriela Mistral, estudio crítico," *Hispania* (Stanford U., California), VI (1923), 202-203.

Alba, Pedro de. "Dádivas espirituales de Gabriela Mistral," *La Nueva Democracia* (New York), XXVII (1947), 52-55.

———. "Elogio de la Peregrina Iluminada," *La Nueva Democracia* (New York), XXV (1944), 16-18.

———. "Gabriela Mistral por los caminos de América," *Boletín de la Unión Panamericana* (Washington, D.C.), LXXX (1946), 123-131.

———. "Hispanismo e indigenismo de Gabriela Mistral," *Homenaje,* CXV (1957), 79-80.

———. "Oración por Gabriela Mistral," *Filosofía y Letras* (Quito), XXXI (1957), 237-244.

Alba, Víctor (pseud. Pere Pagés). "Gabriela Mistral: la gran poetisa chilena, que conquistó el premio Nobel, vista por Palma Guillén de Nicolau, que la acompañó en su estancia en nuestro país," *Hoy* (México, D.F.), August 30, 1952, pp. 36-37.

———. "La Mistral vista por su amiga y secretaria," *Homenaje,* CXV (1957), 91-94.

Albareda, Ginés de. "Figuras literarias del mundo hispánico: Gabriela Mistral," *Revista Javeriana* (Bogotá), XXXII (1949), 149-152.

Aleixandre, Vicente. "A Gabriela Mistral," *Gabriela Mistral, Premio Nobel.* Madrid, 1946, pp. 85-87.

Allison, Esther M. "Apunte de su sonrisa," *Abside* (México, D.F.), XXI (1957), 158-159.

Alonso, Dámaso. "Canción," *Gabriela Mistral, Premio Nobel.* Madrid, 1946, pp. 91-92.

———. "Gabriela Mistral," *Homenaje,* CXV (1957), 103.

Amador Sánchez, Luis. "El existencialismo cristiano de Gabriela," *La Nueva Democracia* (New York), XXXVII (1957), 43-49.

———. "Lucila y Gabriela," *La Nueva Democracia* (New York), XXXVII (1957), 31-33.

Ambía, Isabel de. "Ante Gabriela Mistral," *Gabriela Mistral, Premio Nobel.* Madrid, 1946, pp. 15-18.

Amunátegui Solar, D. "Gabriela Mistral," *Las letras chilenas,* 2nd ed. Santiago, Chile, 1931, pp. 297-302.

Araneda, Fidel. "Gabriela Mistral," *La Revista Católica* (Santiago, Chile), LXXIV (1938), 337-338.

Araquistain, Luis, "Magisterio y poesía," *Repertorio Americano* (San José, Costa Rica), X (1925), 52-53.

Arce, Magda. "Presencia de Gabriela Mistral," *Homenaje,* CXV (1957), 31-38.

Arce de Vázquez, Margot. *Gabriela Mistral: persona y poesía.* San Juan, Puerto Rico, 1958.

———. *Gabriela Mistral, the Poet and her Work,* trans. Helene Masslo Anderson. New York, 1964.

———. "Libros de Gabriela Mistral," *Revista de la Asociación de Mujeres Graduadas* (San Juan, Puerto Rico), III (1940), 24-32.

Arciniegas, Germán. Personal correspondence. August 19, 1964.

Arias, Augusto. "Recuerdo de Gabriela Mistral," *Universidad de Antioquia* (Medellín, Colombia), XXXIV (1958), 513-516.

———. "Zweig y Gabriela Mistral," *Letras del Ecuador* (Quito), XII (1957), 1, 8, 23.

Arnao, Luz Machado de. "Yo conocí a Gabriela Mistral," *Homenaje,* CXV (1957), 81-83.

Arrigoitia, Luis de. "Pensamiento y forma en la prosa de Gabriela Mistral," Ph.D. dissertation. University of Madrid, 1963.

Artel, Jorge. "El Papa, el indio, Gabriela y Germán," *Vida Universitaria* (Monterrey), VIII (1959), no pagination.

Athayde, T. de. "Las tres poetisas del Sur," trans. A. Vieira. *Atenea* (Concepción, Chile), II (1925), 227-239.

Azócar, R. "Gabriela Mistral," *La poesía chilena moderna.* Santiago, Chile, 1931, pp. 115-116.

Barrenechea, Julio. "Gabriela Mistral en Monte Grande," *Cuadernos* (Paris), XLIII (1960), 96.

Barrios, Eduardo. "El primer libro de Gabriela Mistral," *Homenaje,* CXV (1957), 26-30.

Bates, Margaret. "Apropos an article on Gabriela Mistral," *The Americas* (Washington, D.C.), XIV (1957), 145-151.

———. "Gabriela Mistral," *The Americas* (Washington, D.C.), III (1946), 168-189.

———. "Gabriela Mistral's 'Poema de Chile,' " *The Americas* (Washington, D.C.), XVII (1961), 261-276.

Belmas, Antonio Oliver. "Proyección de Gabriela Mistral," *Gabriela Mistral, Premio Nobel.* Madrid, 1946, pp. 61-66.

Benvignat, Fernando. "Cantad sus rondas floridas," *Atenea* (Concepción, Chile), CXXIX (1957), 8-14.

Berchmans, Sister John, O.P. "Gabriela Mistral and the Franciscan Concept of Life," *Renascence* (Milwaukee), V (1952), 40-46, 95.

Berges, Consuelo. "Surco de Gabriela Mistral," *Gabriela*

Mistral, Premio Nobel. Madrid, 1946, pp. 21-34.

Bietti, Oscar. "Evolución de la poesía de Gabriela Mistral," *Nosotros* (Buenos Aires), XV (1941), 187-193.

Blackwell, Alice Stone. "A Spanish American Poet," *The Lexington Herald* (Kentucky), May 11, 1924, no pagination.

Bousoño, Carlos. "Dos poemas sobre la muerte," *Gabriela Mistral, Premio Nobel.* Madrid, 1946, pp. 95-96.

Brenes-Mesén, Roberto. "Gabriela Mistral," *Nosotros* (Buenos Aires), XXII (1929), 5-22.

Bueno, Salvador. "La actualidad literaria: la muerte de Gabriela Mistral," *Boletín Comisión Cubana de la UNESCO* (Havana), VI (1957), 20.

———. "Aproximaciones a Gabriela Mistral," *Homenaje,* CXV (1957), 58-67.

Bussche, Gastón von dem. "Visión de una poesía," *Homenaje,* CXV (1957), 176-194.

C.A. "Significación de un triunfo," *Boletín Informativo* (Bahía Blanca), I (1945), 73.

———. "La Universidad de Chile y Gabriela Mistral," *Boletín Informativo* (Bahía Blanca), I (1945), 74-75.

Cáceres, Ester de. Personal correspondence. December 15, 1965.

Caltofen, R. "Gabriela Mistral, Dichterin menschlichen Leids," *Deutsche Rundschau* (Baden-Baden), LXXIX (1953), 392-395.

Cañas, Salvador. "Gabriela Mistral, los niños y la escuela," *Cultura* (El Salvador), XIV (1958), 96-100.

Capdevila, Arturo. "¡Paz, Gabriela Mistral!" *La Nueva Democracia* (New York), XXXVII (1957), 18-22.

Caronno, A. E. "A propósito de un artículo de Gabriela Mistral," *Nosotros* (Buenos Aires), LIV (1926), 142-143.

Carrera Andrade, Jorge. "Muerte y gloria de Gabriela Mistral," *Nación* (Santiago, Chile), April 25, 1957, pp. 1, 6.

Carrera, Julieta. "Gabriela Mistral," *Revista Nacional de Cultura* (Caracas), III (1942), 23-31.

Carrión, Benjamín. "Meditación sobre Gabriela Mistral," *Homenaje,* CXV (1957), 70-78.

———. *Santa Gabriela Mistral.* Quito, 1956.

———. "Sí, Santa Gabriela Mistral," *Cuadernos Americanos* (México, D.F.), XVI (1957), 238-244.

Cash, M. J. "Libros: Gabriela Mistral: Los poemas de las madres," *Política y Espíritu* (Santiago, Chile), VI (1950), 56-58.

Castillo, Homero. "Gabriela Mistral (1889-1957)," *Revista Iberoamericana* (Albuquerque, N. M.), XXIII (1958), 449-451.

Chacón y Calvo, José Maria. "Gabriela Mistral en una asamblea franciscana," *Boletín de la Academia Cubana de la Lengua* (Havana), VI (1957), 111-118.

———. "Gabriela Mistral: Premio Nobel, 1945," *Revista Cubana* (Havana), XX (1945), 219-224.

Clavería, Carlos. "Biografía de Gabriela Mistral por N. Pinilla," *Hispanic Review* (Philadelphia), XV (1947), 400-402.

———. "El americanismo de Gabriela Mistral," *Bulletin of Hispanic Studies* (Liverpool), XXIII (1946), 116-127.

Clulow, Alfred S. "Desolación," *Nuestra América* (Buenos Aires), VII (1923), 366-372.

Colín, Eduardo. "Gabriela Mistral," *Nosotros* (Buenos Aires), L (1925), 481-484.

Conde, Carmen. "Canto a Gabriela Mistral," *Gabriela Mistral, Premio Nobel.* Madrid, 1946, pp. 99-103.

Dana, Doris. Personal correspondence. October 15, 1965.

October 22, 1965. November 7, 1965. Interview. October 30, 1965.

Díaz Arrieta, Hernán (pseud. Alone). *Gabriela Mistral*. Santiago, Chile, 1946.

———. "Gabriela Mistral," *Las cien mejores poesías chilenas*. Santiago, Chile, 1957, pp. 61-79.

———. "Gabriela Mistral," *Los cuatro grandes de la literatura chilena*. Santiago, Chile, 1963, pp. 119-172.

———. "Historia de Gabriela Mistral," *Gabriela Mistral, Premio Nobel de literatura: Antología*. Santiago, Chile, 1945, pp. i-xxiv.

———. "Interpretación de Gabriela Mistral," *Homenaje*, CXV (1957), 15-18.

———. "Los últimos libros de Pablo Neruda y Gabriela Mistral," *Revista Nacional de Cultura* (Caracas), XVII (1955), 102-109.

———. "Prólogo," *Antología*. Santiago, Chile, 1953.

———. "Prólogo," *Desolación*, 3rd ed. Santiago, Chile, 1926, pp. 9-14.

Diego, Gerardo. "Imperfección y albricia," *Gabriela Mistral, Premio Nobel*. Madrid, 1946, pp. 37-42.

Dinamarca, Salvador. "Gabriela Mistral y su obra poética," *Hispania*, XLI (1958), 48-50.

Donoso, Armando. "Gabriela Mistral," *Nuestros poetas: Antología chilena moderna*. Santiago, Chile, 1924, pp. xxii-xxiv and 296-297.

Donoso González, Francisco. "Gabriela Mistral," *Al margen de la poesía: Ensayos sobre poesía moderna e hispanoamericana*. Paris, 1927, pp. 101-104.

Doyle, Henry Grattan. "Gabriela Mistral: Nobel Prize-Winner," *Hispania* (Menasha, Wisconsin), XXIX (1946), 69.

Edwards Matte, Ismael. "Prólogo," *Antología*. Santiago, Chile, 1946, pp. 7-27.

Escobar Veluda, Oswaldo. "Referencias sobre Gabriela Mistral," *Universidad San Salvador* (El Salvador), LXXXVI (1961), 160-164.

Escudero, Alfonso. "Prólogo," *Recados: Contando a Chile*. Santiago, Chile, 1957, pp. 7-8.

Espina, Antonio. "Luz-Voz de la poesía," *Gabriela Mistral, Premio Nobel*. Madrid, 1946, pp. 45-47.

Espinosa, Aurelio Macedonia. "Gabriela Mistral," *The Americas* (Washington, D.C.), VIII (1951), 3, 40.

Espinoza, Enrique. "Gabriela Mistral y el espíritu de la Biblia," *Homenaje*, CXV (1957), 99-101.

Estenger, Rafael. "Gabriela Mistral, Virgen y Madre," *Cuba Contemporánea* (Havana), XLIV (1927), 219-224.

Feder, E. "Gabriela Mistral as I know her," *Books Abroad* (Norman, Oklahoma), XX (1946), 153-154.

Fernández-Cuervo, Luis. "Gabriela Mistral en la tierra de su infancia," *Mundo Hispánico* (Madrid), XII (1960), 13-15.

Fernández Moreno, César. "Norberto Pinilla: Biografía de Gabriela Mistral," *Sur* (Buenos Aires), XV (1946), 70-72.

Ferrer, Jesús Alfonso. "Romance para Gabriela Mistral," *Ciencia y Cultura* (Maracaibo), II (1957), 225-226.

Ferro, Hellén. "Gabriela Mistral," *Historia de la poesía hispanoamericana*. New York, 1964, pp. 335-342.

Figueira, Gastón. *De la vida y la obra de Gabriela Mistral*. Montevideo, 1959.

———. "Evocación de Gabriela Mistral," *La Nueva Democracia* (New York), XXXVII (1957), 14-24.

———. "Gabriela Mistral," *Revista Iberoamericana* (México, D.F.), XVI (1951), 233-244.

———. "Gabriela Mistral, *Lagar.*" *Revista Iberoamericana* (México, D.F.), XX (1955), 353-354.

Figueroa, Virgilio. *La divina Gabriela.* Santiago, Chile, 1933.

Finlayson, Clarence. "Spanish American Poets: The Life and Ideas of Gabriela Mistral," *The Commonweal* (New York), XXXV (1941), 160-163.

Florit, Eugenio. "Landscape in the poetry of Gabriela Mistral," Lecture delivered at Ladycliff College, N. Y., April 28, 1964.

———. "Poetisa de una era," *The Americas* (Washington, D.C.), III (1951), 37.

Fuenzalida, Héctor. "Gabriela Mistral en la última vuelta," *Homenaje,* CXV (1957), 84-90.

Gallegos, Rómulo. "Ejemplo de dignidad espiritual," *Cuadernos* (Paris), XXIII (1957), 24-25.

García Oldini, Fernando. "Gabriela Mistral," *Doce escritores hasta el año 1925.* Santiago de Chile, 1929, pp. 109-122.

García Prada, C. "Gabriela Mistral, poetisa chilena," *Revista Chilena* (Santiago, Chile), XII (1928), 377-397.

Gatica Martínez, T. "Gabriela Mistral," *Ensayos sobre literatura hispanoamericana: La poesía lírica de Chile, Argentina y Perú,* I. Santiago, Chile, 1930, pp. 84-90.

Godoy, Emma. "Esencia y potencia de Gabriela Mistral," *Libro y el Pueblo* (México, D.F.), IV (1963), 11-12.

Goldberg, I. "Literary Ladies of the South," *The American Mercury* (New York), VII (1926), 448-452.

Gómez Millas, Juan. "Oración del Rector de la Universidad de Chile," *Homenaje,* CXV (1957), 7-9.

González, Manuel Pedro. "Profile of a Great Woman," *Hispania* (Menasha, Wisconsin), XLI (1958), 427-430.

González Lanuza, Eduardo. "Poesía y sexo: A propósito de *Tala,*" *Sur* (Buenos Aires), VIII (1938), 55-62.

González Vera, José Santos. "Comienzos de Gabriela Mistral," *Homenaje,* CXV (1957), 22-25.

Guerra, A. "Vida interior en Gabriela Mistral," *Grafos* (Havana), IV (1936), 1.

Gullberg, M. Hj. "Discours," *Les Prix Nobel en 1945*. Stockholm, 1947, pp. 47-50.

Gutiérrez, Fermín Estrella. "Gabriela Mistral, Maestra," *La Nueva Democracia* (New York), XXXVII (1957), 46-49.

Hamilton, Carlos D. "Gabriela de Hispanoamérica," *Revista Iberoamericana* (Albuquerque, New Mexico), XXIII (1958), 83-92.

———. "Raíces bíblicas de la poesía de Gabriela Mistral," *Cuadernos Americanos* (México, D.F.), XX (1961), 201-210.

Henríquez Ureña, Max. "Vida y angustia de Gabriela Mistral," *Revista Cubana* (Havana), XXXI (1957), 47-69.

Herrera Palacios, Oscar. "Discurso del señor Ministro de Educación en el homenaje a Gabriela Mistral," *Revista de Educación* (Santiago, Chile), XIV (1954), 2-5.

Hughes, Langston. *Selected Poems of Gabriela Mistral.* Bloomington, Indiana, 1957.

Ibarbourou, Juana de. "Mis amados recuerdos: Gabriela Mistral," *Alcor* (Asunción), XX (1962), 1, 9.

Iduarte, Andrés. "En torno a Gabriela Mistral," *Cuadernos Americanos* (México, D.F.), XVI (1946), 240-256.

Iglesias, Augusto. *Gabriela Mistral y el modernismo en Chile.* Santiago, Chile, 1950.

I. I. "Ese premio Nobel de la literatura," *Cuadernos* (Paris), XVI (1956), 113-114.

Illanes Adaro, Graciela. "Elqui en la obra de Gabriela Mistral," *Atenea* (Concepción, Chile), LXXXIII (1946), 171-180.

Labarca, Eugenio. "Literatura femenina chilena," *Atenea* (Concepción, Chile), I (1924), 357-361.

Labarthe, Pedro Juan. "Gabriela, ¡Cómo te recuerdo!" *La Nueva Democracia* (New York), XXXVII (1957), 13-19.

Labrador Ruíz, Enrique. "Gabriela Mistral (Para un estudio de su carácter)," *La Nueva Democracia* (New York), XXXVII (1957), 38-44.

Ladrón de Guevara, Matilde. *Gabriela Mistral, rebelde magnífica.* Santiago, Chile, 1957.

Lago, Tomás. "Gabriela y el nardo de las Parábolas," *Homenaje,* CXV (1957), 95-98.

Lagos Carmona, Guillermo. *Gabriela Mistral en México.* México, 1945.

Lamothe, Luis. "Gabriela Mistral en la poesía hispanoamericana," *El Nacional* (México, D.F.), June 2, 1957, p. 2.

Latcham, Ricardo A. "El sentimiento americano de Gabriela Mistral," *La Nación* (Buenos Aires), January 31, 1957, p. 1.

Larco Herrera, Rafael. "Con Gabriela Mistral, símbolo de América," *La Voz de Atlántida* (La Ceiba, Honduras), XIII (1948), 8.

Lecourt, Eduardo. "La Biblia era su aljibe que le daba agua pura diariamente," *El Mercurio* (Santiago, Chile), January 22, 1957, p. 15.

Lida, Raimundo. "Palabras de Gabriela," *Cuadernos Americanos* (México, D.F.), XVI (1957), 234-237.

Lihn, Enrique. "Elegía a Gabriela Mistral," *Homenaje,* CXV (1957), 105.

López Zanelli, Luisa. "Gabriela Mistral," *Mujeres chilenas de letras,* I. Santiago, Chile, 1917. pp. 151-154.

Loynaz, Dulce María. "Gabriela y Lucila," *Poesías completas.* Madrid, 1962, pp. cxv-cxxxix.

Luigi, Juan de. "Gabriela Mistral en su primera época," *Homenaje,* CXV (1957), 39-43.

Luisi, Luisa. "Two South American Poets: Gabriela Mistral and Juana de Ibarbourou," *Bulletin of the Pan American Union* (Washington, D.C.), LXIV (1930), 588-590.

Mac Dermot, I. K. "Gabriela Mistral and Inter-American Spiritual Understanding," *Bulletin of the Pan American Union* (Washington, D.C.), LVIII (1924), 647-661.

Madariaga, Salvador de. "Homenaje a Gabriela Mistral," *Diamante* (London), VII (1958), 1-20.

Maeztu, María de. "De la vida de Gabriela Mistral," *Raza Española* (Madrid), XXXVIII (1924), 53-55.

Mañach, Jorge. "Gabriela: Alma y Tierra," *Revista Hispánica Moderna* (New York), III (1937), 106-110.

———. "Gabriela y Juan Ramón: La poesía nobelable," *Cuadernos* (Paris), XC (1960), 57-61.

Marañón, Gregorio. "Una sola vez," *Gabriela Mistral, Premio Nobel.* Madrid, 1946, pp. 51-52.

Marín, Juan. "Recuerdo de Gabriela Mistral," *Gabriela Mistral.* Washington, D.C., 1958, pp. 7-13.

Marinello Vidaurreta, Juan. "Gabriela Mistral y José Martí," *Sur* (Buenos Aires), I (1931), 156-163.

Maritain, Jacques. Personal correspondence. November 18, 1965.

Massiani, Felipe. "Recuerdo y ejercicio de Gabriela Mistral," *Revista Nacional de Cultura* (Caracas), VII (1945), 3-12.

Mayo, Margarita de. "Gabriela Mistral, Maestra," *Cuadernos Hispanoamericanos* (Madrid), XXXIII (1958), 360-366.

Medina, José Ramón. "La humana figura de Gabriela Mistral," *Arco* (Bogotá), II (1960), 44-47.

Meléndez, Concha. "América hispana en la poesía de

Gabriela Mistral," *Asomante* (San Juan, Puerto Rico), II (1946), 17-20.

———. "El magisterio de Gabriela Mistral," *Indice* (Madrid), II (1931), 14-15.

Mengod, Vicente. "Gabriela Mistral en mi recuerdo," *Atenea* (Concepción, Chile), XXXI (1954), 57-60.

Mercado, Julio. "Gabriela Mistral," *Cuba Contemporánea* (Havana), XXXII (1923), 154-161.

Miomandre, Francisco de. "*Tala*—Gabriela Mistral y América latina," *Atenea* (Concepción, Chile), LVI (1939), 458-465.

Miranda S., Estela. "El sentimiento de la naturaleza en Gabriela Mistral," *Algunas poetisas de Chile y Uruguay*. Santiago, Chile, 1937, pp. 24-63.

Miró, Clemencia. "Viento de cumbres," *Gabriela Mistral, Premio Nobel*. Madrid, 1946, pp. 55-58.

Mitchell, Edna. "Chilean Poetess Wins Nobel Prize," *The Grace Log* (New York), XXI (1946), 17.

Molina Müller, Julio. "Naturaleza americana y estilo en Gabriela Mistral," *Homenaje*, CXV (1957), 109-124.

Monsalve, Josué. *Gabriela Mistral, la errante solitaria*. Santiago, Chile, 1958.

Montenegro, E. "En el pináculo de la fama en la América latina (sobre *Desolación*)," Revista de Revistas (México, D.F.), XIV (1923), 36.

———. "La maestra Gabriela Mistral," *Cuba Contemporánea* (Havana), XXIX (1922), 351-354.

Monterde, Francisco. "Notas—Gabriela Mistral," *Revista Iberoamericana* (Albuquerque, New Mexico), XXII (1958), 333-337.

Mora, José A. "Las ideas americanistas de Gabriela Mistral," *Gabriela Mistral*. Washington, D.C., 1958, pp. 43-48.

Morley, Sister Maria Leonard, O.S.F. "Franciscan Simplicity

in Gabriela Mistral," M.A. Thesis, St. John's University, Jamaica, New York, 1959.

Mujica, Juan. "Aventura y gloria de Gabriela Mistral," *Mundo Hispánico* (Madrid), X (1957), 13-17.

Núñez, Ana Rosa. *Gabriela Mistral, amor que hirió*. Havana, 1961.

Onis, Federico de. "Gabriela Mistral," *Antología de la poesía española e hispanoamericana,* rev. ed. New York, 1961, pp. 920-922.

———. "Gabriela Mistral," *Homenaje,* CXV (1957), 20-21.

———. Personal correspondence. August 24, 1964.

Ortiz-Vargas, A. "Gabriela Mistral," *Hispanic American Historical Review* (Durham, N. C.), XI (1931), 99-102.

———. "Gabriela Mistral, Chile's Teacher Poet," *Poet Lore* (Boston), XLVI (1940), 339-352.

Oyarzún, Luis. "Discurso en honor de Gabriela Mistral," *Anales de la Universidad de Chile* (Santiago, Chile), CXIII (1954), 109-111.

———. "El mundo poético de Gabriela Mistral," *Pequeña Antología.* Santiago, Chile, 1950, pp. 15-16.

———. "Gabriela Mistral en su poesía," *Homenaje,* CXV (1957), 11-14.

———. "Sus palabras modificaron nuestro idoma y cambiaron el orden de nuestro corazón," *El Mercurio* (Santiago, Chile), January 22, 1957, p. 17.

Paz Paredes, Margarita. "Gabriela Mistral—vida y poesía de un alma," *Cultura* (El Salvador), XVII (1959), 160-168.

Peers, E. Allison. "Gabriela Mistral, the Chilean Schoolmistress who won the Nobel Prize for Literature," *Lectures and Addresses, Institute of Hispanic Studies* (Liverpool), III (1946), 1-16.

Pego, Aurelio. "Penetración—Gabriela Mistral, gaucha," *Hoy* (México), III (1960), 7-8.

Peralta Peralta, Jaime. "El paisaje original de Gabriela Mistral," *Cuadernos Hispanoamericanos* (Madrid), LIII (1963), 471-481.

Pérez Galo, Rene. "La poesía de Gabriela Mistral," *Anales de la Universidad Central del Ecuador* (Quito), XC (1961), 241-265.

Picón-Salas, Mariano. "Homenaje a Gabriela Mistral," *La Nación* (Santiago, Chile), January 17, 1957, p. 1.

———. "Crítica de *Santa Gabriela* por Benjamín Carrión," *Homenaje,* CXV (1957), 301.

Pinilla, Norberto. "Biografía de Gabriela Mistral," *Revista de Educación* (Quito), VI (1946), 60-64.

———. *Biografía de Gabriela Mistral.* Santiago, Chile, 1946.

———. "Boceto crítico sobre Gabriela Mistral," *Revista Iberoamericana* (México, D.F.), XI (1946), 55-62.

Pillement, G. "Sobre Desolación," *Revista de América Latina* (Bogotá), V (1923), 170-171.

Pomés, Mathilde. *Gabriela Mistral.* Paris, 1964.

Porter, Katherine Anne. "Latin America's Mystic Poet," *The Literary Digest International Book Review* (New York), IV (1926), 307-308.

Portilla de Galindo, Antonia. "Juicio sobre Gabriela Mistral," *Ateneo* (El Salvador), XLVIII (1961), 14-18.

Posada, Germán. "Recuerdo a Gabriela Mistral," *Cuadernos Hispanoamericanos* (Madrid), XXXI (1957), 102-104.

Préndez Saldías, C. "Poetas chilenos en 'Atenea,'" *Atenea* (Concepción, Chile), X (1933), 294-305.

Preston, Sister Mary Charles Ann, S.S.N.D. *A Study of the Significant Variants in the Poetry of Gabriela Mistral.* Washington, D.C., 1964.

Quevedo-Hijosa, F. "Una entrevista con Gabriela Mistral,"

Revista de Educación (Santiago, Chile), I (1926), 29-37.

Reyes, Alfonso. "Himno a Gabriela," *Homenaje,* CXV (1957), 19.

Rheinfelder, Hans. "Gabriela Mistral," *Homenaje,* CXV (1957), 44-57.

———. "Gabriela Mistral—Motive ihrer Lyrik," *Razón y Fe* (Madrid), LXVIII (1956), 233-235.

Rincón, César David. "Gabriela Mistral, mística del futuro," *Ciencia y Cultura* (Maracaibo), II (1957), 135-148.

Ríos Espejo, Rebeca. "La sintaxis en la expresión poética de Gabriela Mistral," *Boletín del Instituto de Filología de la Universidad de Chile* (Santiago, Chile), IX (1958), 121-176.

Rodig, Laura. "Presencia de Gabriela Mistral," *Homenaje,* CXV (1957), 282-292.

Rodríguez Embil, Luis. "Los silencios de Gabriela Mistral," *Revista Cubana* (Havana), XI (1938), 221-224.

Rosa, Amira de la and Albareda, Ginés de. "Anticipo de un libro sobre Gabriela Mistral," *Gabriela Mistral, Premio Nobel.* Madrid, 1946, pp. 69-74.

Rosenbaum, Sidonia C. "Criollismo y casticismo en Gabriela Mistral," *Cuadernos Americanos* (México, D.F.), XII (1953), 296-300.

———. "Gabriela Mistral," *Modern Women Poets of Spanish America.* New York, 1945, pp. 171-203.

Saavedra Molina, Julio. "Gabriela Mistral: su vida y su obra," *Poesías completas.* Madrid, 1962, pp. xv-cviii.

Sabat Ercasty, Carlos de. "Homenaje de la Universidad de Montevideo a Gabriela Mistral," *Repertorio Americano* (San José, Costa Rica), XLIX (1957), 209-213.

Sabella, Andrés. "El hijo desconocido de Gabriela Mistral," *Atenea* (Concepción, Chile), XXII (1945), 228-236.

Sánchez, Luis Alberto. "Gabriela Mistral," *Asomante* (San Juan, Puerto Rico), XII (1956), 39-47.

———. "Sobre Gabriela Mistral," *Revista de América* (Bogotá), V (1946), 55-56.

———. "Un ser y una voz inconfundibles," *Cuadernos* (Paris), XXIII (1957), 22-23.

Santandreu, Cora. "Aspectos del estilo en la poesía de Gabriela Mistral," *Homenaje,* CXV (1957), 125-175.

Savoia, Alicia Raquel. "El mundo infantil de Gabriela Mistral," *Universidad Nacional del Litoral* (Santa Fe, Argentina), XLVI (1960), 215-240.

Scrill, Rev. William R. Personal correspondence. August 15, 1964.

Sedgwick, Ruth. "Gabriela Mistral's Elqui Valley," *Hispania* (Baltimore, Maryland), XXXV (1952), 310-314.

Silva, Ana Margarita. "A mi maestra, Gabriela Mistral," *Revista de la Asociación de Mujeres Graduadas* (San Juan, Puerto Rico), III (1940), 48-49.

Silva Castro, Raúl. "Algunos aspectos de la poesía de Gabriela Mistral," *La Nueva Democracia* (New York), V (1923), 8-9, 30.

———. *Estudios sobre Gabriela Mistral.* Santiago, Chile, 1935.

———. "Gabriela Mistral," *Antología general de la poesía chilena.* Santiago, Chile, 1959, pp. 400-407.

———. "Los papeles de Gabriela Mistral," *Atenea* (Concepción, Chile), CXXXVI (1959), 249-251.

———. "Notas sobre los sonetos de la muerte de Gabriela Mistral," *Hispanic Review* (Philadelphia), XXXIII (1965), 57-62.

———. *Producción de Gabriela Mistral de 1912 a 1918.* Santiago, Chile, 1957.

———. "Gabriela Mistral," *Retratos literarios*. Santiago, Chile, 1932, pp. 151-162.

Soiza Reilly, J. J. de. "Gabriela Mistral," *Mujeres de América*. Buenos Aires, 1934, pp. 40-46.

Solar Correa, E. "Gabriela Mistral," *Poetas de Hispano-America*. Santiago, Chile, 1926, pp. 229, 279-281.

Sotomayor de Concha, Graciela. "Gabriela Mistral," *La labor literaria de las mujeres chilenas*. Santiago, Chile, 1928, pp. 718-721.

Suárez Calimano, E. "Sobre *Desolación*," *Nosotros* (Buenos Aires), XLIV (1923), 496-503.

Tapia de Renedo, Dom Benito. "Gabriela Mistral," *Mundo Hispánico* (Madrid), XIII (1960), 50.

Taylor, Martin C. Personal correspondence. April 2, 1965.

———. *Religious Sensibility in the Life and Poetry of Gabriela Mistral*. University Microfilms, Ann Arbor, Michigan, 1964.

Tomic, Rodomiro. "Homenaje a Gabriela Mistral," *Política y Espíritu* (Santiago, Chile), XIII (1957), 10-11.

Torres Ríoseco, Arturo. *Gabriela Mistral*. Valencia, 1962.

———. "Gabriela Mistral, el premio Nobel y su significado," *Revísta de America* (Bogotá), V (1946), 127-128.

———. "Gabriela Mistral, Nobel Prize-Winner at Home," *Hispania* (Menasha, Wisconsin), XXIX (1946), 72-73.

———. "Ultimos recuerdos de Gabriela Mistral," *Insula* (Madrid), XVII (1962), 1, 16.

Turina, Pepita. "Gabriela y sus recados," *Atenea* (Concepción, Chile), XCIV (1949), 289-290.

Undurraga, Antonio de. "Fueron doce los sonetos de la Muerte," *La Nueva Democracia* (New York), XXXIII (1953), 36-41.

———. "Gabriela Mistral, la gran juglaresca," *La Nueva Democracia* (New York), XXXVII (1957), 75-77.

Uribe Echevarría, Juan. "Gabriela Mistral; Aspectos de su vida y de su obra," *Gabriela Mistral.* Washington, D.C., 1958, pp. 15-30.
Valbuena Briones, Angel. "El verso quemante de Gabriela Mistral," *Literatura Hispanoamericana.* Barcelona, 1965, pp. 390-397.
Valbuena Prat, Angel. "Ofrenda," *Gabriela Mistral, Premio Nobel.* Madrid, 1946, p. 108.
Valdovinos, Hernán. "Falleció Gabriela Mistral y el mundo llora la cantora de América, Ganadora del premio Nobel," *Diario de Nueva York,* January 11, 1957, pp. 1, 21.
Valéry, Paul. "Gabriela Mistral," trans. Luis Oyarzún, *Atenea* (Concepción, Chile), LXXXVIII (1947), 313-322.
Valle, Carmen. "Gabriela y su palabra del dolor," *Política y Espíritu* (Santiago Chile), XIII (1957), 12-13.
Valle, Rafael Heliodoro. "Alabanza de Gabriela Mistral," *Gabriela Mistral.* Washington, D.C., 1958, pp. 31-41.
———. "Gabriela Mistral en mis recuerdos," *Homenaje,* CXV (1957), 68-69.
———. "Una charla olvidada con Gabriela Mistral," *Vida Universitaria* (Monterrey), VIII (1958), 6-8.
Varela, Lorenzo. "Las astillas olorosas de *Tala,*" *Taller* (México, D.F.), I (1939), 60-63.
Vasconcelos, José. "Carta a Gabriela Mistral," *Repertorio Americano* (San José, Costa Rica), V (1922), 113-114.
———. "Gabriela Mistral en México," *Revista da Educación Nacional* (Santiago, Chile), XVIII (1922), 123-127.
Vergara, Marta. "Gabriela Mistral," *Memorias de una mujer irreverente.* Santiago, Chile, 1963, pp. 262-269.
Vitier, Cintio. *La voz de Gabriela Mistral.* Cuba, 1957.
Vivanco, Luis Felipe. "Gabriela Mistral, nada más que en su

palabra," *Cuadernos Hispanoamericanos* (Madrid), VIII (1954), 227-232.

Young, Robert J. "Reseñas sobre 'Aspectos del estilo en la poesía de Gabriela Mistral' de Cora Santandreu," *Revista Iberoamericana* (Albuquerque, New Mexico), XXVI (1961), 209-210.

Zamorano Baier, Antonio. "Gabriela Mistral y la crítica," *Atenea* (Concepción, Chile), XXIII (1946), 183-199.

Zardoya, Concha. "Daguerrotipos de recuerdo (A través de un rostro)," *Gabriela Mistral, Premio Nobel*. Madrid, 1946, pp. 77-82.

———. "Desde *Desolación* a *Lagar*," *Revista Hispánica Moderna* (New York), XXII (1956), 137-138.

Zum Felde, Alberto. "Poetisas de América: Gabriela Mistral," *La Pluma* (Montevideo), IV (1928), 13-15.

Zúñiga, Luis Palma. "Gabriela Mistral," *Sociedad de Escritores de Chile* (Santiago, Chile), I (1945), 9-10.

Anonymous Articles

———. "Autores contemporáneos: Gabriela Mistral," *Hoy* (México, D.F.), LXXV (1937), 69-74.

———. "Chile y Gabriela Mistral," *Política y Espíritu* (Santiago, Chile), VII (1951), 325-326.

———. "El premio Nobel," *Atenea* (Concepción, Chile), LXXXI (1945), 205-206.

———. "El regreso de Gabriela Mistral," *Atenea* (Concepción, Chile), XLII (1936), 177-178.

———. "Gabriela Mistral," *Boletín Oficial de la Secretaría de Estado de la República de Cuba* (Havana), XXXV (1938), 289-290.

———. "Gabriela Mistral conquista novos lauréis," *Bolétin de União Panamericana* (Washington, D.C.), XLVIII (1946), 261-267.

———. "Gabriela Mistral entre nosotros," *Raza Española* (Madrid), VI (1924), 47-48.
———. "Gabriela Mistral: Los poemas de las madres," *Política y Espíritu* (Santiago, Chile), VI (1950), 56.
———. "Gloria de Gabriela Mistral," *Sociedad de Escritores de Chile* (Santiago, Chile), I (1945), 5-7.
———. "Habla Gabriela Mistral," *Revista de América* (Bogotá), IV (1945), 462-463.
———. "Homenaje a Gabriela Mistral," *Revista de Educación Nacional* (Santiago, Chile), XXI (1925), 52-54.
———. "Inter-American Notes: The Serra Award," *The Americas* (Washington, D.C.), VII (1951), 281-282.
———. "Mensaje de Gabriela Mistral," *Las Américas* (Washington, D.C.), IX (1957), 24-28.
———. "Noción de la poetisa," *Revista de las Indias* (Bogotá), XXVI (1945), 310-311.
———. "Puntos de vista," *Atenea* (Concepción, Chile), XXXIV (1957), 1-7.
———. "The Serra Award of the Americas for 1950," *Books Abroad* (Norman, Oklahoma), XXV (1951), 219.

III Studies on Mysticism, Religion, Psychology, and Poetry

A Benedictine of Stanbrook Abbey. *Medieval Mystical Tradition and Saint John of the Cross*. London, 1954.
"A Cristo crucificado," *Ten Centuries of Spanish Poetry,* ed. Pedro Salinas and Eleanor L. Turnbull. Baltimore, 1955, p. 236.
Adam, A. Irving. "Francis Thompson," *Poetry Review* (London), II (1913), 221-226.
Aguirre, J. M. "Béquer y lo evanescente," *Bulletin of Hispanic Studies* (Liverpool), XLI (1964), 28-39.
Agustini, Delmira. *Cantos de la mañana*. Montevideo, 1907.

———. *El libro blanco*. Montevideo, 1910.
———. *Los cálices vacíos*. Montevideo, 1913.
Alonso, Amado. *Materia y forma en poesía*. Madrid, 1955.
———. *Poesía y estilo de Pablo Neruda*. Buenos Aires, 1951.
Alonso, Dámaso. *Ensayos sobre poesía española*. Buenos Aires, 1946.
———. *La poesía de San Juan de la Cruz*. Madrid, 1946.
———. *Poesía española: Ensayo de métodos y límites estilísticos*. Madrid, 1957.
Altamira, Rafael. *Los elementos de la civilización y del carácter españoles*, 2nd ed. Buenos Aires, 1950.
Altizer, Thomas. *Oriental Mysticism and Biblical Eschatology*. Philadelphia, 1962.
Anastasi, Anne. *Differential Psychology*, 3rd ed. New York, 1958.
Anderson, Charles R. *Emily Dickinson's Poetry: Stairway of Surprise*. New York, 1960.
An English Mystic of the Fourteenth Century. *The Cloud of Unknowing and Other Treatises*, ed. Justin McCann, O.S.B., 6th ed. Westminster, Maryland, 1952.
Angels, John of the, O.F.M. *Conquest of the Kingdom of God*, trans. C. F. Crowley. St. Louis, 1957.
Aquinas, St. Thomas. *Summa Theologica*, trans. Fathers of the English Dominican Province. 3 vols. New York, 1947.
Arintero, John G., O.P. *Stages in Prayer*, trans. Kathleen Pond. St. Louis, 1957.
———. *The Mystical Evolution in the Development and Vitality of the Church*, trans. J. A. Aumann, O.P. St. Louis, 1951.
Armstrong, Martin D. "The Poetry of Francis Thompson," *Forum* (London), L (1913), 721-723.
Arnould, Edmond. *Essais de théorie et d'histoire littéraire*. London, 1927.

Angustine. *The Confessions,* ed. J. M. Lelen. New York, 1952.

Avila, Teresa de. *Camino de perfección. Clásicos Castellanos,* ed José María Aguado. 2 vols. Madrid 1956, 1958.

———. *Interior Castle,* trans. E. Allison Peers. Garden City, 1961.

———. *Las moradas. Clásicos Castellanos,* ed. Tomás Navarro Tomás, 7th ed. Madrid, 1962.

———. *Libro de las fundaciones. Clásicos Castellanos,* ed. José María Aguado. 2 vols. Madrid, 1931, 1957.

———. *Life,* trans. David Lewis. London, 1962.

———. *Way of Perfection,* trans. Alice Alexander. Westminster, Maryland, 1946.

Bannon, John F. and Dunne, Peter M., S.J. *Latin America: An Historical Survey,* rev. ed. Milwaukee, 1958.

Barja, César. *Libros y autores contemporáneos.* New York, 1935.

Baruzi, Jean. *St. Jean de la Croix et le problème de l'expérience mystique.* Paris, 1931.

Battenhouse, Henry M. *Poets of Christian Thought: Evaluations from Dante to T. S. Eliot.* New York, 1947.

Baumgardt, David. *Great Western Mystics, Their Lasting Significance.* New York, 1961.

Béguin, Albert. *Gérard de Nerval, suivi de poésie et mystique.* Paris, 1937.

———. *L'Ame romantique et le rêve.* Marseille, 1937.

Bell, Aubrey Fitzgerald. *Luis de León: A Study of the Spanish Renaissance.* Oxford, 1925.

Bennett, Charles A. *A Philosophical Study of Mysticism,* 2nd ed. New Haven, 1923.

Bergson, Henri. *Les deux sources de la morale et de la religion,* 13ème ed. Paris, 1933.

Bernard. *On the Love of God,* trans. Terence L. Connolly, S.J. Westminster, Maryland, 1951.

Besant, Annie Wood. *The Changing World and Lectures to Theosophical Students.* London, 1910.

"Bhagavad-Gita, The Song Celestial," trans. Edwin Arnold. *A Guide to the World's Religions.* Englewood Cliffs, New Jersey, 1936, p. 99.

Blackmur, Richard P. *Form and Value in Modern Poetry.* New York, 1957.

Blake, William. *Selected Poetry and Prose,* ed. Northrop Frye. New York, 1953.

———. *Symbolic Poems,* ed. Frederick E. Pierce. New Haven, 1915.

Bloy, Leon. *Pilgrim of the Absolute,* trans. John Coleman and Harry Lorin Binsse. New York, 1947.

Bodkin, Maud. *Archetypal Patterns in Poetry: Psychological Studies of Imagination,* 2nd ed. London, 1963.

Bowra, C. M. *Inspiration and Poetry.* New York, 1955.

Bradley, David G. *A Guide to the World's Religions.* Englewood Cliffs, New Jersey, 1963.

Brémond, Henri. *La Provence mystique au XVIIe siècle.* Paris, 1908.

———. *Prière et poésie.* Paris, 1926.

Brockington, A. Allen. *Mysticism and Poetry.* London, 1934.

Bruno de J. M., O.D.C. *Three mystics: El Greco, St. John of the Cross, St. Teresa of Avila.* New York, 1949.

Butter, P. *Francis Thompson.* London, 1961.

Caimano, Sister Rose Aquin, O.P. "The Antithetical Parallelism between 'El cántico espiritual' of San Juan de la Cruz and 'The Hound of Heaven' of Francis Thompson," M.A. Thesis, Fordham University, New York, 1958.

Carmichael, Montgomery. "The Works of St. John of the Cross," *Dublin Review,* CLXXIV (1924), 84-97.

Carmignac, Jean. *Christ and the Teacher of Righteousness,* trans. Katherine Greenleaf Pedley. Baltimore, 1962.
Carol, Juniper B., O.F.M. *Fundamentals of Mariology: The Study of Our Lady.* New York, 1956.
Cassou, Jean. *Trois poètes: Rilke, Milosz, Machado.* Paris, 1954.
Castro, Américo. *Santa Teresa de Jesús y otros ensayos.* Madrid, 1929.
Chardon, Louis, O.P. *The Cross of Jesus,* trans. R. T. Murphy, O.P. 2 vols. St. Louis, 1957.
Cheney, Sheldon. *Men Who Have Walked With God.* New York, 1946.
Clark, James M. *The Great German Mystics: Eckhart, Tauler, Suso.* Oxford, 1949.
Claudel, Paul. *Poetic Art,* trans. Renée Spodheim. New York, 1948.
Coester, Alfred L. *The Literary History of Spanish America.* New York, 1928.
Cognet, L. *Crépuscule des mystiques.* Tournai, Belgium, 1958.
Coleman, William J., M.M. *Latin-American Catholicism, A Self-Evaluation.* Maryknoll, New York, 1958.
Colledge, Eric. *The Medieval Mystics of England.* New York, 1961.
Conde, Carmen. "Poetisas de lengua española," *Mundo Hispánico* (Madrid), XIII (1960), 29.
Connell, F. M., S.J. *The Study of Poetry.* Boston, 1913.
Connolly, Francis Xavier, S.J. *Poetry, Its Power and Wisdom, An Introductory Study.* New York, 1960.
Connolly, Terence L., S.J. *Literary Criticism.* New York, 1948.
———. *Coventry Patmore, Mystical Poems of Nuptial Love.* Boston, 1938.
Conze, Edward. *Buddhist Meditation.* London, 1959.

Correa, Carlos Rene. *Poetas chilenos.* Santiago, Chile, 1944.

Corvalán, Octavio. *El Modernismo.* New York, 1961.

Craig, G. D. *The Modernist Trend in Spanish American Poetry.* Berkeley, 1934.

Crashaw, Richard. *Poems,* ed. A. R. Waller. Cambridge, England, 1904.

Cruz, San Juan de la. *El cántico espiritual: Clásicos Castellanos,* ed. M. Martínez Burgos. Madrid, 1936.

———. *Obras del beato padre San Juan de la Cruz,* ed. Biblioteca de Autores Españoles. Madrid, 1934.

———. *Poesías completas y otras páginas,* ed. José Manuel Blecua, 4th ed. Madrid, 1961.

———. *Subida del Monte Carmelo,* ed. Father Brice, C.P. New York, 1945.

———. *The Collected Works,* trans. Kieran Cavanaugh and Otilio Rodríguez. Garden City, 1964.

———. *The Works of St. John of the Cross,* trans. David Lewis. London, 1934.

Daly, James J., S.J. *The Hound of Heaven,* New York, 1922.

D'Arcy, Martin C., S.J. *Come, South Wind. A Collection of Contemplatives,* ed. L. M. Shrady. New York, 1957.

———. *The Pain of this World and the Providence of God.* New York, 1952.

Darío, Rubén. *Azul.* Valparaiso, 1888.

———. *Cantos de vida y esperanza.* Buenos Aires, 1905.

———. *Canto errante.* Madrid, 1907.

———. *Poema del otoño y otros poemas.* Madrid, 1910.

———. *Prosas profanas y otros poemas.* Buenos Aires, 1896.

Davies, John Gordon. *The Theology of William Blake.* Oxford, 1948.

Davies, Trevor H. *Spiritual Voices in Modern Literature.* New York, 1919.

Díaz Arrieta, Hernán. *Panorama de la literatura chilena durante el siglo XX*. Santiago, Chile, 1931.

Díez Echarri, Emiliano y Roca Franquesa, José María. *Historia de la literatura española e hispanoamericana*. Madrid, 1960.

Dimock, Marshall E. *Creative Religion*. Boston, 1963.

Dionysius, the Areopagite. *On the Divine Names and the Mystical Theology,* trans. C. E. Rolt. London, 1940.

Dostoievsky, Fedor M. *Crime and Punishment,* trans. Constance Garnett. New York, 1950.

———. *The Brothers Karamazov,* trans. Constance Garnett. New York, 1950.

———. *The Idiot,* trans. Constance Garnett. New York, 1958.

———. *The Possessed,* trans. Constance Garnett. New York, 1936.

Dubay, Thomas, S.M. "Virginial Motherhood," *Review for Religious* (Baltimore, Maryland), XXIV (1965), 744-759.

Fandel, John. "Poets and Mystics," *The Commonweal* (New York), LXXIX (1963), 309-310.

Fausset, Hugh L'Anson. *Fruits of Silence*. London, 1963.

Fein, John M. *Modernism in Chilean Literature, The Second Period*. Durham, N. C., 1965.

Fiore, Dolores Ackel. *Rubén Darío in Search of Inspiration*. New York, 1963.

Flynn, Gerard Cox. "The Alleged Mysticism of Sor Juana Inés de la Cruz," *Hispanic Review* (Philadelphia), XXVIII (1960), 233-244.

Fonseca, Jaime. *Latin America, A Challenge to Catholics*. Washington, D.C., 1960.

Friedman, Norman. *Poetry: An Introduction to its Form and Art*. New York, 1963.

Frost, Bede, *St. John of the Cross, Doctor of Divine Love*. London, 1937.

Füllop-Millen, René. *The Saints that Moved the World*. Manchester, England, 1945.

Gandillac, Maurice de. *Valeur du temps dans la pédagogie spirituelle de Jean Tauler*. Paris, 1956.

Gautrey, Robert M. *This Tremendous Lover*. London, 1937.

Ghose, Sisirkumer. *The Later Poems of Tagore*. New York, 1961.

Gibson, Elsie. "Mary and the Protestant Mind," *Review for Religious* (Baltimore, Maryland), XXIV (1965), 383-398.

Gil-Albert, Juan. *Poetas místicas españoles*. Mexico, 1942.

Gilson, Etienne. *The Mystical Theology of St. Bernard,* trans. A. H. C. Downes, 2nd ed. New York, 1955.

Giusti, Roberto Fernando. *Poetas de América y otros ensayos*. Buenos Aires, 1956.

Godferneaux, A. "Sur la psychologie du mysticisme," *Revue Philosophique* (Paris), LIII (1902), 158-170.

Godoy, Armand. *Trois poèmes de St. Jean de la Croix*. Paris, 1937.

González Martínez, Enrique. "Tuércele el cuello al cisne," *Spanish American Poetry,* ed. Seymour Resnick. Irvington-on-Hudson, N. Y., 1964, p. 71.

Graef, Hilda C. *The Scholar and the Cross: The Life and Work of Edith Stein*. Westminster, Maryland, 1956.

———. *The Way of the Mystics,* Westminster, Maryland, 1947.

Graff, W. L. *Rainer Maria Rilke, Creative Anguish of a Modern Poet*. Princeton, N. J., 1956.

Guillen, Jorge. *Language and Poetry*. Cambridge, Mass., 1961.

———. *Lenguaje y poesía*. Madrid, 1962.

Hand, Thomas A., O.S.A. *St. Augustine on Prayer*. Westminster, Maryland, 1963.

Haring, Clarence H. *The Spanish Empire in America*. New York, 1947.

Hartman, Geoffrey H. *The Unmediated Vision: An Interpretation of Wordsworth, Hopkins, Rilke, and Valéry*. New Haven, 1954.

Hausherr, Irenée. "Les orienteaux connaissent-ils les nuits de Saint Jean de la Croix?" *Orientalia Christiana Periodica* (Rome), XII (1946), 5-46.

Hatzfeld, Helmut. *Estudios literarios sobre mística española*. Madrid, 1950.

Heidegger, Martin. *Being and Time,* 2nd ed., trans. John Macquarrie and Edward Robinson. London, 1962.

Henríquez Ureña, Pedro. *Ensayos en busca de nuestra expresión*. Buenos Aires, 1952.

———. "Las fórmulas del Americanismo," *Obra crítica,* ed. Emma Susana Speratti Piñero. Buenos Aires, 1960, pp. 246-249.

Herrera y Reissig, Julio. *Los éxtasis de la montaña*. Montevideo, 1904-1907.

Hillyer, Robert Silliman. *In Pursuit of Poetry*. New York, 1960.

Hinnebusch, Paul, O.P. "The Hidden King of Peace," *Cross and Crown* (Dubuque, Iowa), XVI (1964), 389-395.

Hoffman, Dominic M., O.P. *The Life Within: The Prayer of Union*. New York, 1965.

Hopper, Stanley R. *Spiritual Problems in Contemporary Literature*. New York, 1957.

Hoyt, Arthur S. *The Spiritual Message of Modern English Poetry*. New York, 1924.

Hull, Ernest R., S.J. *Theosophy and Christianity*. London, 1905.

Ibarbourou, Juana de. *La rosa de los vientos*. Montevideo, 1930.

———. *Las lenguas de diamante*. Buenos Aires, 1919.

———. *Los loores de Nuestra Señora*. Montevideo, 1934.

———. *Raíz salvaje*. Montevideo, 1922.

Inge, Very Rev. W. R., C.V.O. "Plotinus," *British Academy Proceedings* (London), XV (1929), 19-43.

Jaimes Freyre, Ricardo. *Castalia bárbara*. Buenos Aires, 1897.

Jimenez, Juan Ramon. *El Modernismo,* ed. Ricardo Gullón y Eugenio Fernández Méndez. Madrid, 1962.

Johnson, Mildred E. *Swan, Cygnets, and Owl*. Columbia, Mo., 1956.

Judson, Jerome. *The Poet and the Poem*. Cincinnati, 1963.

Kaufmann, Walter. *Religion from Tolstoy to Camus*. New York, 1961.

Keller, Werner. *The Bible as History,* 12th ed. New York, 1963.

———. *The Bible as History in Pictures*. New York, 1964.

Kerr, Walter. *The Decline of Pleasure*. New York, 1962.

Koenig, John H. "College Theology and Community Worship," *Worship* (Collegeville, Minnesota), XXXVIII-XXXIX (1964), 633-644.

Koplowitz, I. *A Manual of the Jewish Religion,* trans. from the German of Rabbi F. Feilchenfeld. Richmond, Va., 1894.

Kripalani, Krishna. *Rabindranath Tagore*. New York, 1962.

Krishnamurti, Jiddu. *Life in Freedom*. New York, 1928.

Latorre, Mariano. "Coquimbo o el misticismo en la poesía chilena," *La literatura de Chile,* IV. Buenos Aires, 1941, 168-174.

———. "El sentido de la naturaleza en la poesía chilena," *Atenea* (Concepción, Chile), XIV (1930), 832-849.

Lavelle, Louis. *The Meaning of Holiness,* trans. D. O'Sullivan. New York, 1954.

Lefebvre, Dom Georges, O.S.B. *The Mystery of God's Love,* trans. Geoffrey Chapman. New York, 1961.

Lejeune, Abbé P. *An Introduction to the Mystical Life,* trans. Basil Levett. London, 1924.

Lenglart, Marcel. *The Mystic Life of Graces.* London, 1936.

León, Fray Luis de. *De los nombres de Cristo: Clásicos Castellanos, prólogo y notas de Federico de Onís.* 3 vols. Madrid, 1956.

———. *La perfecta casada,* ed. Bonilla y San Martín. Madrid, 1917.

———. *Obras completas castellanas,* ed. Félix García, O.S.A., 3 vols. Madrid, 1944.

Lewis, C. S. *The Problem of Pain.* London, 1961.

Lewis, David and Zimmerman, Dom Benedict, O.C.D. *The Mystical Doctrine of St. John of the Cross.* New York, 1935.

Lewis, Eve. *Children and Their Religion.* New York, 1962.

Lizaso, Félix. *Martí, Martyr of Cuban Independence,* trans. Esther Elise Shuler. Albuquerque, New Mexico, 1953.

Lorraine, Lilith. *Warriors of Eternity.* Corpus Christi, Texas, 1963.

Louismet, Dom. S., O.S.B. *The Mystical Life,* 4th ed. London, 1917.

Lowry, Nelson Jr. "The Rhetoric of Ineffability: Toward a Definition of Mystical Poetry," *Comparative Literature* (Eugene, Oregon), VIII (1956), 323-336.

Loyola, Ignatius of. *The Spiritual Exercises,* trans. W. H. Longridge. London, 1922.

Lugan, Abate A. *Fray Luis de León.* New York, 1924.

Lugones, Leopoldo. *Los crepúsculos del jardín.* Buenos Aires, 1905.

———. *Lunario sentimental*. Buenos Aires, 1909.
———. *Odas seculares*. Buenos Aires, 1910.
Macklin, Sister Mary de Lourdes. *An Interpretation of Francis Thompson's "Hound of Heaven."* New York, 1930.
Maiorana, María Teresa. "Bergson y el misticismo cristiano," *Criterio* (Buenos Aires), XXXIII (1961), 94-96.
Mallarmé, Stéphane. "L'Azur," *The Poems of Mallarmé,* ed. Charles Mauron. Binghamton, New York, 1951, pp. 137-138.
Marechal, Joseph, S.J. *Studies in the Psychology of the Mystics*. New York, 1927.
Marías, Julián. "Prologue," *The Christ of Velásquez,* trans. Eleanor L. Turnbull. Baltimore, Maryland, 1951, pp. xii-xiii.
Marín, Diego. *Poesía española y textos, siglos XV al XX*. México, 1958.
Maritain, Jacques. *A Christian Looks at the Jewish Question*. New York, 1939.
———. *Approaches to God,* trans. Peter O'Reilly. New York, 1954.
———. *Art and Poetry,* trans. E. de P. Matthews. New York. 1943.
———. "La poésie, l'homme et les choses," *La Table Ronde* (Paris), CCXV (1965), 7-30.
Maritain, Jacques et Raïssa. *Liturgy and Contemplation,* trans. Joseph W. Evans. New York, 1960.
———. *Situation de la poéie*. Paris, 1938.
———. *The Situation of Poetry,* trans. Marshall Suther. New York, 1955.
———. *We Have Been Friends Together,* trans. Julie Kernan, New York, 1942.
Maritain, Raïssa. *Adventures in Grace,* trans. Julie Kernan. New York, 1945.

Martindale, C. C. "St. John of the Cross," *Month* (London), CXXX (1917), 481-492.

McMahon, J. J. *The Divine Union in the "Subida del Monte Carmelo" and the "Noche oscura" of St. John of the Cross*. Washington, D.C., 1941.

Mecham, J. Lloyd. *Church and State in Latin America, A History of Politico-Ecclesiastical Relations*. Chapel Hill, N. C., 1934.

Medina, J. T. *La literatura femenina en Chile*. Santiago, Chile, 1923.

Metzidakis, Philip. "Unamuno frente a la poesía de Rubén Darío," *Revista Iberoamericana* (Albuquerque, New Mexico), XXV (1960), 229-249.

Mednick, M. T. and S. A. *Research in Personality*. New York, 1963.

Menéndez y Pelayo, Marcelino. "Chile," *Historia de la poesía hispanoamericana,* II, ed. Enrique Sánchez Reyes. Santander, 1948, 219-299.

———. *La mística española*. Madrid, 1956.

———. "Prólogo," *San Juan de la Cruz, el cántico espiritual,* ed. M. Martínez Burgos. Madrid, 1936, pp. vii-xl.

Merlan, Philip. *Monopsychism, Mysticism, Metaconsciousness: Problems of the Soul in the Neoaristotelian and Neoplatonic Tradition*. The Hague, 1963.

Merton, Thomas. *A. Thomas Merton Reader,* ed. Thomas P. McDonnell. New York, 1962.

———. *Disputed Questions*. New York, 1960.

———. *New Seeds of Contemplation*. Norfolk, Conn., 1961.

———. Personal correspondence. February 24, 1965.

———. *The New Man*. New York, 1961.

Miranda, Marta Elba. *Mujeres chilenas*. Santiago, Chile, 1940.

Molina, Roderick A., O.F.M. "Amado Nervo: His Mysticism

and Franciscan Influence," *The Americas* (Washington, D.C.), VI (1949), 173-196.

Monguió, Luis, "Sobre la caracterización del modernismo," *Revista Iberoamericana* (Albuquerque, New Mexico), VII (1943), 68-90.

Moody, Joseph N. "The Dechristianization of the French Working Class," *Review of Politics* (Notre Dame, Indiana), XX (1958), 46-69.

Moore, Thomas Verner, O.S.B. *The Driving Forces of Human Nature and Their Adjustment*. New York, 1948.

———. *The Life of Man with God*. New York, 1955.

More, Paul Elmer. *The Catholic Faith*. Princeton, New Jersey, 1931.

Morison, Stanley. *Some Fruits of Theosophy*. London, 1919.

Morris, Leon. *The Biblical Doctrine of Judgment*. Grand Rapids, Michigan, 1960.

Müller, Frederich Max. *Theosophy or Psychological Religion*. London, 1893.

Muñoz, Matilde. *Antología de poetisas hispanoamericanas*. Madrid, 1946.

Nervo, Amado. *El éxodo y las flores del camino*. México, 1902.

———. *Místicas*. Paris, 1904.

Neubert, Emil, S.M. *Mary in Doctrine*, 3rd ed. New York, 1954.

Nicholson, D. H. S. *The Mysticism of St. Francis of Assisi*. Boston, 1938.

Nicholson, Reynold A. *The Mystics of Islam*. London, 1963.

Noël, Marie. *Le Rosaire des Joies*. Paris, 1930.

———. *Les chansons et les fleurs*. Paris, 1938.

Norwich, Julian of. *The Revelations of Divine Love*, trans. James Walsh, S.J. London, 1961.

Orozco Díaz, Emilio. *Poesía y mística, introducción a la lírica de San Juan de la Cruz*. Madrid, 1959.
Osmond, Percy H. *The Mystical Poets of the English Church*. London, 1919.
Parrinder, Geoffrey. *Worship in the World's Religions*. London, 1961.
Peers, E. Allison. *El misticismo español*. Buenos Aires, 1947.
———. *Fool of Love. The Life of Ramón Lull*. London, 1946.
———. *Handbook to the Life and Times of St. Teresa and St. John of the Cross*. London, 1954.
———. "Mysticism in the Poetry of Lope de Vega," *Estudios dedicados a Menéndez Pidal,* I. Madrid, 1950, 349-358.
———. *Saint John of the Cross and other Lectures and Addresses*. London, 1945.
———. *Spain*. London, 1930.
———. *Spirit of Flame, A Study of St. John of the Cross*. New York, 1944.
———. *Studies of the Spanish Mystics*. 3 vols. London, 1927, 1930, 1960.
Pegis, Anton C. *The Wisdom of Catholicism*. New York, 1949.
Percas, Elena. *La poesía femenina argentina*. Madrid, 1958.
Philipon, M. M., O.P. *The Mother of God,* trans. John A. Otto, 2nd ed. Westminster, Maryland, 1954.
Plus, Raoul. *God Within Us*. New York, 1926.
Poesía Hebraica, trans. J. Millas Vallicrosa. Barcelona, 1953.
Pond, Kathleen. *The Spirit of the Spanish Mystics*. New York, 1958.
"Pope Meets Indian Sects, Commends Hindu Prayer," Anon. rev., *Daily News,* December 4, 1964, p. 20.
Posselt, Teresia Renata de Spiritu Sancto. *Edith Stein,* trans. Cecily Hastings and Donald Michell. New York, 1952.

Powers, Perry J. "Lope de Vega and las lágrimas de la Madalena," *Comparative Literature* (Eugene, Oregon), VIII (1956), 273-290.

Preston, Thomas R. "Christabel and the Mystical Tradition," *Essays and Studies in Language and Literature,* ed. Herbert H. Petit. Louvain, 1964, pp. 138-157.

Price, C. P. *Teresa, John and Thérèse.* New York, 1946.

Rahner, Karl. *Mary, Mother of the Lord.* New York, 1963.

"Rainer Maria Rilke," *Studies in Modern European Literature and Thought,* ed. Erich Heller. New Haven, 1952.

Ravier, André, S.J. *La mystique et les mystiques.* Paris, 1965.

Rethlingshafer, D. *Motivation as Related to Personality.* New York, 1963.

Rilke, Rainer Maria. *Selected Works.* 2 vols., trans. J. B. Leishman. London, 1960.

Rivet, Mother Mary Majella, O.S.U. *The Influence of the Spanish Mystics on the Works of St. Francis de Sales.* Washington, D.C., 1941.

Rodó, José Enrique. *Ariel.* Montevideo, 1900.

Roganski, Ralph, O.P. "Informing Christians in Latin America," *Our Sunday Visitor* (Huntington, Indiana), LIII (1964), 1, 8.

Rubio, David, O.S.A. *The Mystic Soul of Spain.* New York, 1946.

Ryan, Edwin. *The Church in the South American Republics.* New York, 1932.

Sales, François de. *Traité de l'amour de Dieu,* I. Paris, 1925.

Salinas, Pedro. "The escape from reality—Fray Luis and San Juan," *Reality and the Poet in Spanish Literature.* Baltimore, 1940, pp. 97-128.

Sandoval, Adolfo de. *San Juan de la Cruz, el santo, el doctor místico, el poeta.* Madrid, 1942.

Sansom, Clive. *The World of Poetry.* London, 1959.

Sanson, Henri. *L'esprit humain selon St. Jean de la Croix*. Paris, 1953.

Santos Chocane, José. *Alma América*. Madrid, 1906.

Sandreau, Auguste. *The Life of Union with God,* trans. E. J. Strickland. London, 1926.

———. *The Mystical State, Its Nature and Phases,* trans. D. M. B. New York, 1924.

Sarason, Irwin G. *Contemporary Research in Personality*. Princeton, New Jersey, 1962.

Schweitzer, A. *Quest of the Historical Jesus*. New York, 1959.

Sencourt, Robert. *Carmelite and Poet, A Framed Portrait of St. John of the Cross*. New York, 1944.

Sepich, Juan R. *San Juan de la Cruz, místico y poeta*. Buenos Aires, 1942.

Setien, Emeterio G. *Las raíces de la poesía sanjuanista y Dámaso Alonso*. Burgos, 1950.

Sewell, Elizabeth. *The Human Metaphor*. Notre Dame, Indiana, 1964.

Shapiro, Karl J. *Beyond Criticism*. Lincoln, Nebraska, 1953.

Sharp, A. B. *Mysticism, Its True Nature and Value*. London, 1910.

Sheets, John R., S.J. "The Mystery of the Church and the Liturgy," *Worship* (Collegeville, Minnesota), XXXVIII-XXXIX (1964), 612-620.

Shen, Sampson C. *Confucius and Tagore, A Comparative Study*. Taipei, 1960.

Siena, Catherine of. *The Dialogue of the Seraphic Virgin,* trans. Algar Thorold. London, 1896.

Silva Castro, Raúl. *Antología general de la poesía chilena*. Santiago, Chile, 1959.

Sitwell, Gerard, O.S.B. *Spiritual Writers of the Middle Ages*. New York, 1961.

St. Rose, Sister Mary, S.N.D. "St. John of the Cross, Doctor of the Cross, Doctor of Divine Love," *Review for Religious* (Baltimore, Maryland), XVI (1957), 193-210.

Suso, Blessed Henry. *Little Book of Eternal Wisdom and Little Book of Truth,* trans. James Clark. New York, 1953.

———. *The Exemplar,* ed. Nicholas Heller, trans. Sister M. Ann Edward, O.P. 2 vols. Dubuque, Iowa, 1962.

Suzuki, D. T. *Mysticism: Christian and Buddhist*. New York, 1957.

Symonds, John. *The Lady with the Magic Eyes: Madame Blavatsky, Medium and Magician*. New York, 1959.

Synagogue Service: New Year and Atonement. New York, n.d.

Tagore, Rabindranath. *A Tagore Reader,* ed. Aniya Chakravarty. New York, 1961.

———. *Gitanjali—Song Offerings*. New York, 1916.

Tanquerey, Adolphe. *The Spiritual Life, A Treatise on Ascetical and Mystical Theology,* trans. Herman Branderis, S.S. Tournai, Belgium, 1930.

Teilhard de Chardin, Pierre. *Building the Earth,* trans. Noël Lindsay. Wilkes-Barre, 1965.

———. *Hymn to the Universe,* trans. Simon Bartholomew. New York, 1961.

Théry, P. G., O.P. "Scot Erigène, introducteur de Denys," *The New Scholasticism* (Baltimore, Maryand), VII (1933), 91-108.

The Book of Psalms, trans. Ronald Knox. New York, 1955.

The Catholic Encyclopedia, X, ed. C. G. Herbermann. New York, 1913, 663-665.

The Constitution on the Sacred Liturgy of the Second Vatican Council, ed. Paulist Fathers. Glen Rock, New Jersey, 1964.

The Essential Plotinus, trans. Elmer O'Brien. New York, 1964.

The Holy Bible, trans. from the Latin Vulgate. New York, 1949-1950.

Thomas, George Inger. *Poetry, Religion and the Spiritual Life.* Houston, 1951.

Thompson, Edward J. *Rabindranath Tagore, His Life and Work.* Calcutta, 1921.

———. *Rabindranath Tagore, Poet and Dramatist.* Oxford, 1926.

Thompson, Francis. *Poems,* ed. Terence L. Connolly, S.J. New York, 1932.

———. *Works.* 3 vols., ed. W. Meynell. New York, 1913.

Tolstoy, Leo N. *The Death of Ivan Ilyich,* trans. Aylmer Maude. New York, 1960.

Trapp, Jacob A. *A Contemporary Anthology of Modern Religious Poems.* New York, 1964.

Unamuno, Miguel de. *El Cristo de Velázquez.* Madrid, 1920.

———. *The Christ of Velazquez,* trans. Eleanor L. Turnbull. Baltimore, Maryland, 1951.

Underhill, Evelyn. *Mysticism,* 2nd ed. London, 1911.

———. *The Essentials of Mysticism,* 12th ed. New York, 1960.

———. *The Life of the Spirit and the Life of Today.* New York, 1922.

———. *The Mount of Purification with Meditations and Prayers.* New York, 1960.

———. *The School of Charity—The Mystery of Sacrifice,* 2nd ed. New York, 1956.

Valbuena Briones, Angel. "El lugar de Amado Nervo en el modernismo," *Literatura hispanoamericana.* Barcelona, 1965, pp. 215-228.

Valbuena Prat, Angel. *La poesia española contemporánea.* Madrid, 1930.

Van Kaam, Adrian, C.S.Sp. *Religion and Personality*. Englewood Cliffs, New Jersey, 1964.

Vann, Gerald, O.P. *The Heart of Man*. New York, 1945.

Van Zeller, Dom Hubert, O.S.B. *The Inner Search*. New York, 1956.

Vaughn, Robert Alfred. *Hours With the Mystics: The Spanish Mystics,* IX. London, 1895.

Very, Francis. "Rubén Darío y la Biblia," *Revista Iberoamericana* (Albuquerque, New Mexico), XVIII (1952), 141-155.

Viatte, Auguste. *Les sources occultes du romantisme, illuminisme, théosophie*. Paris, 1928.

Vilnet, Jean. *Bible et mystique chez Saint Jean de la Croix*. Bruges, 1949.

Vossler, Karl. *La soledad en la poesía española*. Madrid, 1941.

Wach, Joachim. *The comparative Study of Religions,* ed. Joseph N. Kitagawa. New York, 1958.

Walker, Kenneth, F.R.C.P. *The Mystic Mind*. New York, 1965.

Walsh, Thomas. "Menéndez y Pelayo on Spanish Mystical Poetry," *Thought* (New York), XVI (1941), 102-121.

Watkin, Edward Ingram. *The Philosophy of Mysticism*. New York, 1920.

Weigel, Gustave, S.J. *The Modern God—Faith in a Secular Culture*. London, 1963.

Wepman, Joseph M. and Heine, Ralph W. *Concepts of Personality*. Chicago, 1963.

White, Helen C. *The Mysticism of William Blake*. Madison, Wisconsin, 1927.

Whiteman, J. H. M. *The Mystical Life*. London, 1961.

Wright, George Thaddeus. *The Poet in the Poem; the Persons of Eliot, Yeats, and Pound*. Berkeley, 1962.

Young, Howard T. *The Victorious Expression*. Madison, Wisconsin, 1964.

Zardoya, Concha. *Poesía española contemporánea*. Madrid, 1961.

———. "Twentieth Century Spanish Poetry," Lecture delivered at Barnard College, N. Y., April 24, 1966.

Zéréga-Fombona, A. *Le symbolisme français et la poésie espagnole moderne*. Paris, 1919.

Zweig, Stefan. *The World of Yesterday*, 2nd ed. Lincoln, Nebraska, 1964.